TWENTY BUILDINGS *every architect*

Have you ever wondered how the ideas behind the world's greatest architecture came about? What process does an architect go through to design buildings which become world-renowned for their excellence?

In this book Simon Unwin reveals the secrets behind twenty such buildings. He asks you to 'read' the building and understand its starting point by analysing its final form through drawing. By this gradual process of understanding the thinking behind architectural form, you learn a unique methodology which can be used every time you look at a building.

Analysing buildings from throughout the twentieth century and across the globe including the US, France, Italy, Mexico, Switzerland, Spain, Finland, Australia, Norway, Sweden and Japan, this book is essential reading for every architect.

Simon Unwin is Emeritus Professor of Architecture at the University of Dundee, UK. He has lived in the UK and Australia, and taught or lectured on his work in China, Israel, India, Sweden, Turkey and the US. His previous books, including *Analysing Architecture,* are used in schools of architecture around the world.

Some reviews of Simon Unwin's previous book, *Analysing Architecture*:

'What is striking about the book is the thoughtfulness and consideration which is present in each phrase, each sentence, each plan, each section and each view, all contributing to an overarching quality which makes the book particularly applicable and appropriate to students in their efforts to make sense of the complex and diverse aspects of architecture... Unwin writes with an architect's sensibility and draws with an accomplished architect's hand.'

Susan Rice, Rice and Ewald Architects, *Architectural Science Review*

'Unwin chooses to look at the underlying elements of architecture rather than, as is more usual, at the famous names, styles, movements and chronology of the genre. This rejection of the conventional art-historical approach can lead to interesting conclusions... it is all presented cogently and convincingly through the medium of Unwin's own drawings.'

Hugh Pearman, *The Sunday Times*

'This is an excellent book, recommended to anyone seriously interested in architecture. Its starting point is Unwin's ability to draw well – to think through his hands, as it were. This is fundamental to architectural skill and Unwin has used it to "talk back to himself" and describe the architecture around him. He uses this skill to romp through a huge number and variety of buildings and architectural situations in order to describe architectural strategies. Unwin has at the heart of his book a definition and understanding of architecture that we thoroughly endorse: to be dealt with in terms of its conceptual organisation and intellectual structure. But he adds to this potentially dry definition an emotive overlay or parallel: architecture as the identification of place ("Place is to architecture as meaning is to language"). Thus he takes on the issue of why we value architecture.'

http://www.architecturelink.org.uk/GMoreSerious2.html

'In clear, precise diagrams and thoughtful text, author Simon Unwin offers an engaging methodology for the study of architecture and aesthetic systems. Time-tested buildings from classical temples to traditional Japanese homes and early modernist masterpieces, are explored in this wide ranging, but focused study. Unwin demonstrates that while architectural styles change over time, the underlying principles that organize quality designs remain remarkably consistent. This book is a must for all architectural students interested in acquiring the visual skills needed to understand a wide variety of design methodologies.'

Diane78 (New York), *Amazon.com website*

'The text has been carefully written to avoid the use of jargon and it introduces architectural ideas in a straightforward fashion. This, I suspect, will give it a well-deserved market beyond that of architects and architectural students.'

Barry Russell, *Environments BY DESIGN*

'From the campsites of primitive man to the sophisticated structures of the late twentieth century, architecture as an essential function of human activity is explained clearly, and illustrated with the author's own excellent drawings. Highly recommended as a well-organized and readable introduction.'

medals@win-95.com, *Amazon.com website*

'This book establishes a systematic method in analyzing architecture. It explains how architectural elements are combined together to form designs that could relate an appropriate sense of "place" specific to the programme as well as the environment surrounding it. The book is well illustrated with diagrams and examples. An extremely useful introductory guide for those who want to learn more about the basics of architecture.'

nikana99@hotmail.com, *Amazon.com website*

'*Analysing Architecture* should become an essential part of all architectural education and an informative guide to the powerful analytical tool of architectural drawing.'

Howard Ray Lawrence, Pennsylvania State University

'Excellent in every way – a core book, along with *An Architecture Notebook*.'

Terry Robson, Teaching Fellow, University of Bath, UK

'I think this is an excellent book and I will continue to recommend it to my students.'

Professor Donald Hanlon,
University of Wisconsin-Milwaukee, US

'Probably the best introductory book on architecture.'

Andrew Higgott, Lecturer in Architecture,
University of East London, UK

'One would have no hesitation in recommending this book to new students: it introduces many ideas and references central to the study of architecture. The case studies are particularly informative. A student would find this a useful aid to identifying the many important issues seriously engaged with in Architecture.'

Lorraine Farrelly, *Architectural Design*

'The most lucid and readable introduction to architecture I have read.'

Professor Roger Stonehouse,
Manchester School of Architecture

Architecture Notebooks *by Simon Unwin:*

 www.routledge.com/textbooks/9780415489287/

TWENTY BUILDINGS
every architect should understand

Simon Unwin

Routledge
Taylor & Francis Group

London and New York

First published 2010 by Routledge
2 Park Square, Milton Park, Abingdon, Oxon, OX14 4RN

Simultaneously published in the USA and Canada by Routledge
270 Madison Avenue, New York, NY 10016

Routledge is an imprint of the Taylor & Francis Group, an informa business

First edition © 2010 Simon Unwin

Designed and typeset in Adobe Garamond Pro by Simon Unwin

Printed and bound in Great Britain by The Cromwell Press Group, Trowbridge, Wiltshire

British Library Cataloguing in Publication Data
A catalogue record for this book is available from the British Library

Library of Congress Cataloging-in-Publication Data
Unwin, Simon, 1952-
Twenty buildings every architect should understand / Simon Unwin.
    p. cm.
  Includes bibliographical references and index.
  1. Architecture, Modern—20th century. I. Title.
NA680.U59 2010
724'.6–dc22   2009051181

ISBN10 0-415-55251-6 (hbk)
ISBN10 0-415-55252-4 (pbk)
ISBN10 0-203-84939-6 (ebk)

ISBN13 978-0-415-55251-6 (hbk)
ISBN13 978-0-415-55252-3 (pbk)
ISBN13 978-0-203-84939-2 (ebk)

for Emily

CONTENTS

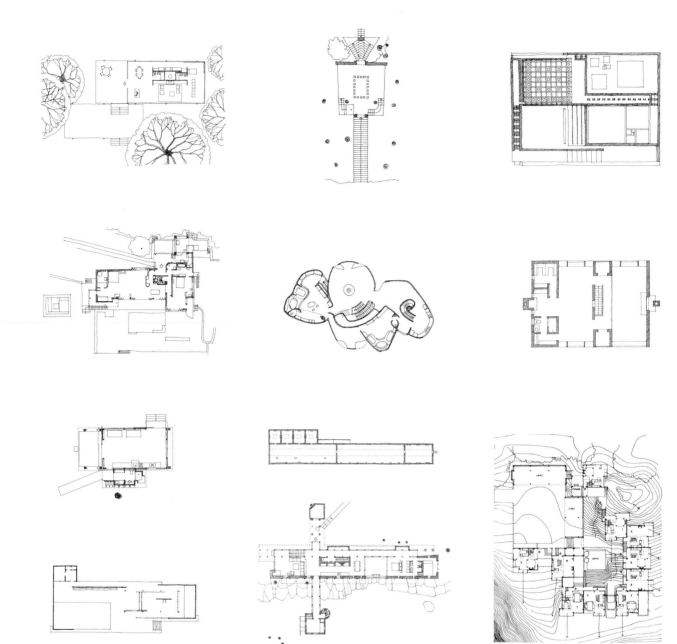

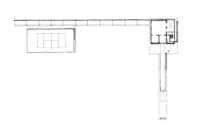

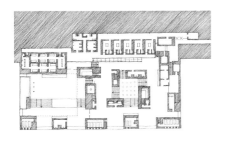

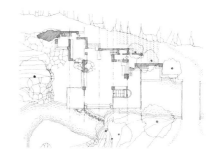
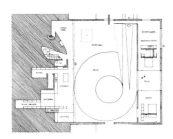

TWENTY BUILDINGS

every architect should understand

'Architecture is open to analysis like any other aspect of experience, and is made more vivid by comparison. Analysis includes the breaking up of architecture into elements, a technique I frequently use even though it is the opposite of the integration which is the final goal of art. However paradoxical it appears, and despite the suspicions of many Modern architects, such disintegration is a process present in all creation, and it is essential to understanding.'

Robert Venturi – *Complexity and Contradiction in Architecture*, Museum of Modern Art, New York, 1966, p. 18.

'Originality may often express itself suddenly but never without some previous experience with form... Imitation is a method of assimilation. In accepting it as such the student gains knowledge and experience and is quicker thereby to discover his own originality.'

'Comments of Harwell Hamilton Harris to the Faculty, May 25, 1954' (written by Bernhard Hoesli and Colin Rowe) printed in **Colin Rowe**, edited by Caragonne – *As I was Saying: Recollections and Miscellaneous Essays*, MIT Press, Cambridge, MA, 1996, p. 48.

'One uses one's eyes and draws so as to fix deep down in one's experience what is seen. Once the impression is recorded by the pencil it stays for good, entered, registered, inscribed... To draw oneself, to trace the lines, handle the volumes, organize the surface... all this means first to look, and then to observe and finally perhaps to discover... and it is then that inspiration may come. Inventing, creating, one's whole being is drawn into action, and it is this action that counts.'

Le Corbusier, translated by Palmes – *Creation is a Patient Search*, quoted in Le Corbusier, translated by Žaknić – *Journey to the East* (1966), MIT Press, Cambridge, MA, 1977, p. xiii.

'Positing a designing mind behind the architectural reality lets the analyst explain architectural change. The person who will be a maker of houses travels through architectural experiences from the beginning of his life... Like the learning singer of epics or chanter of sermons, he passes through an apprenticeship of imitation. But at maturity, like the best of the epic singers, he is reliant not on one original, but on a competence constructed out of numerous originals.'

Henry H. Glassie – *Folk Housing in Middle Virginia: A Structural Analysis of Historic Artifacts*, University of Tennessee Press, Knoxville, TN, 1975.

'Remember the impression given by good architecture, that it expresses a thought. It makes one want to respond with a gesture.'

Ludwig Wittgenstein, edited by von Wright and Nyman, translated by Winch – *Culture and Value* (1977), Blackwell Publishing, Oxford, 1998, p. 16e.

INTRODUCTION

'Obeying laws, the maker works like his creator; not obeying law, he is such a fool as heaps a pile of stones and calls it a church.' **George MacDonald**, 1893.

You cannot understand architecture merely by looking at photographs. You cannot understand architecture by only reading words. Yet many books on architecture have only words and/or photographs. The only way to understand architecture is through the medium used in its creation – drawing. Long ago architecture was made by drawing directly on the ground, maybe first with a stick and then by digging trenches or piling stones into walls. For many centuries architecture was drawn at a small scale on paper before it was built. Now the same happens on computer screens. These are the fields, the grounds – sand, paper, screens – where architects have created and continue to create architecture.

It is not possible to write instructions for how to do architecture without restricting its possibilities, any more than it is possible to write instructions for how to speak without constraining what may be said. When we begin, we learn by attending to and imitating how others (parents, friends, teachers…) do these things. Gradually we find our own voices, in architecture as in language.

Architecture resides in the drawings (and nowadays in the computer-generated models) of buildings. It is here that you can find the intellectual structure given to designs by their architects. It is here that you, as an architect, give form to your own ideas. It is through drawing that you must study and imitate how others do architecture so that you can learn to do it yourself and find your own architectural voice.

In learning to do architecture the study of plans and sections takes precedence even over visiting buildings; though visits to buildings are enjoyable and provide a chance to see how architecture, conceived through the abstraction of drawing, changes the real world and makes places for life. Visiting buildings gives you the best chance to experience architecture in relation to the world of light, sound, setting, people… and to assess the performance of the abstraction when made real. But to understand the underlying architecture of buildings you need to study them through drawing.

Architecture is about changing the world; making it better, more comfortable, more beautiful, more efficient… according to people's aspirations and beliefs. Architects do not deal in truth, they deal in a kind of fantasy (dreams, philosophical propositions, political manifestoes), though sometimes those fantasies are about what they think of as ordinary everyday pragmatism. Architects often try to suggest that their fantasy is the truth of how the world should be. But different architects come up with different answers. And they can become frustrated when the people for whom they design fail to use their buildings in the ways they think they should. Architecture is a matter of proposal and evaluation, call and response. It depends on ideas.

This book is about architectural ideas developed and communicated through drawing. We tend to think of ideas as things we express in words. Architectural ideas are expressed in line, and in solid and space. They are the intellectual structures (one might call them self-generated 'laws') by which architects conceive and design buildings. In his 1893 essay, 'The Fantastic Imagination' (quoted above), George MacDonald theorised about how to write stories. He suggested that however fantastic and far from natural reality a story might stray, to be plausible it must obey its own (predetermined) laws; to make a story without discipline was like throwing a pile of stones on the ground and calling it a church. MacDonald's use of an architectural metaphor is useful: it is an architectural idea that turns a pile of stones into a church.

MacDonald, Queen Victoria's favourite writer of fairy tales, lived in the nineteenth century. Nowadays we live in times when a pile of stones can be considered a work of art in that merely the *decision* to throw the stones into a pile or even to leave a found pile of stones undisturbed can be asserted as a generative idea. But the point of MacDonald's parable remains valid: that the creative activity of human beings depends upon the generation and application of ideas that give discipline to their work. This argument holds even if the idea is one of formlessness, indiscipline, mystery, emptiness… Without an idea nothing, not even the undisturbed pile of stones, can be said to have form. It is in the mind – the realm of ideas – that architecture comes into being and exists.

The present book is related to another. *Analysing Architecture* first appeared in 1997 and has subsequently been published in second (2003) and third editions (2009). It has been translated into Chinese, Japanese, Korean, Spanish, Persian and is being translated into Arabic. As one reviewer commented (gratifyingly and reassuringly), *Analysing Architecture* 'establishes a systematic method for analyzing architecture'. The present book explores and tests that method by applying it in analysing twenty buildings of diverse character, in different countries, and dating from various times during the last eight decades of the twentieth century. Architecture has never been more diverse than during that period.

Of course there are rather more than twenty buildings that any architect should understand to underpin their fluency in the language of architecture and connoisseurship of the canon of great works. The collection here is diverse but not random. Not all are 'great'; some may be familiar, others less so. All are of a size and complexity of brief (program) that might be presented to architectural students during the early years of their architectural education.

Two particular themes have informed the choice of examples analysed. They are themes around which many architectural ideas cluster. The first concerns the different types of space in which architects deal. You might think that there is only one sort of space. In one sense there is. But architects mould and engineer space. We can leave it open to infinity or close it off from everywhere else. We can emphasise its horizontal dimensions or its vertical. We can give it focus and definition or leave it vague and diverse. We can excavate it from solid matter or even from itself. We can give it direction or make it suggest wandering. Architects can make space that is static or dynamic, or both at the same time. We can make space that

works in straight lines and right angles or space that curves and flows. Architects have even tried to warp space.

The second theme concerns the different ways in which architects think of the human being as an ingredient/component/recipient of architecture. In music the person who receives is called the listener; in art the viewer or observer; in sport the spectator; in television the watcher… But in architecture we do not have a word for the person who experiences a building: 'user' is too functional; 'visitor' too transient; 'dweller', 'resident' or 'inhabitant' too domestic; 'man' or 'woman' too gender specific; 'owner' too possessive; 'experiencer' too ugly. I have had to resort to just using the word 'person', which may occasionally, in the following analyses, sound a little clunky. A person sees, hears, touches, smells (and occasionally tastes), walks around, uses, and may be emotionally affected by a building, whether he or she is a member of an audience, family, work force, congregation, tour party or whatever. But architects sometimes also use the person as the model on which to base their architecture, whether in terms of biology, dimensions, skeletal structure and articulation, mobility… I have not covered all of these in the following analyses but the ways in which architects have sought to accommodate or have found inspiration in the person remains one of the themes by which their subjects were chosen.

This book has been written for those for whom the generation of architectural ideas is a repeated challenge. It seeks to extract, by analysis, the ideas underlying works of architecture in ways that keep uppermost in the consciousness the astonishing (miraculous) ability of the human mind to conceive intellectually. There is no other faculty that makes human beings more human than our ability to come up with ideas. The question of where they come from and how they come into being is a mystery that science has made no progress in answering. But perhaps 'where they come from' can be partly answered by suggesting that our critical and mischievous playfulness, when it encounters the ideas of others, has an ability to distort, reinterpret, contradict and reinvent them in such a way as to produce what passes for new ones. Certainly it is difficult to find ideas that are radically and essentially novel. Usually they may be interpreted as developments from or contradictions of previous ideas evident in the work of other people or apparent in nature. Such links will be apparent in the following analyses.

This book begins with buildings and tries to understand the thought processes and decisions behind their conception. As far as is possible, it puts the reader (of the drawings as well as the words) in the position of the architect. It asks the question 'what moves did I make when designing this building?' By doing so it gives insight into the processes of design and language of architecture.

The analyses are not presented in chronological order. There is a benign mischief to this. It is consciously intended to subvert the orthodox historical interpretation usually overlaid on the discussion of architecture. I do not mean to suggest that such interpretation is irrelevant. But I do share the concern, expressed a century ago by W.R. Lethaby (as quoted at the beginning of *Analysing Architecture*), that the labels and classifications of architectural history can distract from appreciation of the fundamental powers of architecture as the medium through which people build their world.

The analyses that follow show that architects do not always do the obvious, straightforward and direct thing. Sometimes it seems that architecture consists in wilful deviation from some undefined norm. If the variety of approaches exposed in the following pages does not make the task of design any easier, it will perhaps illustrate some of those powers available to the architect and make those who want to design buildings aware of some of the possibilities and potential of this richest of all arts.

A note on methods of study

The intention of this book is not only to provide ready analyses of buildings but also to show how such analyses might be done. Readers of this book will probably learn more about the workings of architecture by doing their own analyses than merely by following those offered here. Together with *Analysing Architecture*, the analyses offered here suggest the sorts of things analysts might look for and that architects might try in their own work.

In preparing analyses one is dependent necessarily upon published material. In working from published sources the analyst is likely, if not certain, to encounter inaccuracies in drawings and possibly be thrown off course by the occasional cases where photographs have been printed the wrong way around. Even architects' own drawings usually (not sometimes) differ from what is built because variations are often made during construction or because architects sometimes would prefer to record an idealised version of their architecture. This is a practice that goes back at least to Palladio in the sixteenth century, whose published version of the house known as the Villa Rotonda in his *Four Books on Architecture* is different from the actual building to be found on a hillside just outside Vicenza. Amongst the analyses present in this book, the plan of *Le Cabanon* published by Le Corbusier in Volume Five of his *Œuvre Complète* is different from the plan of the shed as built.

Interrogating published material is part of the analytical process. And redrawing the plans and sections of buildings under scrutiny is an essential part of that interrogation. It is through redrawing that the analyst is able to correct mistakes in published material and acquire a deeper perception of what the architect has been up to and how decisions might have been made. It is of course impossible to get inside the mind of an architect but it is arguable that one may get closer by redrawing their architecture than by reading the words they write or say. This is not to suggest that architects intend to be disingenuous in the ways they sometimes obfuscate their architecture with words. But, as has already been suggested, it is impossible to explain architecture fully in words.

Understanding how other architects have made decisions helps you understand what is possible in your own work. Understanding the variety of ways in which architects have made decisions, the variety of criteria they use, introduces you to the problem of deciding your own values and priorities in design. In the analyses contained in this book you will see that in each of the twenty buildings a different approach to design was adopted, different values and ideas were in play. By looking carefully at the work of others you can ask yourself the questions, 'Do I find this way of designing interesting, pertinent, sustainable… or vacuous, irresponsible, self-indulgent…?' and 'Can I learn something from this that I can use (emulate) in, or makes me reflect critically on, my own work?' The answers to these question are yours.

The following analyses use the conceptual framework offered in *Analysing Architecture*. Nevertheless the present book may be read on its own. The only slight problem may relate to abbreviations used for some concepts that are explained in detail in the earlier book. Those that may need explanation are:

'identification of place' – the realisation that architecture, distinct from other art forms, begins with the desire or need to establish a place or places in the world;

'basic elements' – wall, floor, roof, defined area of ground, pit, platform, doorway, window…; i.e. the basic elements of the 'language' of architecture;

'modifying elements' – light, temperature, scale, ventilation, texture, time…; i.e. elements that come into play once a work of architecture is built, and which modify the person's experience of it;

'primitive place types' – place types, usually with their own accepted names, timelessly part of human inhabitation of the world, e.g. bed, altar, hearth, pulpit…;

'temples and cottages' – a complex dimension of attitudes architects adopt towards aspects of the world (site, materials, climate, people, history, the future…) ranging, roughly speaking, from one of control to one of acceptance or responsiveness;

'geometries of being' – geometry that is innate to materials, the ways in which they are made, to human form and movement…;

'ideal geometry' – geometry that is imposed onto materials, the ways in which they are made, human form and movement…, i.e. perfect squares, circles, rectangles with particular mathematical proportions, computer-generated formulae…;

'stratification' – the organisation of buildings in the vertical dimension, the differing relationships between different levels of a building and the ground;

'space and structure' – the various relationships between structural order and spatial organisation in architecture;

'parallel walls' – spatial organisation based in the use of parallel, and usually load-bearing, walls;

'transition, hierarchy, heart' – the progressive zoning of the spatial organisation of a building, e.g. between public and private, sacred and secular, etc.;

others, such as 'framing', 'using things that are there' and 'elements doing more than one thing', are self-explanatory.

Simon Unwin, September 2009

References and other relevant publications, websites, broadcasts:

Simon Unwin – *Analysing Architecture*, third edition, Routledge, Abingdon, 2009.

Simon Unwin – 'Analysing Architecture through Drawing', in *Building Research and Information*, 35(1), 2007, pp. 101-110.

Simon Unwin – *An Architecture Notebook: Wall*, Routledge, London, 2000.

Simon Unwin – *Doorway*, Routledge, Abingdon, 2007.

Simon Unwin – 'Notebook Architecture', in Wendy Gunn, editor – *Fieldnotes and Sketchbooks: Challenging the Boundaries between Descriptions and Processes of Describing*, Peter Lang GmbH, Frankfurt am Main, 2009, pp. 37-59.

Simon Unwin – 'Teaching Architects', in Elisabeth Dunne, editor, *The Learning Society*, Kogan Page, London, 1999, pp. 187-196.

LA CASA DEL OJO DE AGUA

CHORA

*'We must start our new description of
the universe by making a fuller
subdivision than we did before; we
then distinguished two forms of reality
– we must now add a third. Two were
enough at an earlier stage, when we
postulated on the one hand an
intelligible and unchanging model and
on the other a visible and changing copy
of it. We did not distinguish a third
form, considering two would be enough;
but now the argument compels us to try
to describe in words a form that is
difficult and obscure. What must we
suppose its powers and nature to be?
In general terms, it is the receptacle
and, as it were, the nurse of all
becoming and change.'*

Plato, translated by Lee – *Timaeus* (c.360BC)
16, Penguin, Harmondsworth, 1971, p. 66.

LA CASA DEL OJO DE AGUA

A house in the Mexican jungle
ADA DEWES and SERGIO PUENTE, 1985-90

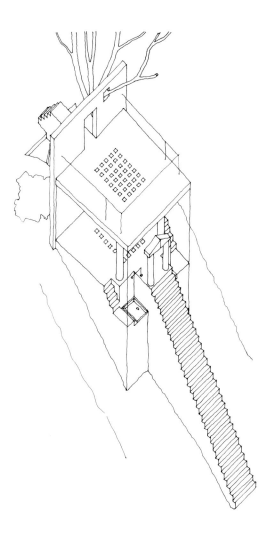

This is not a cutaway drawing. It is of a house with two floors, one wall (instead of the usual four) and no roof, though the floor of the upper room acts as a roof to the lower, or *vice versa*. The two rooms of *La Casa del Ojo de Agua* ('house of the waterhole', which I think is the equivalent in Spanish of a 'bolthole' or 'weekend house') were designed as a bedroom and a dining room. The other spaces of the house – kitchen etc. – are accommodated in a separate building nearby, also designed by Ada Dewes and Sergio Puente.

Basic elements and identification of place

La Casa del Ojo de Agua is an example of how the idea of a house might be rethought from first principles. Although it will be seen to be reminiscent of a particular historic precedent apt to Mexico, its form is a composition of basic elements of architecture composed according to context and content. Rather than accept the orthodox architectural idea of 'house' the architects have reassessed each

1

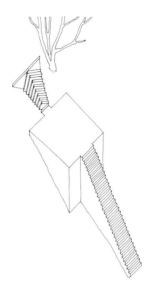

2

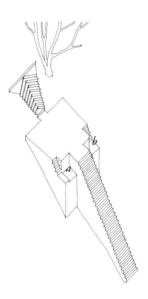

3

element according to what it does and whether or not it is actually needed. The elements of an orthodox house that are absent from this design have been omitted for particular reasons that make the house a more interesting place to be.

The best way to understand the architecture of a building is by analysing its conceptual build-up or composition. The order in which one explores the conceptual build-up of a work of architecture is not necessarily the same as the order in which the building was actually constructed physically. Such analysis is also usually something of a *post hoc* rationalisation because the processes of design are rarely simple and straightforward; they depend on ideas that sometimes seem to come from nowhere and refinements that can go through many iterations. Nevertheless, analysis exposes the ideas manifest in the resultant work.

La Casa del Ojo de Agua begins with an almost rectangular platform built by a large mango tree on a steep hillside (*1*). For clarity I have left out most of the context but you should imagine this platform amongst large exposed rocks and surrounded by dense vegetation. It also stands just above a stream at the bottom of the slope; small tributaries to the stream run alongside the platform.

The platform is the starting point for the house. It relates to the tree that is already there but represents the generative moment when things change. It establishes architecture in the midst of the forest, rocks and stream. It manifests the presence of the mind of the architect. It identifies a place where things can happen – *chora*. It changes the world.

The place the platform establishes is one for human habitation. It is by creating this level area, amongst the general irregularity of

the ground, that a certain sort of habitation is made possible. The platform makes a horizontal surface, which is more comfortable; you can stand there steady and certain of where you are. You can move around on the platform easily. It makes possible the use of furniture, which needs a flat surface to stand upon. Immediately the platform makes a place distinct from the world around, a rudimentary 'temple' dedicated to the human presence in the world.

The next stage in the conceptual generation of the architecture of this house is the provision of steps (*2*). Steps in chevron lead down the slope to the platform and a long straight flight leads down from the platform to the stream. The steps, acting as pathways to and from the platform, extend its presence into the land around. Their

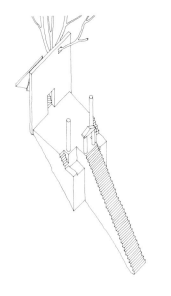

4

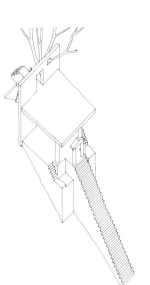

5

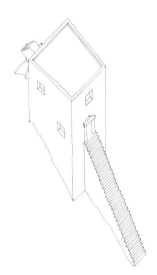

6

position establishes thresholds – specific points of entry onto and exit from the platform. They also make the platform into an in-between place, a point of stasis on a route between the hill and the stream or *vice versa*. Imagine stepping down onto the platform, pausing to survey the scene, and seeing the flight of steps suggesting/offering a precarious descent to the stream below. Imagine too the effort of climbing back up the long flight of steps, achieving the level surface of the platform, the 'temple' above, where you can pause and rest. This platform is the bedroom of the house.

The first two stages in the conceptual development of this house are elemental, timeless in their architectural power. The third is more particular (*3*). The corners of the platform are taken away to

make a small place for a shower (*a*) and to provide access down to a lavatory under the top of the long flight of steps (*b*).

The fourth stage returns to the elemental, evoking the timeless powers of architecture (*4*). A wall is built across the uphill threshold onto the platform, screening it from the approach, providing privacy but also making the platform even more like a stage on which the performances of domestic life happen. The wall also frames the threshold from the chevron steps, providing it with a doorway for entrances and exits. A small opening in the wall accommodates one large branch of the mango tree. Another doorway frames the threshold to the steps leading down to the stream. This doorway is like a temple in itself, composed of two columns and a triangular pediment.

Two other columns stand further onto the platform. These frame the doorway to the long flight of steps and also, with the wall, help to frame the space of the bedroom. They also support the upper floor (*5*), which has its own doorway through the wall. Steps and a small bridge over the chevron steps lead to this doorway. This upper floor is the dining room. The inner surface of the wall, in the dining room and the bedroom below, is plastered as if it was an interior wall. The other walls of these two rooms are provided by trees around, though the three open faces of the bedroom are provided with mosquito mesh screens. The roof of the dining room is the canopy of the mango tree.

In a more conventional arrangement the house would have four walls, with windows and a roof (*6*). The character of the rooms and their relationship with their surroundings would be very different. *La Casa del Ojo de Agua* is as simple in its conception as a

1

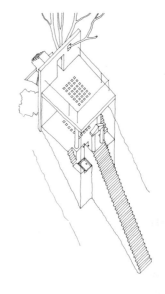

2

child's drawing of a house (*1*) but without three of the walls and with no roof other than that provided by the tree.

Finally, in addition to the mosquito mesh enclosing the bedroom, the dining room is provided with a thin steel rail as a balustrade (*2*). Glass blocks are let into the floors; those in the floor of the dining room help to light the bedroom below. In his description of *La Casa del Ojo de Agua* in *Modern House* (1995, p. 146), John Welsh suggests those in the floor of the bedroom allow views of a stream passing under the house.

Stratification; transition, hierarchy and heart

La Casa del Ojo de Agua is more or less symmetrical about one central longitudinal axis that stretches through the chevron steps and the steps up to the dining room, through the bedroom and doorway at the top of the long flight of steps, and down to the stream (*4*). Along this axis there are various levels, with different characteristics (*3*). The dining room is at the uppermost level, open to the canopy of the mango tree above and to the forest on three of four sides. The bedroom is at the middle, in-between level. It has a ceiling above, and is open on three sides to the forest. But that openness is modified by the columns and the free-standing doorway, and veiled by the mesh of the mosquito screen. The stream is the lowest level.

This arrangement produces a hierarchy of spaces, with the dining room and bedroom vying to be the heart of the house. The status probably alternates according to weather and time of day.

There are three different transitions. First there is that from the hill, up the short flight of steps, across the bridge and through the doorway into the dining room, where one finds oneself on an elevated platform amongst the trees. Second is that from the hill down the chevron steps and through the doorway into the bedroom, where one finds oneself in a space more like a room. Third is the passage out through the free-standing doorway and down the precarious steps to the stream below.

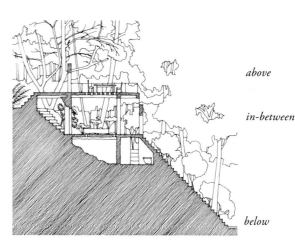

above

in-between

below

3

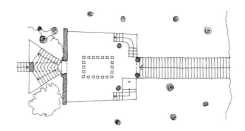

4

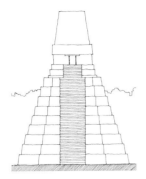

5

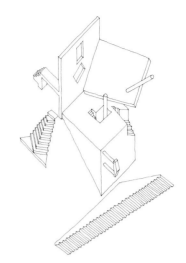

6

Primitive place types

Appropriately, the arrangement of *La Casa del Ojo de Agua* is reminiscent of a Mayan or Inca temple (*5*) with its long flight of steep steps leading up to a doorway into a cell at the top. Whereas such temples were places of sacrifice – with severed heads being thrown still bleeding down the steps – *La Casa del Ojo de Agua* is a temple to the things one does in a dining room or bedroom, with table and bed as altars for different purposes.

Conclusion: notes on sense in architecture

The words and punctuation of the present sentence could be rearranged to produce nonsense. The effect of losing grammar is unnerving, irritating, unsatisfactory:

punctuation words The the nonsense of and could. present produce be sentence to rearranged

Without the grammar there is no meaning. The assemblage of words becomes more a puzzle, a challenge to our sense of sense. As the philosopher Ludwig Wittgenstein suggested, meaning in language resides less in the individual words themselves and more in the grammar of the ways in which those words are put together.

Something similar can happen in architecture. The equivalents of words in architecture are the basic architectural elements of floor, wall, roof etc. The equivalent of meaning (at one conceptual level at least) is place – a place for eating, a place for sleeping, a place for entering etc.

Even though it is hardly a conventional house, the elements of *La Casa del Ojo de Agua* are arranged to make architectural sense. They could be rearranged to make architectural nonsense (*6*). The nonsense in this drawing is in various dimensions. There is constructional nonsense in that some elements defy gravity and constructional pragmatism. But there is also spatial nonsense: steps leading nowhere; doorways out of place; spaces that deny rather than accommodate inhabitation (i.e. they do not make places for the various activities of, in this case, domestic life).

By contrast the actual *Casa del Ojo de Agua* is like a neat, well-constructed sentence which progresses along its longitudinal axis. You approach, either ascend or descend steps, pass through a doorway which is like a colon: then you find yourself in another situation. Ascending to the dining room you reach a full-stop. Going down into the bedroom there is a further (optional) clause through another 'colon': you can pass through the free-standing doorway and descend to the stream below.

In language, nonsense and the breaking of grammar are used in various ways. Lewis Carroll wrote nonsense poems such as 'Jaberwocky' (1872) –

'Twas brillig and the slithy toves
Did gyre and gimble in the wabe:
All mimsy were the borogoves,
And the mome raths outgrabe.

– which, because of its grammar and evocative invented words, still manages to conjure images in the mind.

James Joyce, in *Ulysses* (1922), wrote whole chapters without punctuation –

'… I tasted one with my finger dipped out of that American that had the squirrel talking stamps with father he had all he could do to keep himself from falling asleep after the last time we took the port and…'

13

– mimicking the ways thoughts stream through our conscious minds.

As in language, architectural nonsense can be used as a 'literary' device or for philosophical comment. Examples include: Robert Venturi's Vanna Venturi House (see *Analysing Architecture*, Case Study 7), which contains a staircase to nowhere, and Peter Eisenman's House VI (*Analysing Architecture*, Case Study 9), which as well as having an inverted staircase to nowhere in the ceiling, has a column that gets in the way of the dining table and a glazed slot in the bedroom floor that (initially at least) prevented the clients from using a double bed.

But in *La Casa del Ojo de Agua*, despite it being an unusual house, we are presented with architectural sense.

References and other relevant publications, websites, broadcasts:

Frances Anderton – 'Jungle House', in *AR Architectural Review*, June 1991, pp. 42-47.

John Welsh – *Modern House*, Phaidon, London, 1995, pp. 144-147.

NEUENDORF HOUSE

'I know of no more beautiful effect than to be secluded on all sides, insulated against the turmoil of the world, and to see above, free, the sky. In the evening.'

Friedrich Gilly, quoted in Neumeyer
– *The Artless Word*, 1991, p. 217.

NEUENDORF HOUSE

A holiday home on the island of Mallorca
JOHN PAWSON and CLAUDIO SILVESTRIN, 1987-89

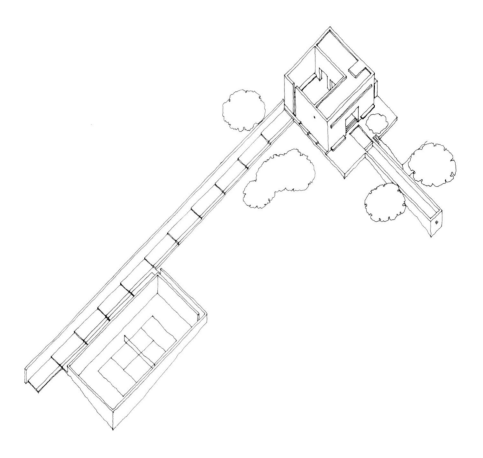

Musicians write *études* (studies) to explore what is possible within a particular form or set of musical parameters. John Pawson and Claudio Silvestrin's house on the island of Mallorca is an architectural *étude*. The possibilities it explores are those of the wall. Using little more than this most basic of basic architectural elements, the architecture of the Neuendorf House takes the person through a series of experiences. The house has an introduction – a slow drawn-out crescendo. It has a moment of transition – an instant when mounting anticipation is replaced with trepidation, a change of key. Through the transition the mood changes – movement along a clear direction is replaced with relative stasis, it slows, uncertain, trying to find a centre. The climax, which projects the mind into the far distance, into a world changed by the experience of entrance,

is a moment of revelation. Experiencing the house is the spatial equivalent of listening to a short passage of music.

If architecture is like language, then wall is a verb. 'To wall' is the process of building – placing stone upon stone, brick upon brick – but a wall remains a verb when it is finished. Architecturally, a wall achieves its status as a verb once it is built. Walls are often thought of as dumb and immobile. But to an architect a wall is an instrument. Walls do things. They are powerful. They set the rules by which space is organised and experienced. The Neuendorf House is an exercise in what walls can do.

The architecture of John Pawson, and of Claudio Silvestrin, who since building this house together have worked separately, is usually characterised as minimalist, austere. They make buildings

1 section along entrance path

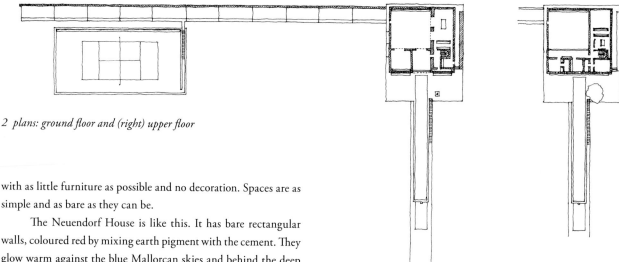

2 plans: ground floor and (right) upper floor

with as little furniture as possible and no decoration. Spaces are as simple and as bare as they can be.

The Neuendorf House is like this. It has bare rectangular walls, coloured red by mixing earth pigment with the cement. They glow warm against the blue Mallorcan skies and behind the deep green Mediterranean trees. There are almost no windows; those there are are tiny rectangular openings in the walls. Some walls have no more than one tiny window. One has a regularly spaced row of them, like an insistent beat. Others are camouflaged, hidden in a long horizontal slit like the visor of a helmet (3). More than austere, the architecture of the Neuendorf House is severe, even daunting. Inscrutable on its hilltop, it is more like a castle than a house. Except that it has a tennis court, a terrace for sunbathing and a swimming pool, internally it makes very few concessions to the fact that it is for vacations.

Geometry

The form of the house is strictly orthogonal. Apart from a curved wall screening off the bathroom upstairs and the winding stair hidden away, excavated from its own block of solid matter, everything is rectangular, perfect, sharp-edged. The approach path is straight, climbing regular steps. The roof is horizontal, the walls vertical. The swimming pool is a long rectangle stretching along an axis. The small windows are square. Even the bath is a rectangular block.

As one might expect, the house appears to have been designed on a ideal geometric matrix (6 and 7). The main block is based on a square divided into thirds to make nine smaller squares. A courtyard,

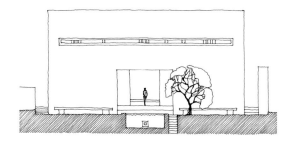

3 south elevation

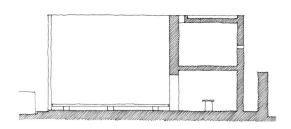

4 section through entrance slit, courtyard and dining room

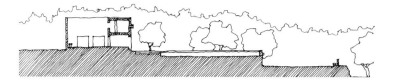

5 section through courtyard and swimming pool

open to the sky, occupies four of these. The living accommodation – dining room, bedrooms, utility spaces etc. – takes up the other five. On the south side, the middle third is an open loggia facing the swimming pool. The courtyard too is divided into thirds, with its entrance from the approach path – a thin slit, the full height of the wall – situated on one of the 'third' lines.

As is usual, the precision of the ideal geometry is confused by the thicknesses of the walls. Ideal geometry can be a crutch, a help in making decisions about the relative positions and sizes of things when no other deciding criteria are apparent. In the Neuendorf House it appears to have been used to achieve the repose and calmness thought to be lent to spaces that are proportioned according to simple geometric ratios.

Basic element: wall

Although the Neuendorf House might be interpreted as an abstract composition of elements – a 'masterly, correct and magnificent play of masses brought together in light' – its architecture operates in other dimensions too. Most notably it involves the modifying element of time, the time it takes. It is not a building merely to be looked at, but experienced. As has already been suggested, it is a building that takes the person 'by the hand' and leads them on a journey equivalent to hearing a piece of music.

And, as has also already been mentioned, the instrument by which the Neuendorf House orchestrates experience is the wall. As in listening to music, the journey is emotional.

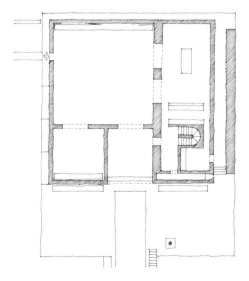

6 ground floor plan

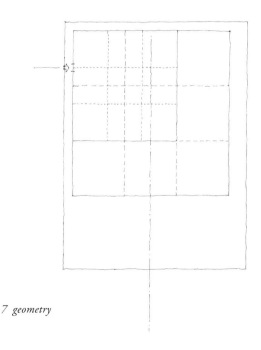

7 geometry

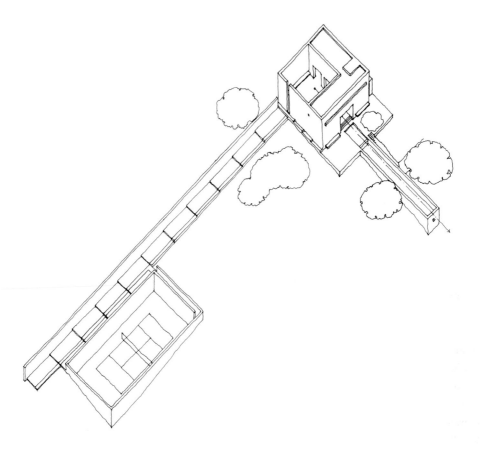

The journey begins when the house sends out, metaphorically projects, a 'telescopic' pathway to meet you on arrival. It is as if the hosts have come to meet you at the entrance to their estate, and to lead you to the house. The path, with steps widely spaced, determines your line of approach. The wall alongside ushers you forward, managing what you see and what you do not. Just as the host would, the wall takes you by the arm and gently accompanies you on the climb.

On your right as you begin the ascent is the pit of the tennis court within its own high blank walls (see the later analysis of *Il Danteum*), accessed down a stair confined in a narrow space between two parallel walls. The wall of the tennis court, along with the wall that accompanies the pathway to the house, suggests a gateway into the castle's domain.

The stepped pathway with the perspective of the wall alongside, gradually diminishing in height as you climb higher, is focused directly on the tall narrow slit in the wall of the house in front of you. It is a geometrically perfect crevice in the cliff face that is the wall. The wall is a barrier but the slit offers the possibility of penetration.

This slit is your goal. Apart from one tiny square window high on the right this wall has no other features. In the evening it blazes with the reflected orange light of the setting sun.

You approach the wall and its slit with anticipation. The climb is slow and slightly arduous. The architect, like a film director, engineers suspense. As you near the slit there is one last step up onto a platform. Then, between the walls, there is another, the threshold into the courtyard. As you tend to at any threshold into someone else's world, you hesitate. The wall has, until you got near, hidden what is inside. Now you can peer through the slit to see if it is safe to enter. It takes a slight effort of will to go in.

Once you pass through the wall you are in a different place. The threshold is a fault line in space. The courtyard is separated from the world, almost completely. There is nothing natural about this space. It is the space of a mind, a bare stage set. Here the stories are not of the mindless processes of nature but of human will and relationships. You look up and see the blue or starry sky. The walls of the house are around you, but they are hardly less severe and uncompromising than the external walls. There are two rectangular

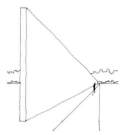

1

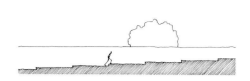

2

openings in front of you, leading into the bare dining room with its altar-like table at its centre. On the upper floor to your right is a balcony. Perhaps someone greets you from there.

Becoming more confident, and looking around at the enigmatic space in which you find yourself, you wander further into the square courtyard. You see, under the balcony, a broad doorway. You position yourself to look through it and are confronted by the climax: the long swimming pool stretching into space. The house frames you at its very centre as you are spellbound by the perspective – the perfectly level surface of the water reflecting the sky with the deep dark green of the trees beyond – all set like a perfectly composed picture within the rectangle of the loggia, a subtly moving image projected onto a wall that is not there.

As a coda, following the climax of the piece, you go through the wide doorway into the loggia, between the courtyard and the pool. You find at its edge two very high steps that make it uncomfortable, if not impossible, to descend to the terrace and swimming pool outside. You are caught in the mind-world of the house. It insists you remain in its matrix as a spectator of the framed moving image of the pool and landscape outside. (Intermediate steps were later installed to make the descent from the loggia to the terrace easier.)

Conclusion: the powers of the wall

All architects are like gods. They make worlds for people to inhabit. In the Neuendorf House, John Pawson and Claudio Silvestrin are manipulative gods. Like puppeteers, they dangle people by strings, playing with their emotions, leading them along pathways and across thresholds, testing and astonishing them. Like composers and film directors they build suspense, provoke uncertainty, and provide resolution. Architecture is the means by which they do this. And in this house their chief instrument is the wall.

First there is the wall that greets you at the beginning and guides and accompanies you on the climb up the steps towards the

house (*1*). The top of this wall is horizontal so the effective height of the wall diminishes as you get nearer to the house; it becomes less dominating (*2*).

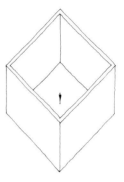

3

The house is contained within a square enclosure of walls all the same height (*3*). These walls define a special zone separated from everywhere else, a zone which is artificial, determined by the minds of its architects. The tennis court alongside the approach path is a walled enclosure too. It is accessed by steps channelled down a narrow passage between two parallel walls (*4*). These become higher as you descend. They release you at the bottom into the space of the court, defined by its high walls and with the sun casting slanting shadows.

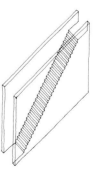

4

1

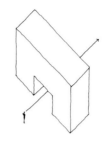

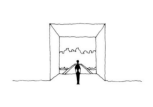

2

The only way through the barrier of the walls of the house, the only access into the enclosure, is through a narrow gap – the slit (*1*). The high walls define this fault line between outside and inside.

Inside, the courtyard is walled on two sides by the living accommodation. Through one of these is a large opening, the loggia, establishing an axis that strikes out into the landscape and framing the perspective of the long swimming pool (*2*). Elsewhere small square openings in the walls make tiny pictures of the world outside (*3*).

3

As well as providing the screens onto which the light of the sun and shadows are projected, walls also screen (in a different sense) the interiors. The wall between the courtyard and the dining room is perforated by two large openings (*4*). This wall is thicker than the rest to make the whole building appear more substantial. It plays its part in a relationship between the inside, the controlled outside of the courtyard, and the narrow entrance slit that gives a view of the approach path. The one curved wall in the house screens the bathroom upstairs (*5*).

Walls also provide the back rests to the benches (*6*).

6

The Neuendorf House is an object lesson in using walls to do things. It makes clear that, like other art forms, architecture involves time. It need not be comfortable. It may presume the lifestyle of a monk. But this is a house incomplete without the person. It is a transaction between the architects and those who visit and use it.

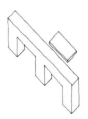

4   *5*

References and other relevant publications, websites, broadcasts:

Mark Alden Branch – 'Light architecture', in *Progressive Architecture* Volume 73, Number 11, November 1992, pp. 76-79.

John Welsh – *Modern House*, Phaidon, London, 1995, pp. 28-35.

http://www.johnpawson.com/architecture/residential/europe/neuendorfhouse

http://www.claudiosilvestrin.com/
  (follow the links to 'Projects', 'Buildings', 'Neuendorf Villa')

BARCELONA PAVILION

'Before my eyes there seems to emerge, as a vision, a hitherto unimagined mode of superlative historical research that is truly Western… a comprehensive Physiognomic of all existence, a morphology of becoming for all *humanity that drives onward to the highest and last ideas… This philosophic view – to which we and we alone are entitled by virtue of our analytic mathematic, our contrapunctal music and our perspective painting – in that its scope far transcends the scheme of the systematist, presupposes the eye of an artist, and of an artist who can feel the whole sensible and apprehensible environment dissolve into a deep infinity of mysterious relationships.'*

Oswald Spengler, translated by Atkinson
– *The Decline of the West* (1918), 1932, p. 224.

BARCELONA PAVILION

Built as the German Pavilion at the Barcelona Universal Exposition
MIES VAN DER ROHE, 1929

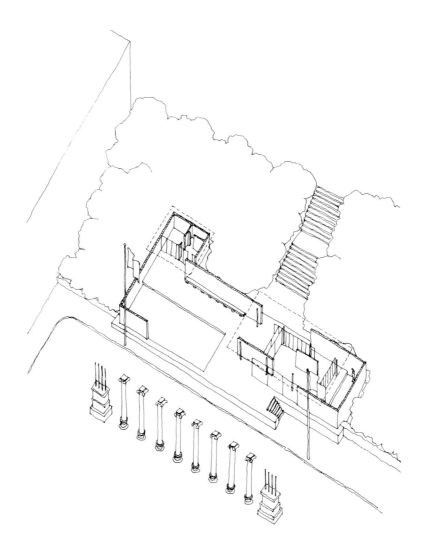

Mies van der Rohe's German Pavilion at the Barcelona Universal Exposition of 1929, known simply as the Barcelona Pavilion, was designed and built some twenty years before his Farnsworth House (see pages 61-80). Though the Farnsworth House has been identified as a significant work of architecture in the twentieth century, the Barcelona Pavilion is even more so; it is one of the seminal works of all time; its power and influence has grown rather than dissipated in the eighty years since it was built.

The pavilion's broad context – in Europe midway between the two World Wars in which Germany was a principal protagonist – was infinitely more charged politically than that of the later Farnsworth House built in the peaceful sylvan landscape of rural Illinois. As a contribution to an international exposition, set in juxtaposition to pavilions of other countries, the Barcelona Pavilion was intended as a symbol for a nation that had reinvented itself – as what is historically know as the Weimar Republic – after the social and cultural

* For an account of the research into the original Barcelona Pavilion and of its reconstruction in the 1980s see: **Ignasi de Solà Morales, Cristian Cirici and Fernando Ramos** – *Mies van der Rohe: Barcelona Pavilion*, Editorial Gustavo Gili SA, Barcelona, 1993.

upheaval of the First World War. These challenges and conditions, perhaps assisted by the short time in which the project had to be designed and completed, stimulated Mies to produce one of the most startling works of architecture in history.

Only a few years after the pavilion was built, in 1933, political power in Germany was taken by the National Socialist movement and its dictatorial leader Adolf Hitler. The Nazis rejected modernism as an expression of German identity in favour of an austere and monumental classicism for public and governmental buildings, and domestic building derived from traditional folk architecture. Four years later, in 1937, Mies moved to the United States.

From inception to completion Mies had less than a year to negotiate a site for, design and supervise the construction of the Barcelona Pavilion. The commission provided him with an opportunity to bring to realisation in built form architectural ideas he (and others) had been exploring during the preceding decade. These ideas concerned the use of new materials and construction techniques, as well as no less than a reinvention of architectural space. After the horrors of the First World War, they were ideas that promised a new cultural language of architecture, a new way of making sense of the world.

Mies van der Rohe's own development of these ideas was conditioned by his self-education in classical architecture and philosophy, and fed by contemporary archaeological discoveries. It exploited the fresh possibilities of materials such as steel and large sheets of glass put together without applied ornament. In the Barcelona Pavilion, Mies also employed more traditional materials, used in architecture of all times, such as travertine (a sedimentary rock quarried in Italy and used by Mies in relatively thin slabs as paving and to clad some of the walls), polished marble (two types – one from Greece, the other from the Valle d'Aosta in north-west Italy – both with a strong ingrained pattern, also used as relatively thin wall cladding) and rare onyx (from North Africa, used for one particular wall at the core of the pavilion).

The Barcelona Pavilion is a poem in architectural form. Its underlying theme relates to how Western culture could achieve, through expression in space, the 'Destiny Idea' (as Oswald Spengler had called it after the First World War in his then popular book *The Decline of the West*) towards which it had (according to Spengler and other theorists of history) been striving for nearly a millennium. Whether or not that political/historical aspiration was ever met, the Barcelona Pavilion has influenced generations of architects not only as an example of fluid spatial composition and minimalist detailing using highly finished materials, but also as an example of how an individual architect can promulgate ideas, through the medium of architecture, that aspire to philosophical propositions.

The pavilion was dismantled almost immediately after the Exposition. For the following half-century its existence persisted only in a collection of black and white photographs and some preparatory design drawings. But, in its absence and consequent mythic status, the building's reputation grew through the following decades until in the 1980s, after the fiftieth anniversary of its first manifestation and leading up to the centenary of Mies's birth in 1986, moves were made to recreate it. The building now standing on the original site at the western end of the Gran Plaza de la Fuente Mágica in Barcelona is a carefully researched reincarnation.*

The Barcelona Pavilion is one of the most enigmatic, engaging and hence most extensively discussed buildings in all of architectural literature. The bibliography at the end of this analysis has room for no more than a small selection of the many essays and books that attempt to understand what it is about.

Using things that are there

When the opportunity is there, the first architectural decision in any project is to decide on a specific location; orientation and relationships to what is already there are essential ingredients in every work of architecture that is built (or does not move). Although the

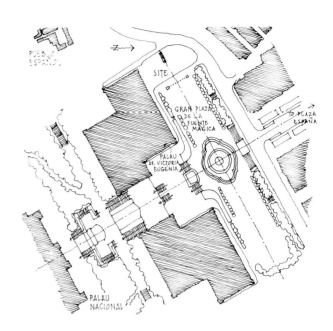

1 (north is to the right)

Barcelona Pavilion is often presented in drawings as an abstract composition free of context (and which would therefore be more or less the same anywhere) it was, in its original form and in its recreation (though missing one significant element), tied firmly into its location. Mies negotiated with the Exposition authorities to obtain a particular site in preference to the one they had allocated. His choice shows how he was attracted by features that were already there and to which he related his own design, using them as part of the overall composition.

The Exposition was held in and around the monumental buildings, designed according to Beaux Arts principles (generally neo-classical, arranged according to axes of symmetry) rising up grand flights of steps to the Palau Nacional, a museum of Catalonian art. According to de Solà Morales,* the Germans were first offered a site for their pavilion at the bottom of the steps. Mies rejected this in favour of a site at the western end of the Gran Plaza de la Fuente Mágica (1). This site had features conducive to the architectural ideas Mies wanted to explore (2). It gave him something to work with; he did not design the Barcelona Pavilion in a vacuum.

Apart from the way the site looks out across the esplanade of the Gran Plaza, there were four existing elements that contributed to Mies's design. First was the slope, upwards away from the Gran Plaza, which would place the pavilion on a raised level like a precious object on its own podium. Second was the route across the site, rising up some short flights of steps aligned with the central axis of the Gran Plaza and leading in the direction of the Pueblo Español (a permanent exhibition of traditional Spanish buildings). Third was the massive north wall of the adjacent Palau Victoria Eugenia, almost always in shadow. And fourth was a row of Ionic columns also centred on the axis of the Gran Plaza, but now gone. These elements formed what might be called a 'Miesian' composition in their own right. A 'Miesian' composition might be defined as consisting in distinct architectural elements – in this case a route, a wall and a row of columns – arranged in an orthogonal relationship

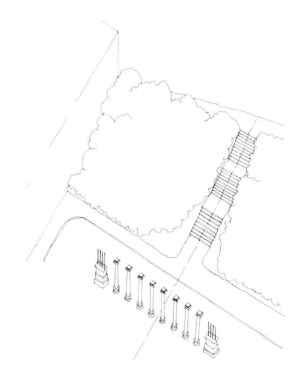

2 (the orientation of this drawing is rotated, approximately 60° to the right, in relation to the site plan above.)

27

but not touching. It is understandable that Mies saw here a setting sympathetic to his own ideas.

First move

Mies's first design move was to make a platform (*1*) – a stage on which to perform his architecture. Veiled from the Gran Plaza by the curtain of Ionic columns, this platform was rectangular and bedded into the slope. It was oriented at right angles to the wall of the Palau Victoria Eugenia and parallel to the row of Ionic columns but was not centred on the axis of the Gran Plaza. Drawings prepared for the scheme (some of which are published in de Solà Morales, 1993) suggest that Mies mused on whether this platform should be

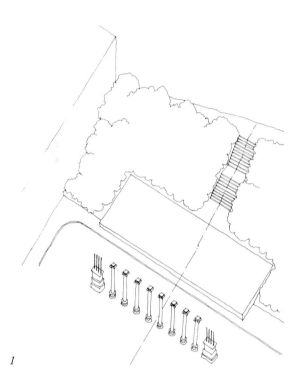

1

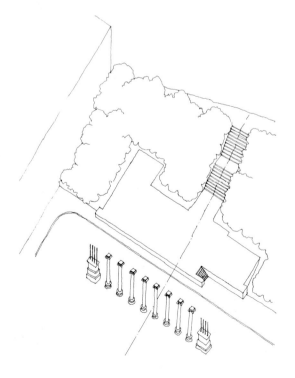

2

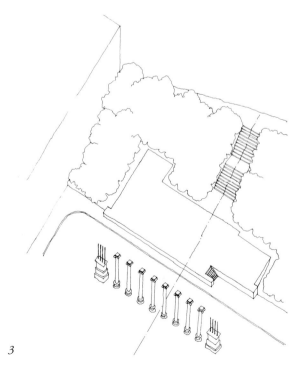

3

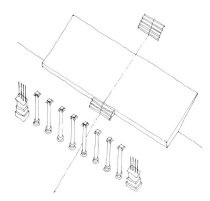

4

thought of as a discrete platform (as shown in *1*) or as the equivalent of a rocky outcrop/ledge emerging from the slope (*2*) and with its surface reaching to the steps. The platform needed its own access steps, also avoiding the Gran Plaza's axis.

The rule of asymmetry – playing with an axis rather than following its authority – is essential to the seminal character of the Barcelona Pavilion. In a Beaux Arts scheme both the platform and the approach steps would be aligned on the axis (*4*). Although Mies acknowledged the axis of the Gran Plaza – he drew it onto his design drawings – he dealt with it in subtle ways.

The platform as built is shown in *3*. Its rectangle is modified in a number of places to accommodate an office (at the back left corner) and to avoid its travertine cladding running into the slope

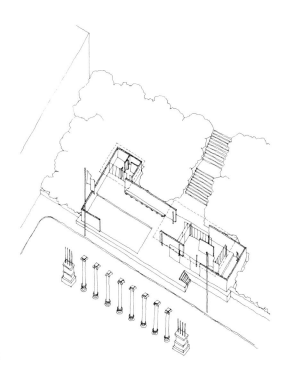

5

(the two nibs extending sideways at the front corners of the platform). Generally these deviations from the rectangle are not noticed when one visits the pavilion; it appears a discrete and rectangular platform. On its upper side, away from the Gran Plaza, the paving stops at the notional edge of the platform's rectangle rather than reaching to the bottom of the steps. Though this might appear to be a minor detail, it is significant; this threshold (a slight step) between the paving of the platform and the ground's surface affirms the platform as a discrete entity and reinforces the sense that the pavilion exists in its own special realm somehow apart from the real world. Mies's musing on extending the paving to the steps suggests he was thinking about the platform as part of the route from the Gran Plaza up towards the Pueblo Español. He decided against emphasising this rôle, though it was not dismissed completely.

The superstructure of the pavilion is erected on this platform (*5*). The drawing shows it as a composition related to the features already there. The route provided a line of movement on which the pavilion could create an event. The massive wall of the Palau Victoria Eugenia provided the pavilion with a backdrop, almost always in shade and appearing in many iconic photographs of the building as a glowering 'sky' enhancing the pavilion's brightness. And the line of Ionic columns separated the pavilion from the Gran Plaza de la Fuente Mágica. As one approached across the plaza, the columns would have created a sense of mystery and anticipation, reinforcing the pavilion's otherness – its difference from the Beaux Arts buildings around. Once on the pavilion's platform they would have been the equivalent of the screen of trees along the riverbank by the Farnsworth House (see page 68), providing an extra layer through which the outside world was seen. The columns defined a threshold between an outside and an inside – between the open esplanade of the Gran Plaza and the pavilion's own special domain. They gave the pavilion a detached portico, such as one would see on a neo-classical building. They are redolent of the loggia/portico along the front of one of the nineteenth century buildings by Karl

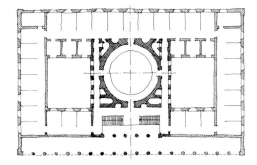

1

2 the stair of the Altes Museum, seen in cutaway from inside

Friedrich Schinkel, whose work Mies admired – the Altes Museum in Berlin (*1*), which also has Ionic columns. To suggest Mies had this precedent in mind is speculation but it seems plausible, in regard to the Barcelona Pavilion, that he did see the dramatic potential of situating his building behind a row of columns; in a way similar to that in which the celebrated stair of the Altes Museum is screened behind its columns (*2*).

Basic elements

The Miesian composition of existing features (*3*), along with the platform (*4*), constitute the first basic elements of the Barcelona Pavilion. Subsequent elements are arranged on the horizontal surface of the platform – the blank sheet of paper Mies created as the artificially perfect ground for his composition of walls, columns, pits, roofs…. This composition may be deconstructed into its component elements (*5-9*). This is not the order in which Mies conceived the

design nor is it the sequence in which the pavilion was constructed but breaking it up in this way and building up the composition in steps helps describe how the design is organised conceptually.

The first element is a flat rectangular roof, floating parallel to the platform's top surface and supported on eight evenly spaced columns (*5*). There is also a smaller roof over the area to be occupied by the office. Spatially, these roofs establish a horizontal layer of space – between ground and sky – within which Mies makes his spatial composition with walls. The roof on its columns is an aedicule that might be thought of as a temple or propylon (*6*) across the route. Although this aedicule is symmetrical in itself, it follows the rule of asymmetry in that it is positioned off the axis of the plaza, which passes approximately two fifths the way across the first intercolumnar space.

The next element is the solid (non-glass) wall (*7*). Most of these solid walls wrap around the edge of the platform, forming a fragmented enclosure like a temenos around its temple or a courtyard

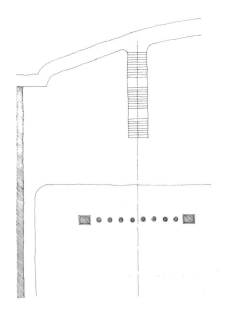

3

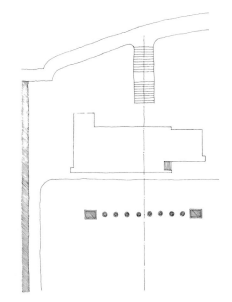

4

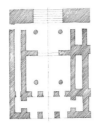

6 a propylon – a building that straddles a route – in the Palace of Minos, Knossos, Crete

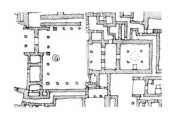

8 the megaron with its courtyard at the heart of the palace of Tiryns; it too has a propylon at the left

in front of a Mycenean or Minoan megaron (*8*). But two shorter walls, without corners, stand free. The longer of these (*a*) does not merely play with the plaza's axis, it blocks it. On its own, this wall asserts the underlying principle of the spatial composition. By interrupting the axis of movement it makes a place to linger. Together with the arrangement of the access steps onto the platform, this wall controls the way a person is allowed to move across the site. While the position and orientation of the access steps insist that you cannot ascend to the platform along the line of axis, this wall prevents you, once on the platform, regaining that axis; it insists you go either to the left or the right. The age old use of architecture to establish a reliable axis – a datum (as provided by many religious and public buildings) onto which one may hold through uncertainty – is contradicted. This wall is a political manifesto.

The labyrinth of the Barcelona Pavilion has begun. To the left is a courtyard open to the sky, to the right a megaron under its roof – a classic juxtaposition, but in this case one where walls have been relieved of their traditional rôles of supporting a roof and isolating a completely enclosed space from everywhere else, and reinforced in their rôles as screens and instruments for managing movement.

The shorter free standing wall (*b*) stands inside, under the roof, alongside the central axis of the megaron. In all the composition, this is the wall that comes closest to establishing a heart for the pavilion. This wall may be compared to the wall behind the throne in the megaron of Tiryns (*8*) (as well as the core of the Farnsworth House). In the 1929 Exposition the pavilion was inaugurated by King Alfonso XIII of Spain. Maybe Mies considered placing one of his specially designed chairs against this wall as a throne? In the event, the contemporary photographs show a table (an altar) against this wall on its central axis (like the fireplace in the Farnsworth House) with a pair of chairs to one side. Ludwig Glaeser reported that 'the principal function (of the pavilion) was the inaugural ceremony in which the Spanish King was to sign his name into a "golden book". The table for the book stood against the onyx wall, which clearly

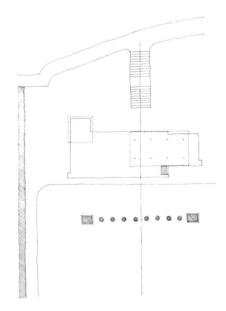

5

7 wall b also appears to be positioned on the centre line of the platform as a whole (without subtractions), i.e. midway between lines x and y (see Psarra, 2009, p. 49)

'Architecture is the will of an epoch translated into space.'

Mies van der Rohe (1923), quoted in Johnson, 1978, p. 188.

identified the ritual center' (Bonta, 1979, p. 208).

All the walls to the courtyard are clad in the same travertine stone as the platform. All those to the megaron are clad in the coloured and highly patterned marbles and onyx mentioned above. This difference suggests Mies wanted a qualitative difference between the two zones. The rarest and most valuable stone – the onyx – was reserved to clad the 'altar' wall.

The next elements in this compositional build up are the walls of clear but tinted glass (*9*). These introduce views through from one space to another: from the platform access steps into the megaron; from the interior of the megaron to the inner courtyard; and from the interior of the megaron up the slope towards the steps. They also form, in concert with the solid walls, the closest the pavilion has to doorways (*a* and *b*). These are the points at which the original pavilion had removable doors used for closing the pavilion up at night, and where the present pavilion has permanent doors. (The permanent doors are anathema to the ideas of fluid space and uncer-

tain separation of inside and out that are intrinsic to the pavilion's design, but necessary for security.) The glass walls also contribute to the labyrinthine quality of the pavilion, breaking up the routes around and through it. A further glass wall encloses the front of the office, allowing it a view over the courtyard.

The last wall to be added to the composition, conceptually that is, is a double wall of translucent white glass (*c*) blocking the axial view from the interior of the megaron out to the courtyard and similarly blocking any exit from or entry to the megaron along that axis (*10*). The double wall also creates a portico (*d*), but one with no doorway, looking out to the courtyard and shaded by the roof. This double wall has a rooflight over its inaccessible cavity, so that its glows mysteriously. It also contains artificial lighting so it glows in the dark.

The glass and polished stone walls are like mirrors. So too are the surfaces of two rectangular pools of water, a small one almost filling the small courtyard and a large one out in the main courtyard

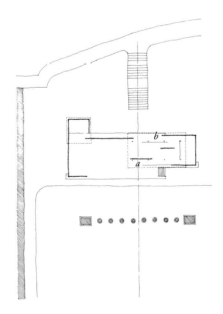

9

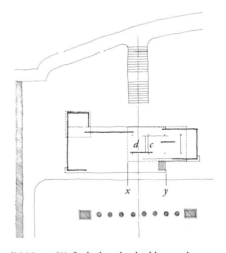

10 Psarra (2009, p. 49) finds that the double translucent wall c is positioned on the centre line between the edge of the roof and the beginning of the steps, i.e. midway between lines x and y

(*11*). These pools add to the labyrinthine quality of the pavilion by creating inaccessible areas where one may only stand at the edge, look across, and maybe look down at one's own reflection. Reflection is an essential element in the Barcelona Pavilion. Here overlapping and confusing reflections make the visual experience of the pavilion complex. They also, as noted by Robin Evans in 'Mies van der Rohe's Paradoxical Symmetries' (1990), introduce symmetries not apparent in the building's drawn composition. Whereas the two halves of a symmetrical building can be said to be mirrored about its central axis, in the Barcelona Pavilion symmetries are literally mirrored, vertically and horizontally, in the reflective surfaces of glass, polished stone and water.

The composition of walls of different types, together with the pools, completes the labyrinth of the Barcelona Pavilion. The final two elements indicated in *11* are: a statue standing on a plinth in the small pool (*e*), apparently shielding her eyes from the sun, and visible in many photographs framed in 'doorway' *b*; and a black carpet (*f*) reinforcing the place-making rôle of the 'altar' wall. The statue provides a focus of attention, and a symbolic representation of 'the person' to whom this 'temple' is dedicated (see also Bonta, 1979, p. 208). In shielding its eyes from the sun the statue draws attention to the upward direction that the generally horizontality of the design denies. The surface of the pool in which she stands reflects her upside down, drawing attention to the downwards direction too. The black carpet by the 'altar' wall is the equivalent of the hearth in the ancient megaron; it defines a special area of ground on which the table stood. (The sandy yellow of the travertine stone pavement and cladding, the black of the carpet and the red of the curtains used to reduce the sun through the east-facing glass wall, approximate to the yellow, black and red of the German national flag. In 1929, Spanish and German flags were flown on the two flagpoles shown in the drawing on the first page of this analysis. Nowadays, they carry the flags of Barcelona and of the European Union.)

Geometry of making

The Barcelona Pavilion is like a stage set in more ways than one. We have seen that it occupies its own transcendent realm separate from the world around (like the stage of a theatre). We have seen too that it sets the rules for a particular type of action; insisting that people explore its space like a labyrinth rather than follow the established axis asserted by the Gran Plaza and existing flight of steps. In its construction the pavilion is like a stage set too; nothing is quite as it seems. The platform is not a solid foundation of stone but hollow. The walls are not built of blocks of stone but consist of veneers of thin stone hung on a steel framework. The roof, with its smooth white soffit, betrays no clue of its structure. This is a building of surface rather than substance.

The pavilion also ignores the conventions of traditional building construction, as might be evident in the reconstructed folk architecture in the Pueblo Español nearby. Unlike the Farnsworth

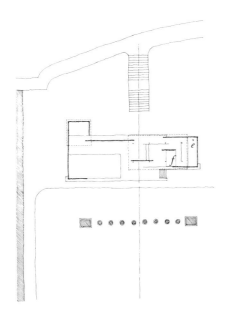

11

1

House, the Barcelona Pavilion is not an exercise in clear and un-equivocal structure and construction. It has even been observed that there is visual confusion about whether the columns or the walls are supporting the roof (Evans, 1997, pp. 240-241). They are not both necessary; either could support the roof alone. Nor are the columns solid; but composed of four steel angles sheathed in chrome covers (*1*) (polished stainless steel was used in the reconstruction).

In the Farnsworth House we shall see that the rectangular travertine paving sets a geometric matrix disciplining the positions of the main elements. At first sight it seems that the same happens in the Barcelona Pavilion (*2*). But if you look more closely you can see something more subtle is happening. The eight columns supporting the megaron roof, for example, are evenly spaced in themselves and aligned along one longitudinal paving joint, but they do not always hit the lateral joints. The end columns do but the middle ones do not. It is as if there is a syncopated rhythm between one beat that belongs to the paving and the other belonging to the columns. They reinforce each other at the ends but are at odds in the middle. The same sort of thing happens elsewhere. The mullions of the large paned glazing by the access steps, for example, begin on a lateral joint but never hit a lateral joint again. The mullions of the glass screen by the small courtyard, which is not aligned along a lateral joint, hit longitudinal joints at each end but not in the middle.

The impression one is left with is musical. It is not that there is no relationship between the beat established by the square paving and the other elements of the composition. It is more that there are complex relationships; off-beat and conflicting rhythms such as one might find in a contemporary piece by Stravinsky, whose 'Rite of Spring' (1913) began to be more performed in the 1920s. Though one cannot compare the primitive drama and violent rhythms of Stravinsky's music with the calm sophistication of the Barcelona Pavilion, Mies's building, in its own cool way, possesses a comparable conflict of varying rhythms overlaid one on another. As will be seen in the Farnsworth House, Mies was concerned with dimensional ordering derived from materials and the ways in which they were put together rather than with the imposition of the ideal geometry of mathematical proportions such as one would find in neo-classical Beaux Arts architecture.

Ideas and influences

Creativity depends on ideas. The Barcelona Pavilion is replete with them. Although it appears, and was, startlingly novel, the design did not crystallise in a vacuum. It was informed by Mies's understanding of classical architecture, his reading of philosophy and his interest in contemporary movements in architecture and the arts. Mies was

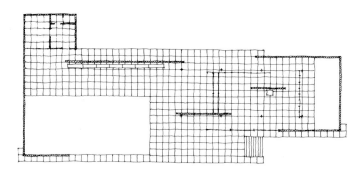

2

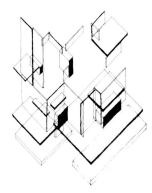

3

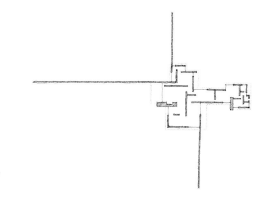

4

generally taciturn about his influences and, like most artist/architects, kept quiet about his working methods. We are left to speculate on where he found the ideas he used in his work.

De Stijl

In his book *Architecture and its Interpretation* (1979), J.P. Bonta used the Barcelona Pavilion as a case study. He devoted a number of pages (pp. 161ff.) to discussing various architectural critics' views on the relationship between Mies van der Rohe and the 1920s Dutch group of painters, architects and furniture designers called De Stijl, which included Theo van Doesburg, Gerrit Rietveld and J.J.P. Oud. The conclusion Bonta draws is that critics were aware that Mies was not formally associated with the De Stijl group and that occasionally there was friction between him and it. But they also thought the De Stijl influence on Mies's work was clear. Mies denied it. When one looks at van Doesburg's spatial studies (*3*), done around 1920, the resemblance seems obvious.

Van Doesburg's studies were part of a movement to liberate space from the straitjackets of traditional and classical ways of defining it. This movement, also represented in the paintings of Piet Mondrian and the furniture and buildings of Rietveld, was called Neo-Plasticism. In 1924 van Doesburg wrote a manifesto, 'Towards a Plastic Architecture'. It seems so relevant to the Barcelona Pavilion that I have included it in full on the following page. As you read it, it is easy to see it as a recipe for the Barcelona Pavilion, so close are its precepts to what may be found in Mies's building.

The rejections of 'form' in paragraphs 1 and 5 of the manifesto are rejections of the formulaic ways of design promulgated by the Beaux Arts neo-classicist architects. Mies himself in 1924 wrote, 'Form as an aim is formalism; and that we reject' but he also realised the semantic problem, since any building – including the Barcelona Pavilion – has form. Mies pondered this semantic problem. In 1927 he wrote, 'My attack is not against form, but against form as an *end*

in itself' (the emphasis is Mies's) (see Johnson, 1978, pp. 188-189 and pp. 192-193). What it seems Mies was saying was that any project should be seen as an opportunity to think things through afresh, allow the particularities of the case to lead the design, rather than resort to established formulaic responses. Certainly this is what Mies did in the Barcelona Pavilion… or was it? He had experimented with this way of managing space before – in his 1924 project for a Brick Country House (*4*) – and would do so again – in the model house he designed for the Berlin Building Exhibition in 1931 (*5*). These suggest Mies was developing (his own) formulaic way of designing rather than allowing circumstances to produce their own solutions. The Barcelona Pavilion certainly offered a way of designing that could be, and was, used by other architects.

Paragraph 2 of van Doesburg's manifesto says the new architecture should be 'elemental'. With its distinct walls, roofs, pits… each with its own material, colour, detailing…, the Barcelona Pavilion is clearly elemental.

In paragraph 3, van Doesburg's word 'economic' might be equated with 'minimal' in twenty-first century usage. And the word 'plastic' in paragraph 6 (and the title) means mouldable, capable of being given shape (according to needs, conditions and material) rather than made of what we now call plastic.

In paragraph 5 van Doesburg suggests that 'plastic' architecture should be 'functional'. Since the Barcelona Pavilion has no more than a cursory function – to accommodate its own inauguration and

5

Theo van Doesburg, 'Towards a plastic architecture', 1924.

1 *Form.* Elimination of all *concept of form* in the sense of *a fixed type* is essential to the healthy development of architecture and art as a whole. Instead of using earlier styles as models and imitating them, the problem of architecture must be posed entirely afresh.

2 The new architecture is *elemental*; that is to say, it develops out of the elements of building in the widest sense. These elements – such as function, mass, surface, time, space, light, colour, material, etc – are *plastic*.

3 The new architecture is *economic*; that is to say, it employs its elemental means as effectively and thriftily as possible and squanders neither these means nor the material.

4 The new architecture is *functional*; that is to say, it develops out of the exact determination of the practical demands, which it contains within clear outlines.

5 The new architecture is *formless* and yet exactly defined; that is to say, it is not subject to any fixed aesthetic formal type. It has no mould (such as confectioners use) in which it produces the functional surfaces arising out of practical, living demands.

In contradistinction to all earlier styles the new architectural methods know no closed type, no *basic type*.

The functional space is strictly divided into rectangular surfaces having no individuality of their own. Although each one is fixed on the basis of the others, they may be visualized as extending infinitely. Thus they form a coordinated system in which all points correspond to the same number of points in the universe. It follows from this that the surfaces have a direct connexion to infinite space.

6 The new architecture has rendered the concept *monumental* independent of large and small (since the word 'monumental' has become hackneyed it is replaced by the word 'plastic'). It has shown that everything exists on the basis of interrelationships.

7 The new architecture possesses no single *passive factor*. It has overcome the *opening* (in the wall). With its *openness* the window plays an active role in opposition to the *closedness* of the wall surface. Nowhere does an opening or a gap occupy the foreground; everything is strictly determined by contrast. Compare the various counter constructions in which the elements that architecture consists of surface, line, and mass are placed without constraint in a three-dimensional relationship.

8 *The ground-plan.* The new architecture has *opened* the walls and so done away with the separation of *inside* and *outside*. *The walls themselves no longer support*; they merely provide supporting points. The result is a new, open ground-plan entirely different from the classical one, since inside and outside now pass over into one another.

9 The new architecture is *open*. The whole structure consists of a space that is divided in accordance with the various functional demands. This division is carried out by means of *dividing surfaces* (in the interior) or *protective surfaces* (externally). The former, which separate the various functional spaces, may be movable; that is to say, the dividing surfaces (formerly the interior walls) may be replaced by movable intermediate surfaces or panels (the same method may be employed for doors). In architecture's next phase of development the ground-plan must disappear completely. The two-dimensional spatial composition *fixed* in a ground-plan will be replaced by an *exact constructional calculation* – a calculation by means of which the supporting capacity is restricted to the simplest but strongest supporting points. For this purpose Euclidean mathematics will be of no further use – but with the aid of calculation that is non-Euclidean and takes into account the four dimensions everything will be very easy.

10 *Space and time.* The new architecture takes account not only of *space* but also of the magnitude *time*. Through the unity of space and time the architectural exterior will acquire a new and completely plastic aspect. (Four-dimensional space-time aspects.)

11 The new architecture is *anti-cubic*; that is to say, it does not attempt to fit all the functional space cells together into a closed cube, but *projects functional space-cells* (as well as overhanging surfaces, balconies, etc) centrifugally from the centre of the cube outwards. Thus height, breadth, and depth plus time gain an entirely new plastic expression. In this way architecture achieves a more or less floating aspect (in so far as this is possible from the constructional standpoint – this is a problem for the engineer!) which operates, as it were, in opposition to natural gravity.

12 *Symmetry and repetition.* The new architecture has eliminated both monotonous repetition and the stiff equality of two halves – the mirror image, symmetry. There is no repetition in time, no street front, no standardization.

A block of houses is just as much a whole as the individual house. The laws that apply to the individual house also apply to the block of houses and to the city. In place of symmetry the new architecture offers a *balanced relationship of unequal parts*; that is to say, of parts that differ from each other by virtue of their functional characteristics as regards position, size, proportion and situation. The equality of these parts rests upon the balance of their dissimilarity, not upon their similarity. Furthermore, the new architecture has rendered front, back, right, left, top, and bottom, factors of equal value.

13 In contrast to frontalism, which had its origin in a rigid, static way of life, the new architecture offers the plastic richness of an all-sided development in space and time.

14 *Colour.* The new architecture has done away with painting as a separate and imaginary expression of harmony, secondarily as representation, primarily as coloured surface.

The new architecture permits colour organically as a direct means of expressing its relationships within space and time. Without colour these relationships are not real, but *invisible*. The balance of organic relationships acquires visible reality only by means of colour. The modern painter's task consists in creating with the aid of colour a harmonious whole in the new four-dimensional realm of space-time – not a surface in two dimensions. In a further phase of development colour may also be replaced by a denaturalized material possessing its own specific colour (a problem for the chemist – but only if practical needs demand this material).

15 The new architecture is *anti-decorative*. Colour (and this is something the colour-shy must try to grasp) is not a decorative part of architecture, but its organic medium of expression.

16 *Architecture as a synthesis of Neo-Plasticism.* Building is a part of the new architecture which, by combining together all the arts in their elemental manifestation, discloses their true nature.

A prerequisite is the ability to think in four dimensions – that is to say: the architects of Plasticism, among whom I also number the painters, must construct within the new realm of space and time.

Since the new architecture permits no images (such as paintings or sculptures as separate elements) its purpose of creating a harmonious whole with all essential means is evident from the *outset*. In this way, every architectural element contributes to the attainment on a practical and logical basis of a maximum of plastic expression, without any disregard of the practical demands.

the signing of a book – this might be considered an aspect in which Mies's building deviates from the precepts of 'neo-plastic' architecture. But the pavilion has fundamental characteristics that make it more 'functional' than van Doesburg's own spatial studies. Mies's building stands on the ground under the influence of gravity with a clear up and down and horizontality, where van Doesburg's study has neither ground nor gravity. The composition of Mies's elements, unlike that of van Doesburg's, is neither abstract nor random but carefully arranged to manage movement and to orchestrate people's experience of space. If these characteristics of Mies's design do not make it exactly 'functional', they do make it real, human, existential, phenomenological in that it accommodates and incorporates the person, human scale, mobility, senses, emotions in ways that could be neglected in abstract formalism. Maybe that is what van Doesburg meant by 'functional'?

Van Doesburg's reference to the 'window' in paragraph 7 of his manifesto suggests that windows should not be seen as objects of attention in themselves (as they can be in the façade of a neo-classical building) but thought of in terms of what they do, i.e. allow views through to space beyond.

Paragraphs 8, 9 and 11 refer to the Neo-Plasticists' aversion, shared by Mies, to the enclosed cell in favour of 'openness' and the gradual spatial blending of 'inside' and 'outside'.

Paragraph 10 suggests that time is as essential a dimension in architecture as depth, width and height. As a stage on a route and as a labyrinth the Barcelona Pavilion provides a frame for movement and incorporates the dimension of time.

Paragraphs 12 and 13 reject axial symmetry (because it was a key characteristic of neo-classical architecture and a symbol of authoritarianism) and 'frontalism'. We have seen that asymmetry and blocking the axis were motives in the design of the Barcelona Pavilion, and that, although it could be said to have a front to the Gran Plaza, it does not have a façade.

Finally (leaving paragraph 16 to speak for itself), paragraphs 14 and 15 suggest that colour and ornamentation in architecture should only be allowed if they are 'organic'. The only colours and ornamentation in the Barcelona Pavilion, apart from the red of the curtains, are the natural organic colours and ingrained patterns of the various stones and tinted glass.

Oswald Spengler's *The Decline of the West*

The Decline of the West by Oswald Spengler was published, in two volumes, in the years after the First World War. Due to its mechanistic view of the cyclic nature of history and because Spengler came to be associated with Hitler's National Socialism it is now a largely discredited text. But in the 1920s Spengler's writing enjoyed huge popularity. Its apparent erudition seemed to explain something about how history worked and the culture of the times. *The Decline of the West* was particularly popular amongst architects because it presented architecture as a key cultural indicator. The fundamental driving conceptions of all great cultures and civilisations – their 'Destiny Ideas' – Spengler argued, were evident most strongly in the ways in which they conceived and dealt with space, i.e. in their architecture. Oscar Schlemmer, a teacher in the Bauhaus in the 1920s, noted in his diary how powerful Spengler's arguments seemed. When he was appointed director of the School of Architecture in Stockholm in 1931, the Swedish architect Eric Gunnar Asplund used Spengler's arguments as the theme for his inaugural lecture. And Mies himself betrayed having read Spengler when he wrote in 1924, 'Greek temples, Roman basilicas and medieval cathedrals are significant to us as creations of a whole epoch rather than as works of individual architects... Their true meaning is that they are symbols of their epoch. Architecture is the will of the epoch translated into space' (in Johnson, 1978, p. 191).

Spengler's work was influenced by many of his German philosophical antecedents. He drew on the thought of Goethe, Hegel, Nietzsche and many others. Hegel, for example, wrote of architecture: 'Its task lies in so manipulating external inorganic nature that it becomes cognate to mind, as an artistic outer world' (Hegel, 1820s, p. 90). Architecture then, rather than being merely a matter of pragmatics, should better be seen as a manifestation of a person's and, by extension, a culture or civilisation's world view – the way in which it made sense of the space of its world. Spengler gave a number of examples of how different civilisations had dealt with space. The 'Destiny Idea' of Greek civilisation was the body in space, as exemplified in Hellenic sculpture and architecturally in the classic Greek temple set in the open landscape. Byzantine architecture turned this idea inside out and produced the architecture of the cave, the basilica, with its focus on the interior. Egyptian architecture, further back in time than either Greek or Byzantine, derived from the idea of the route or path; its pyramids for the dead were the end-points on a journey through temples and along causeways from the Nile. The Chinese 'Destiny Idea' was supposedly dependent on wandering; its houses were, Spengler suggested, like mazes. And, the 'Destiny Idea' of Western culture was its fascination with and drive towards infinite space. According to Spengler this was no recent fascination; it stretched back to medieval times and was evident in such buildings as the Sainte Chapelle in Paris (thirteenth century) with its large stained glass windows. 'The *window as architecture*,' (this is Spengler's own emphasis) 'is peculiar to the Faustian soul' (an idea from Nietzsche) 'and the most significant symbol of its depth-experience. In it can be felt the will to emerge from the interior into the boundless' (Spengler, 1918, p. 199).

It is evident in some of the less transparent things that he said that Mies considered his Barcelona Pavilion not just to be an intriguingly novel composition but to be a philosophical proposition on the management of space as a manifestation of modern culture. Spengler had implied that 'Destiny Ideas' emerged within their cultures organically, without self-conscious intent; but Mies promoted his consciously. The Barcelona Pavilion is informed by the idea of 'emerging from the interior into the boundless'.

Knossos

The late nineteenth and early twentieth century was a period of 'heroic' archaeology. One of the most celebrated excavations was Arthur Evans's work at Knossos, the ancient Palace of King Minos, on the Mediterranean island of Crete. The excavations received great publicity at the time because they appeared to have unearthed the labyrinth at the heart of the ancient Greek myth of the Minotaur. Evans's findings were published, in seven volumes, through the 1920s and into the 1930s.

Though public interest in the findings may have centred on the association of the ruins with myth, architects were fascinated by the plans Evans was publishing of the palace buildings. They did however have a problem with reconciling their avowed proclamation of a 'new epoch' with an interest in ancient architecture. Frank Lloyd Wright, for example, denounced ancient architecture as 'pagan poison' (Wright, 1930, p. 59) even though it is clear he learnt from them.

There is something 'pagan' about the Barcelona Pavilion; perhaps it derived from the Minoan architecture of Knossos. One of the first plans from the excavations to draw attention was that of the palace's Royal Apartments (*1*). The Cretan palaces had no fortifications; they seemed to accommodate democratic city states living in peace with each other. Plans such as those of the Royal Apartments appeared to affirm this view. Axial symmetry, though present, was modulated rather than emphasised by the architecture. The throne, as in the megaron of the Mycenaean palace of Tiryns, did not sit on an axis but against a side wall. Space was layered by screens of columns and pillars. There was no sharp division between inside and outside but a sequence of zones of increasingly interior character, with the most interior part in some cases apparently open to the sky. Some of these features seem driven by a desire on the part of kings to avoid facing the glare of the openings to the bright outside whilst sitting on their thrones and a need for cooling cross

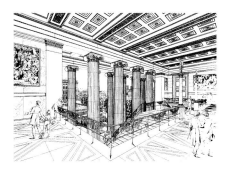

3

ventilation in the heat of the Cretan summer. But visiting these palaces – Knossos, Phaestos, Hagia Triada… – one is struck by the aesthetic investment made in achieving views from high-status apartments out to the god-inhabited landscape beyond: the 'will… (to) the boundless', Spengler might have called it. Spengler himself had observed that Minoan art 'subserves the habit of comfort and the play of intellect' (1918, p. 198).

Placing the plan of the megaron of the Barcelona Pavilion (*2*) alongside that of the Royal Apartments (*1*), and discounting the thickness of walls and columns, one can see the resemblance. The roofed area of the pavilion has similar proportions to the principal part of the Royal Apartments. And the small courtyard of the pavilion is comparable, and again almost identical in proportion, to the light well of the Hall of the Double Axes.

Karl Friedrich Schinkel

One of the most discussed influences on the work of Mies van der Rohe is that of the nineteenth century German neo-classicist Karl Friedrich Schinkel. The possible allusion of the row of Ionic columns in Barcelona to the loggia of Schinkel's Altes Museum in Berlin has already been mentioned. Apart from their shared adherence to orthogonal discipline, two particular characteristics of Schinkel's work seem to have interested Mies: his desire to provide the people who lived in or visited his buildings with subtle spatial experiences; and the relationship of his buildings with their landscape settings. In being to do with content and context, these two characteristics diverted the focus of architectural concern away from the design of façades as two-dimensional graphic compositions and towards

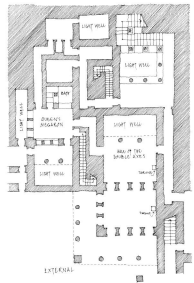

1

2

1

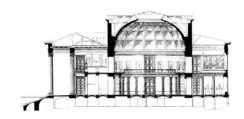

2

ideas exploiting the three dimensions of space together with a fourth, that of movement in time. This implied a richer and more complex conception of architecture, one that was not merely preoccupied with issues of style and proportion.

The stair and entrance to the Altes Museum make a case in point. On the one hand you can look at the front elevation of this building (*1*) and see a regular row of Ionic columns sandwiched between a podium and an entablature. The elevation is something that one may look at, as a spectator, from outside. But by the evidence of his own buildings, Mies's interest in those of Schinkel was not in their superficial stylistic appearance but in the way in which he managed space in relation to the person and to the landscape. As you climb the steps, and pass between the columns into the long loggia, entering the layer of space defined by the platform beneath your feet and the roof over your head, you are no longer a spectator, you become an essential part of the architecture – a participant in its spatial experience. Schinkel plays on this and provides you with options. You may pass through into the circular space – the rotunda (*2*) – at the heart of the building and then into the galleries. Or you can turn left or right up flights of steps that take you under the landing above, around a half-landing and then up to the floor above where you can look out through the double layer of columns to the Lustgarten (see figure *2* on page 30) or inwards into the rotunda. The stair and landing of the Altes Museum was one of the great in-between spaces in all architecture. (It is a pity it was, in the 1990s, enclosed by glass screens between the columns.) This is one example of how Schinkel used architecture as an instrument to orchestrate experience and relationships with the landscape/outside world.

There are others. The Charlottenhof (*3*) is a villa set in the extensive grounds of the Sanssouci Palace in Potsdam on the outskirts of Berlin. Compositionally – raised on a platform with a megaron relating to a partly enclosed courtyard – the Barcelona Pavilion's resemblance is clear. Just as in the case of the pavilion, the 'temple' (house) of the Charlottenhof sends out from its right hand side

an arm, in this case a pergola, to enclose one side of the garden. The pergola strikes out from the main building into the outside world – a precursor of the Miesian wall as in his project for Brick Country House. This arm, in the case of both the Charlottenhof and the pavilion, wraps around at the end, defining a stage with a view across open space.

But there is another characteristic of the Charlottenhof, more profound than mere compositional resemblance, that influenced Mies. It is similar to that noted above in the case of the Altes Museum and relates to the recognition that architecture is not merely a matter of visual appearance and sculptural form but is also an instrument for orchestrating experience. In the case of the Charlottenhof, the house is not just an object sitting in the parkland of the palace, it establishes a zone of transition. It too is a propylon, a gateway through which one passes from the general ground level of the parkland up onto the elevated stage of the garden. By means of his design Schinkel draws out a route that manipulates the person, taking him or her from the parkland, through a doorway, up a flight of stairs, across a landing, through another doorway into a saloon, across the saloon, out through a doorway into a portico, and finally out into the garden where one can wander to the end and look back (just as in the Barcelona Pavilion). Because there is a centre post to the main doorway and the stairs are divided, the person is denied the axis of the composition until the upper level. The architecture implies/asserts that the principle associated with the axis – its backbone – belongs to the morally, intellectually, socially and politically more noble, superior level.

Mies conflates these ideas in the Barcelona Pavilion but in a way that subverts rather than reinforces the dominant axis. In some of his earlier development drawings for the project he drew onto the plan the axis of the Gran Plaza (6, which I have redrawn). In the general compositional resemblance between the pavilion and the Charlottenhof, the axis of the former is at right angles to that of the latter. Both buildings can be thought of as propylons. But whereas

3

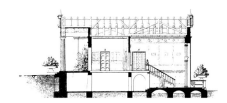

4 *these engravings are from K.F. Schinkel, 1819-1840; they depict designs that were realised but not exactly as they were drawn. Both have also been modified since, in ways that change their architecture*

Schinkel reinforces the axis of authority and nobility, the Mies of the Weimar Republic (though he was to create symmetrical buildings later in his career), denies it, creating his labyrinth. In both cases the intention is to use architecture to manage movement in support of a philosophical proposition or political comment.

In conclusion

Analysing the Barcelona Pavilion illustrates that a work of architecture may be startlingly novel and yet based in ancient ideas at the same time. It suggests that new ideas may be generated by the modification or contradiction of old ones. It shows that architectural concepts may be derived from abstract philosophical ideas and that the design of a building can be a philosophical proposition in itself, expressed in the composition of elements and the organisation of space rather than in words.

The Barcelona Pavilion illustrates an essential part of architecture. It is a building that is almost completely without function and yet it is a work of architecture rather than sculpture. The key difference lies in its accommodation of the human being; Mies's design recognises the person not merely as a spectator but as an ingredient. The game Mies plays is not merely an abstract composition (like that of van Doesburg in his spatial studies); it is a game in which people – the visitors to the pavilion – are the pieces (though they are often left out of architectural photographs of the building) manipulated, though they are free to wander, by the architect. Each wall is positioned not merely for compositional reasons but to deflect people's movement and orchestrate their experience. The pavilion makes people pause on a route so that they may experience the spatial pleasure of architecture; so that they may experience a kind of architectural space that is different from that organised according to an axis of symmetry. The Barcelona Pavilion is a sort of warp field – reinforced by its reflective surfaces – where traditional conceptions of space dissolve. In place of a directional route it

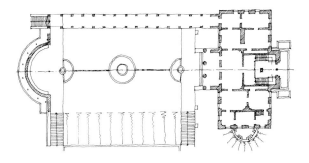

5 *the plan of the Charlottenhof is an instrument for manipulating the person's experience of space; it allows the person to attain the axis at the higher level*

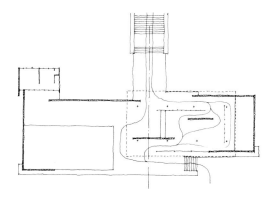

6 *the plan of the Barcelona Pavilion (this is an earlier version than the one built) is also an instrument for manipulating the person's experience of space; here the higher level is a zone of uncertainty, with the axis denied*

substitutes a labyrinth replete with mirages. And as is appropriate in a building that originally had a political purpose, Mies managed to imbue his design with political meaning. As well as being a beautiful and strikingly novel building, it was also a manifesto. Though there is doubt as to whether such things can be consciously promoted, Mies van der Rohe was intent on exemplifying the 'Destiny Idea' of a new age, a new culture.

References and other relevant publications, websites, broadcasts:

Werner Blaser – *Mies van der Rohe*, Thames and Hudson, London, 1972.

Juan Pablo Bonta – *Architecture and its Interpretation*, Lund Humphries, London, 1979. (Contains a number of other useful references.)

Peter Carter – *Mies van der Rohe at Work*, Phaidon, London, 1999.

Caroline Constant – 'The Barcelona Pavilion as Landscape Garden: Modernity and the Picturesque', in *AAFiles* 20, Autumn 1990, pp. 46-54.

Theo van Doesburg – 'Towards a plastic architecture', in *De Stijl*, 12, 6/7, 1924.

Robin Evans – 'Mies van der Rohe's Paradoxical Symmetries' (1990), in *Translations from Drawing to Building and Other Essays*, Janet Evans and Architectural Association, London, 1997.

Georg Wilhelm Friedrich Hegel, translated by Bosanquet – *Introductory Lectures on Aesthetics* (1820s, 1886), Penguin Books, London, 2004.

Robert Hughes – 'Mies van der Rohe – Less is More', *Visions of Space* 4/7, BBC, 2003.

Philip Johnson – *Mies van der Rohe* (1947, 1953), Secker and Warburg, London, 1978.

Fritz Neumeyer – *The Artless Word: Mies van der Rohe on the Building Art*, MIT Press, Cambridge, MA, 1991.

Sophia Psarra – 'Invisible Surface', in *Architecture and Narrative: the Formation of Space and Cultural Meaning*, Routledge, London, 2009, pp. 42-64.

Colin Rowe – 'Neo-"Classicism" and Modern Architecture I' (1973) and 'Neo-"Classicism" and Modern Architecture II' (1973), in *The Mathematics of the Ideal Villa and Other Essays*, MIT Press, Cambridge, MA, 1982, pp. 119-138 and 139-158.

Franz Schulze – *Mies van der Rohe: a Critical Biography*, University of Chicago Press, Chicago and London, 1985.

Franz Schulze – *Mies van der Rohe: Critical Essays*, Museum of Modern Art, New York, 1989.

Ignasi de Solà Morales, Cristian Cirici and Fernando Ramos – *Mies van der Rohe: Barcelona Pavilion*, Gustavo Gili SA, Barcelona, 1993.

K.F. Schinkel – *Sammlung architectonischer Entwürfe (Collected Architectural Designs)*, 1819-1840, also available in facsimile with an Introduction by Doug Clelland, Academy Editions, London, 1982.

David Spaeth – *Mies van der Rohe*, The Architectural Press, London, 1985.

Oswald Spengler, translated by Atkinson – *The Decline of the West* (1918, 1922), George Allen & Unwin, London, 1932.

Wolf Tegethoff – *Mies van der Rohe: the Villas and Country Houses*, MIT Press, Cambridge, MA, 1985.

Frank Lloyd Wright, edited and introduced by Neil Levine – *Modern Architecture; being the Kahn Lectures for 1930* (1930), Princeton University Press, 2008.

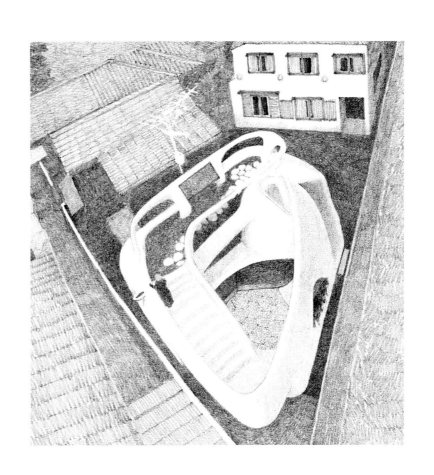

TRUSS WALL HOUSE

'Space is to be experienced most directly
by movement; on a higher level, by the
dance. The dance is at the same time
an elemental means for realization of
space-creative impulses. It can articulate
space, order it.'

Lázló Moholy-Nagy – *The New Vision* (1938,
1947), 2005, p. 163.

TRUSS WALL HOUSE

A house in the Tsurukawa suburb of Machida-City, Japan
KATHRYN FINDLAY and EISAKU USHIDA, 1993

The Truss Wall House is a small residence on a tiny site in a dormitory city on the outskirts of Tokyo in Japan. Its name derives from the way in which it was constructed. It was designed by Kathryn Findlay, an architect from Scotland, and Eisaku Ushida from Japan. The Truss Wall House is distinctive because of its curvilinear form. It is like an architectural squiggle interposed amongst the orthodox rectangular/orthogonal geometry of the suburban villas around it, and set alongside the linear (unidimensionally dynamic) forms of the river to the west and road and railway to the south. In its curved form the Truss Wall House is unorthodox or, at least, it challenges the presumed authority of the orthogonal that has tended to hold sway in architecture since human beings left caves. The presumed authority of the orthogonal, as discussed in *Analysing Architecture* (in the chapter on 'Geometries of Being'), derives from: the geometry of making (i.e. using standard building materials such as bricks and straight lengths of timber it is easier to build orthogonally); and from the six-directions-plus-centre implicit in the human form. The Truss Wall House contradicts both of these: first by employing a construction method based on spraying concrete into and onto an armature of steel reinforcement bars preformed into curved 'trusses' to achieve the complex curvilinear form of the house; and second by recognising that human beings are not constricted to being static cross-shaped creatures – they move in winding ways, they dance.

Identification of place, primitive place types

The house is on three floors. These accommodate the usual places associated with domestic life in unambiguous function-related form. They are clearly identified within the cave-like interior.

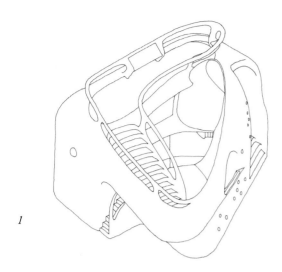

1

2

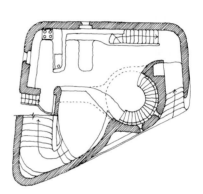

3

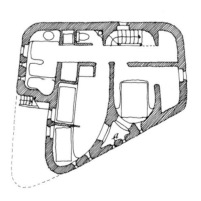

4

The house is entered up a few steps from the road. The entrance floor (*3*) is therefore the middle of the three floors. Here there is a semi-circular sitting area under a sky-lit dome, a fixed dining table and a kitchen for cooking and washing, with its own access to a lane alongside the house. The only free-standing pieces of furniture are some dining chairs (not shown); everything else is built-in, fixed, as it would be in a ship. From this level you can go:

through a small paved courtyard, up a curved external stair onto a roof terrace (*2*) where there are seats and solar panels; this is a place from which guests may survey the city around, with views to the distant hills, and watch the trains go by;

or down, to the sleeping floor (*4*) which is partly sunk into the ground, and where there is a master bedroom with a double bed, a children's bedroom with two bunks, and a bathroom with separate lavatory. (For simplicity of drainage the bathroom is directly below the kitchen.)

Stratification; transition, hierarchy, heart; light

The vertical organisation of the house is different from that of an orthodox house with its day rooms – into which visitors might be invited – on the ground floor and more private bedrooms upstairs. The arrangement of the Truss Wall House allows access from the day rooms to the roof terrace without passing through the more private zone of the bedrooms. The day rooms are nevertheless directly accessible, if up a few steps, from the street. This arrangement also means that the most womb-like spaces on the lowest level are used for sleeping, whilst the day rooms receive, through the small courtyard and the roof light over the sitting area, more light from the sky. The rooms on the lowest level are lit though small windows like the portholes of a ship, and through windows into a tiny triangular light well on the south side of the house (*a* in *4* and *5*).

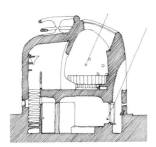

5 the sitting area is lit through a sky light; the bedrooms through the tiny triangular courtyard

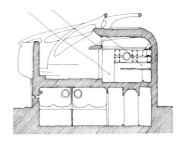

6 the dining area is lit through the small courtyard which is screened from the road and railway by a high wall; a light shelf shades the interior from excessive direct sunlight but also reflects light on to the ceiling, creating a softer light deeper into the space

The heart of the house is the sitting area (though it does not look particularly comfortable as a place to relax). The entrance steps and passageway, together with the small courtyard and steps up to the roof terrace, create an S-shaped route taking the visitor from the road up to the higher level. This route passes through a series of different experiences: up the steps into the tunnel-like entrance; turning left where the interior is revealed, past the sitting and dining areas, through the glass screen to the small courtyard, and up the curving steps up to the roof terrace. It is as if the building makes you do a dance.

A small stair deviates from this route to take you down to the bedrooms and bathroom on the lowest level.

Geometry

All this could be done in a conventional house with right angles, vertical walls and a flat roof. This curvaceous building is expressive and sculptural as well as being organised according to practicality and to orchestrate experience. In this it contravenes the geometry of making in favour of something else. In this case that 'something else' is not ideal geometry. The lines of this building are dynamic, related to movement. It is as if the architects have taken the site as a blank piece of paper and drawn that squiggle (*7*); except that the squiggle is in three dimensions – it spirals up into space and down into the ground.

A squiggle is free and fluid but not random. Its curves are related to the geometry of the hand and arm. Various artists, designers and architects have explored the decorative possibilities of the free line derived from movement and related to gesture, particularly since the movement known as *Art Nouveau* towards the end of the nineteenth century. One was Charles Rennie Mackintosh, the Scottish architect who worked in Glasgow. He produced decorative elements seemingly generated from squiggles in two dimensions, as in this pattern from a fireplace in the Cranston Tea Rooms (*8*), and

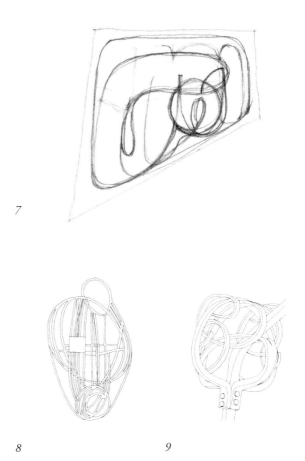

7

8   *9*

in three, as in this finial (*9*) from one of the window brackets on the north elevation of his Glasgow School of Art building. Pablo Picasso too experimented with the free line derived from movement. While a camera shutter was open he quickly drew in the air with a light; the

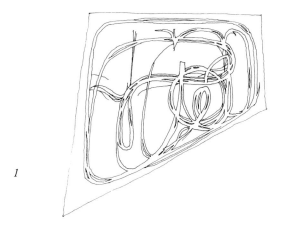

1

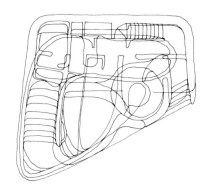

2

image, which for a split second occupied three-dimensional space, was captured on the film. (You can see some of these experiments if you Google 'picasso light drawing'.)

The Truss Wall House is like this, except it is, literally, set in concrete. Its plan, if all three levels are overlaid and reduced to two dimensions, can be compared to a Mackintosh decoration (*1*). The house derives from a flourish, a flamboyant gesture. If an ancient Greek temple is a static body standing in space (*3*) then the Truss Wall House is a body in movement (*4*).

Mackintosh's squiggles and Picasso's light drawings occupy space but do not accommodate anything. Being a house, the Truss Wall House accommodates the places associated with domestic life. These places are inserted into the curves of the spatial flourish (*2*). It is probable that the generative squiggle was drawn with some notion of what the lines might demarcate in terms of places – the entrance and the sitting area are cases in point, and the loops of the roof terrace and of the bedrooms clearly assert places.

Architecture relates to the body in other ways too. The Truss Wall house relates not only to the movement of a hand in drawing; it channels the body in motion too. This idea also has precedents. In the *Bauhaus*, the innovative design school in 1920s Germany, while Paul Klee was interested in 'taking a line for a walk', Lázló Moholy-Nagy and Oscar Schlemmer were interested in the way the body occupied and moved in space. Schlemmer did drawings that took the famous Leonardo da Vinci image of Vitruvian Man a step further by showing the person's potential for movement (*6*) and suggesting that through movement the body projects its energy and dynamism into space (*8*). He designed costumes for dancing and other constructions that represented movement (*7*).

The Truss Wall House is a construction that represents movement in space. Not only are the routes through it like the arms of a posing ballet dancer (*5*), the three-dimensional layout of the house involves the person in moving through space as if dancing, as if leaping and twirling up into the air, and down again.

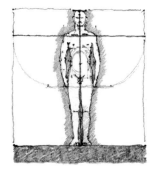

3

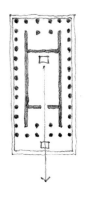

4

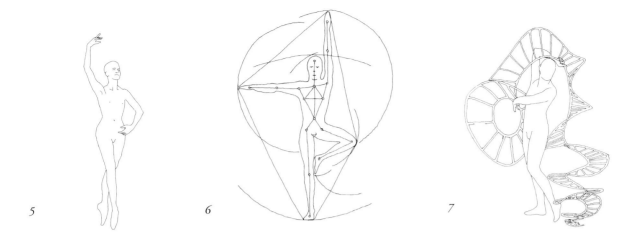

5   6   7

Conclusion: a problem and a question

The Truss Wall House poses a problem and provokes a question. First is the problem that because it contravenes the geometry of making, the house involved a difficult process of construction, with a dense and complex armature of reinforcement – the 'trusses' – covered with concrete and finished by hand. This is a building process for which there are no standard components or well-established crafts.

Second is a question about the relationship between human movement and the form of buildings. The Truss Wall House is a representation of human movement – the hand in drawing and the body dancing. An alternative is to think of a building as a frame for movement rather than a representation of it. The Truss Wall House channels rather than accommodates free movement.

When the sprinters in Martin Creed's *Work No. 850* (2008) ran full pelt the length of the Duveen Gallery in London's Tate Britain (9), they would never take a perfectly straight line down the axis of the space; sometimes they had to deviate around people wandering through the galleries. The line they took played around

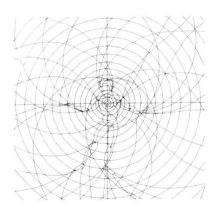

8

the architectural axis rather than being dictated by it. It would only be in the constrained circumstances of a formal procession that people might try to follow the axis of such a space exactly. Normally we wander through such spaces, crossing the axis occasionally, dancing around it rather than being tied to its line.

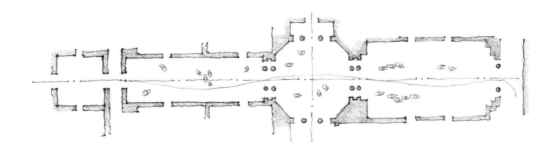

9

'The idea of the three directions is an out-and-out abstraction and is not contained in the immediate extension-feeling of the body (the "soul"). Direction as such, the direction-essence, gives rise to the mysterious animal sense of right and left and also the vegetable characteristic of below-to-above, earth to heaven. The latter is a fact felt dream-wise, the former a truth of waking existence to be learned and therefore capable of being transmuted. Both find expression in architecture, to wit, in the symmetry of the plan and the energy of the elevation, and it is only because of this that we specially distinguish in the "architecture" of the space around us the angle of 90° in preference, for example, to that of 60°. Had it not been so, the conventional number of our "dimensions" would have been quite different.'

Oswald Spengler – *The Decline of the West* (1918, 1922), p. 169 (Note 1).

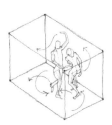

1

3

When we dance it is either in the open landscape or within the freedom of a rectangular room (*1*), when we act out a drama it is in the pristine circle of the *orkestra* of an ancient Greek theatre or the rectangle of an open stage. In 2007, a drug-affected Dutch driver tried to escape from a chasing police car; his tyres drew a chaotic tangle of lines within the bounds of a rectangular field (*2*). When a waitress waits on tables in a café she performs dances in infinite permutations as she moves between the tables (*3*).

It is arguable that architecture's relationship with human movement is as an interplay between the irregularity of that movement and the regularity of the frame it provides, similar to the interplay between the melody and the beat in a piece of music.

Are the curved spaces of the Truss Wall House deterministic, constraining? They do not have the flexibility, in terms of accommodating furniture and human movement, of an orthodox rectangular room.

Evidence that Oswald Spengler (above) may have been wrong in suggesting that the 'three directions' (i.e. the six-directions-plus-centre) are arbitrary is offered by the fact that, in the curvilinear Truss Wall House, which tries to avoid straight lines and rectangles, the floors, steps and shelves are (approximately) level for practicality, the doorways and beds are rectangular (rectangles that accommodate the varying sizes and movements of people) and the dining table has parallel sides. Nevertheless, if *La Casa del Ojo de Agua* is a sentence, then the Truss Wall House is a lyric, and formed of the lines of a dancer's pirouette.

2

References and other relevant publications, websites, broadcasts:

'Ushida Findlay Partnership: Truss-Wall-House', in *Kenchiku Bunka* (Special Issue), August 1993, pp. 29-68.

Paul Klee, translated by Manheim, edited by Spiller – *Notebooks, Volume 1: The Thinking Eye*, Lund Humphries, London, 1961.

Lázló Moholy-Nagy – *The New Vision: Fundamentals of Bauhaus Design, Painting, Sculpture, and Architecture* (1938, 1947), Dover Publications, New York, 2005, p. 163.

Mario Pisani – 'Eisaku Ushida, Kathryn Findlay: Truss Wall House, Tokyo', in *Domus*, number 818, September 1999, pp. 18-25.

Oswald Spengler, translated by Atkinson – *The Decline of the West* (1918, 1922), George Allen & Unwin, London, 1932, p. 169 (Note 1).

Leon Van Schaik – 'Ushida Findlay Partnership', in *Transition*, Number 52-53, 1996, pp. 54-61.

John Welsh – *Modern House*, Phaidon, London, 1995, pp. 188-193.

ENDLESS HOUSE

'when i conduct
the orchestra of space
by grace
of the Unknown
the endless house
has ins and out
without a door
or wall
they change at will
from void to fill
yet standing still
they cannot budge
or billow-bulge
until I
split
with light
reality-illusion
it's simply done
by magic fusion
of what is not
what can
but does not want to be
yet must obey
oh! stay
succumb!
don't play me
dumb

my
scribble
nibbles
crumbs of mine
and Gods and Devils'
fall
in line'

Frederick Kiesler – *'when i conduct'*, 1960.

ENDLESS HOUSE

An unbuilt project for a house based in infinity
FREDERICK KIESLER, 1947-61

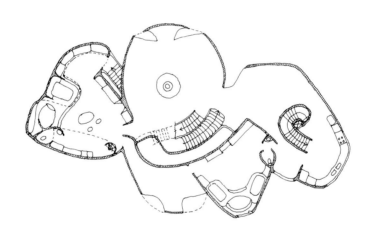

The Japanese artist Katsuhiro Yamaguchi has drawn connections between the Truss Wall House and a project from some thirty years earlier that was never realised (Yamaguchi, 1993). This project was called The Endless House. The architect Frederick Kiesler worked on it for much of the last twenty years of his life. (He was born in 1890 and died in 1965). When, in 1961, a lady called Mary Sisler, from Florida, expressed interest in Kiesler's project, the design of the house was developed to a state in which it might have been built but nothing came of it. During the years Kiesler worked on this project he produced numerous drawings and models.

The project for The Endless House emerged out of a collaboration between Kiesler and some of the Surrealist artists, especially Marcel Duchamp. In 1947 Kiesler designed two exhibitions: *Blood Flames* at the Hugo Gallery in New York; and the *Exposition Internationale du Surréalisme* held at the Maeght Gallery in Paris. Two years later, in a then new architectural magazine called *L'Architecture d'Aujourd'hui*, he published his own manifesto – '*Manifeste du Corréalisme*'. Kiesler's Correalism was something of a reaction against Surrealism's immersion in the psychological realm of dreams. Kiesler argued that human beings and nature are not separate (divorced,

1

distinct entities… as suggested by, for example, the Biblical story of Adam and Eve's eviction from the Garden of Eden) but part of an integrated system, and that architecture should reflect this.

Lines of architecture

In the fifteenth century, the Florentine architect Leon Battista Alberti wrote that architecture is a matter of lines or lineaments (see *Analysing Architecture*, page 153):

> *'The whole matter of building is composed of lineaments and structure. All the intent and purpose of lineaments lies in finding the correct, infallible way of joining and fitting together those lines which define and enclose the surfaces of the building.'*

Alberti tended towards the view that the lines of architecture should be determined by the figures and proportions of ideal geometry: squares; circles; √2 rectangles; and so on. But there are other views. Some of these may be summarised in the following way.

First there is the view that the lines of a building should be governed, or at least strongly influenced, by the size and characteristics of the materials from which it is built (*1*). This is the view expressed in the American architect Louis Kahn's dictum 'a brick knows what it wants to be'. It is exemplified in: the brick wall or column whose geometry is a function of that of the brick itself; the native American teepee, the shape of which is a function of leaning poles against each other; the African hut that influenced Mies van der Rohe (see page 70); and Mies's own Farnsworth House, the form of which is, to a large extent, a function of the character of structural steel (*1*). This is the view explored in *Analysing Architecture* under the heading of the 'Geometry of Making'. Those who subscribe to this view tend to claim moral authority for it on the basis that the form of buildings appear to arise from, or at least be in harmony with, the innate characteristics of the materials being used. These suggest the ways in which they may be put together and the shapes of the buildings that result.

Second there is the view that the purpose of buildings is to accommodate life, and that their lines should therefore follow what might be called the lines, or patterns, of life. An example might be that of an African village (*2*) in which, although component parts might follow the geometry of making, the geometry of the whole is more conditioned by the social structure and practices of the community that live in it.

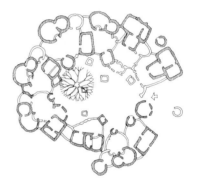

2

Another example would be a house by Hans Scharoun (*3*) in which the shapes of domestic life – eating together, sitting by the fire, playing the piano – hold precedence over the geometry of building the house. Protagonists of this view claim that its moral authority lies in its origination in life as it is lived by people.

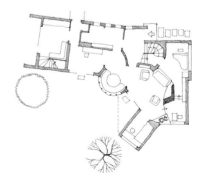

3

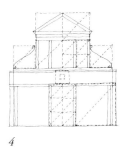

4

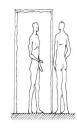
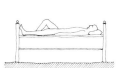

5

A third view would be Alberti's, that the lines of architecture need not be constrained by the geometry of making nor by the patterns of life. The human intellect can strive for higher ideals, even perfection, as apparently provided by the perfect geometric figures of the square, circle and rectangles with specific proportions. This is the view described in *Analysing Architecture* under the heading of 'Ideal Geometry'. It is exemplified in Alberti's own design for the front of Santa Maria Novella in Florence, and in Louis Kahn's Esherick House (which is the subject of a later analysis) (*4*). The authority ascribed to this view derives from the apparently incontrovertible rightness of geometric figures derived from their mathematical formulation – the observation that they are not arbitrary.

A fourth view is that geometric figures are too abstract and that the lines of buildings should be related to the size and characteristics of the human figure. Thus a doorway should be just the right height for average-sized people to pass through and a bed the right size for them to lie upon (*5*). A traditional Japanese house (*6*) would fall into this category since the sizes of the rooms are related to the sizes of the tatami mats on their floors, and the size of the mats is related to that of a person lying down. This view's claim to authority is similar to that of views one and two.

A fifth view would be to combine the third and fourth by suggesting that since it is arguable that geometric figures can be discovered in the human form, as illustrated by Leonardo da Vinci and

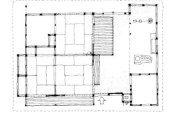

6

Le Corbusier (*7*), a codified system of proportions for architecture can be derived from the human form, as Le Corbusier did in his Modulor system and used in various designs including *Le Cabanon* (also the subject of a later analysis, *8*). This view combines the claims for moral authority of views three and four.

A sixth view is that the principles of architectural geometry should be subverted, perhaps because they introduce an unreal certainty. According to this view, parallel lines are made to converge or diverge, vertical walls are twisted or broken, geometric figures are denied independence and clarity and are made to conflict. By this view sensational forms arise. Moral authority for this source of the lines of architecture is either eschewed or based in claiming resonance with a complex and contradictory world. Alvaro Siza

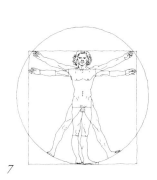

7

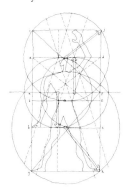

8

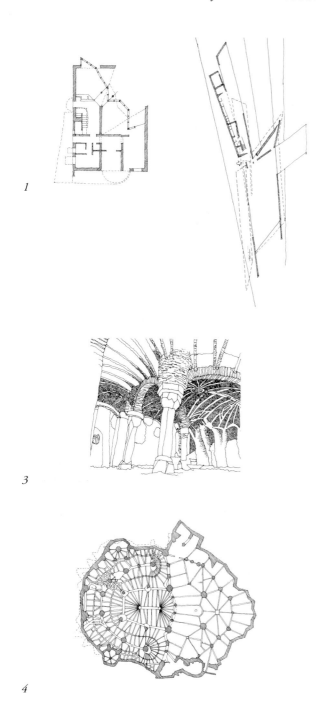

1

2

3

4

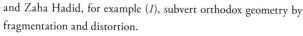

and Zaha Hadid, for example (*1*), subvert orthodox geometry by fragmentation and distortion.

[These various views of the role of geometry in architecture are rarely discrete. Works of architecture are often informed by a combination of them. For example, Le Corbusier's *Cabanon*, though informed by his Modulor system of dimensions does not ignore the geometry of making; and a native American teepee manages quite well to accommodate the social circle of people sitting around a fire. Each view has at various times had claims made for its own overriding authority, moral or otherwise, over the lines of architecture. Perhaps because architecture is complex, too complex for any one view to finally prevail, the field is always open for a fresh view of the role of geometry in architecture.]

A seventh view is that the lines of architecture might be derived from those of natural creations without reducing them to geometric figures and proportions; i.e. that buildings might be like trees and plant tendrils, bones and skeletal structures, shells and rock formations… The Spanish architect Antonio Gaudi, for example, constructed balconies on his *Casa Batlló* in Barcelona derived from the skulls of fish (*2*). He also made columns in the crypt chapel at the Colonia Guell that, made of rough hewn rock, resemble the trunks of trees in a forest (*3*), though the plan (*4*) displays that blend of order and irregularity found in natural creations. An aspiration associated with this view is that people might build as animals do, naturally and unselfconsciously, or even that buildings might be made to grow as if by natural process, like a shell around a mollusc or a pupa around a caterpillar. It is as if architecture might be thought of as an aspect of original sin. The moral authority thought to belong to this view of how the lines of architecture should be generated is perhaps based in an attempt to escape or deny human wilfulness, seen as the root cause of wrong; to return to the innocent state of animals.

There are two corollaries to this seventh view. One is current in architecture in the first decade of the twenty-first century, that computer software may be sophisticated and subtle enough to emulate natural processes in their response to variant conditions. Parametric software, for example, enables architects to modify form by inputting factors such as gravity, loading, sunshine… and assessing how form effectively modifies itself, as a natural creature might respond to changing conditions. In this way forms thought of as natural – the growth of plants, the film of bubbles distorted by

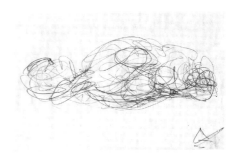

5   6   7   *© 2009 Austrian Frederick and Lillian Kiesler Private Foundation, Vienna*

breeze and gravity, the complex growth curves of shells and bones – might be emulated in human building.

The other corollary has a longer pedigree. It concerns how human wilfulness might be lessened in or obviated from the hand that draws to produce lines that seem more natural or more convincingly similar to the lines of nature – plant tendrils, the flow of water, the flight of a bird through the air, the growth of a shell. This allows the hand (and arm) to move freely. Beginning with a free swirl of lines, for example, it is possible to construct a plausibly natural looking tree (5). This is the sort of method used by Charles Rennie Mackintosh, as mentioned in the analysis of the Truss Wall House. It is also that used by Hector Guimard in, for example, the gate to the Castel Beranger in Paris (6).

Kiesler fits this seventh view of how the lines of architecture might be generated. His desire to find a natural way of creating architecture, uncorrupted by human will, is indicated in the following passage, taken from the beginning of his 1949 essay 'Pseudo-Functionalism in Modern Architecture'. His first sentence is a direct contradiction of Le Corbusier's dictum that 'the plan is the generator' (*Towards a New Architecture*, 1923):

> '*The floor plan is no more than the footprint of the house. From a flat impression of this sort it is difficult to conceive the actual form and content of the building. If God had begun the creation of man with a footprint, a monster all heels and toes would probably have grown up from it, not a man… Fortunately the creation proceeded otherwise, growing out of a nuclear conception. Out of a single germ cell which contained the whole and which slowly developed into the separate floors and rooms of man. This cell, owing its origin to the erotic and creative instinct and not to any intellectual mandate, is the nucleus of the human edifice.*'

Kiesler's antipathy to orthogonal architecture is expressed in the same essay:

> '*The ground plan is only a flat imprint of a volume. The volume of the principal activity to be expected in the house is not taken into consideration; instead, squares and rectangles, long ones, short ones, bent ones, are juxtaposed, or something jumbles – and then superimposed in storeys (elevation plan). This box construction is not in keeping with the practice of living. A house is a volume in which people live polydimensionally. It is the sum of every possible movement its inhabitants can make within it; and these movements are infused with the flux of instinct. Hence it is fallacious to begin with the floor plan. We must strive to capture a general sense of dwelling, and configurate accordingly.*'

The possibilities Kiesler saw in free drawing are described in the following, from his 1959 essay on 'Hazard and the Endless House':

> '*Drafting is grafting vision on paper with lead, ink, or – or. Blindfolded skating rather than designing, significantly keen, directed by experience and will, and channelling one's feelings and thoughts, deliberately proud of pruning them to clarity and definition. Chance drawing and sculpting or painting is an ability to let go, to be entirely tool rather than a guide of tools. It is to design with one's whole body and mind, never mind-ful of either. No, it is not sketching, the bastard version between chance and will.*'

Some of the study sketches for Kiesler's Endless House are scribbles (7). It seems the form of the house (8) was produced, like my drawing of a tree, by the selective editing of a scribble; the free movement of the hand producing curves that could not be determined by conscious decision.

8

'The Endless House *is called the "endless" because all ends meet, and meet continuously. It is endless like the human body – there is no beginning and end to it. The "endless" is rather sensuous, more like the female body in contrast to sharp-angled male architecture… The coming of the Endless House is inevitable in a world coming to an end."*

Frederick Kiesler, 1966.

1 west elevation

The house

The Endless House went through many iterations. The most finished is the one Kiesler prepared for his client Mary Sisler in 1961, hoping that it would be built. It consists of a cluster of interlinked pods supported off the ground on inhabited columns or pedestals (*1*). Kiesler thought of his Endless House as independent of the ground. He wrote that 'it can just as well be on the ground or could be floating on the water or on sand' (in a television interview in 1961). Presumably, if it were not for gravity, the house could float in the air.

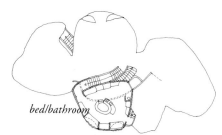

2 top floor plan

The places in the house are not completely clear from the drawings. Each of the three pedestals (4) has an entrance. The sweep of the drive suggests the main entrance is in the middle pedestal. It contains the grandest of the stairs to the middle floor, and a room that is probably a cloakroom. It also contains what appears to be a garden store. The southern pedestal has a stair leading up to the kitchen, and also a space that is presumably for storage. The northern pedestal seems more a way out to the garden at the bottom of an external stair that sweeps down under the pod from the parents' room on the middle floor.

At the head of the grand stair on the middle floor is a large living space (*3*), apparently with a hearth at its centre. The parents' room leads off this and it appears to have a pool. The living space also gives access to the kitchen, through what appears to be a dining space. The final space on this floor appears to be a combined bedroom and bathroom for the children of the family. A stair from the living space leads up to another bed/bathroom on the top floor (*2*). And from that room there appears to be a further external stair climbing up onto the roof of the pod but going nowhere.

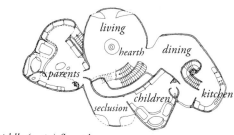

3 middle (main) floor plan

The free form of the house is reminiscent of cave systems carved out of rock by running water (*5*) or of the grottoes built by landscape architects in the eighteenth century (*6*). The space of the Endless House is however carved not out of solid matter but from space itself.

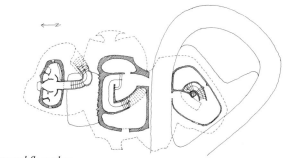

4 ground floor plan

5

6

Infinity

There are many intertwining routes around, into and through the Endless House. Like the Truss Wall House this house is about movement as well as sculptural form. The form of the house sets the lines of the free movement of the hand that drew it but its spaces also frame the movement of a person. The drawing below (*7*) is a superimposition of the house's three floors with possible lines of movement weaving in and out, up and down. The house seems a comment on the restlessness of modern life.

∞

8

Kiesler explained (in that 1961 television interview) that the underlying idea of the house was the mathematical sign for infinity (*8*). The house also seems to have some conceptual affinity with the Klein Bottle (*9*) and the Möbius Strip (*10*) both being objects with a single – i.e. endless – surface.

Conclusion, with a note on light and time

An article on an early version of the Endless House was published in the journal *Interiors* in November 1950. This article focused on the house as an instrument for the manipulation of light, both natural and artificial.

> '*The curving shell of the house provides excellent vantage-points for carefully distributed, built-in filament and gaseous light sources, which send out vertical, diagonal, and horizontal beams adaptable to varied purposes… We now have at our disposal three technical means of controlling daylight: (1) Dimensioning of the cut-outs – more commonly referred to as windows – through which daylight enters the building. We can make them large or small, round or rectangular. (2) Shielding the aperture of path of the light with a diffusing skin of glass, plastic, or a translucent woven material. (3) Masking the aperture with one of any number of disguises to temper or deflect the light.*'

The house also had what Kiesler called a 'color clock':

> '*Daylight is transmitted through a prismatic glass crystal of three basic colours, gradually shifting to each in turn from dawn to dusk. The rays are filtered into the interior through a convex mirror, and the dweller can gauge the hour by the colour of the tinted light around him. Instead of depending solely on a mechanical*

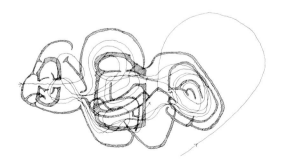

7

9   10

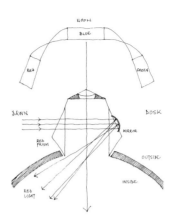

clock, splintering his life into minute particles of time, he becomes aware of the continuity of time and his own dynamic integration with natural forces.'

A diagram of one of the crystals of the colour clock show that it was intended to consist of prisms, lenses and mirrors. At dawn for example (1) light from the east would shine in through a prism that would colour it red; that light would then be dispersed into the room by a concave mirror. In the evening, something similar would happen with the light from the west, except that it would be coloured green. In between, the colour of the light would gradually turn from the red of dawn, through the blue of midday, to the green of evening.

1 the colour clock of the Endless House; Kiesler's own diagram is on page 50 of Bogner, 2003

References and other relevant publications, websites, broadcasts:

'Frederick J. Kiesler's Endless House and its Psychological Lighting', in *Interiors*, November 1950, reprinted in Dieter Bogner, editor – *Friedrich Kiesler: Endless House 1947-1961*, Austrian Frederick and Lillian Kiesler Private Foundation, Vienna, 2003, pp. 50-57.

Interview with Friedrich Kiesler – ' The Endless House', Camera Three, 1960, reprinted in Dieter Bogner, editor – *Friedrich Kiesler: Endless House 1947-1961*, Austrian Frederick and Lillian Kiesler Private Foundation, Vienna, 2003, pp. 85-89.

Website of *The Austrian Frederick and Lillian Kiesler Private Foundation*: http://www.kiesler.org

Dieter Bogner – *Friedrich Kiesler: Inside the Endless House*, Böhlau, Vienna, 1997.

Dieter Bogner, editor – *Friedrich J. Kiesler: Endless Space*, Austrian Frederick and Lillian Kiesler Private Foundation, Vienna, 2001.

Dieter Bogner, editor – *Friedrich Kiesler: Endless House 1947-1961*, Austrian Frederick and Lillian Kiesler Private Foundation, Vienna, 2003.

Le Corbusier, translated by Etchells – *Towards a New Architecture* (1923), John Rodker, London, 1927.

Friedrich Kiesler – 'Pseudo-Functionalism in Modern Architecture', in *Partisan Review*, July 1940, reprinted in Dieter Bogner, editor – *Friedrich Kiesler: Endless House 1947-1961*, Austrian Frederick and Lillian Kiesler Private Foundation, Vienna, 2003, pp. 29-34.

Friedrich Kiesler – 'Hazard and the Endless House', in *Art News*, November 7, 1960, reprinted in Dieter Bogner, editor – *Friedrich Kiesler: Endless House 1947-1961*, Austrian Frederick and Lillian Kiesler Private Foundation, Vienna, 2003, p. 63.

Katsuhiro Yamaguchi – 'Living Media Architecture', in 'Ushida Findlay Partnership: Truss-Wall-House', *Kenchiku Bunka* (Special Issue), August 1993, pp. 66-67.

FARNSWORTH HOUSE

'The most important assignment of life: to begin each day afresh, as if it were the first day – and yet to assemble and have at one's disposal the entire past with all its results and forgotten lessons.'

George Simmel – *Posthumous Fragments and Essays*, 1923 (quoted in Neumeyer, 1991, p. 96; Simmel's book was in Mies van de Rohe's library).

FARNSWORTH HOUSE

On the banks of Fox River near Plano, Illinois, USA
MIES VAN DER ROHE, 1950 (designed c.1945)

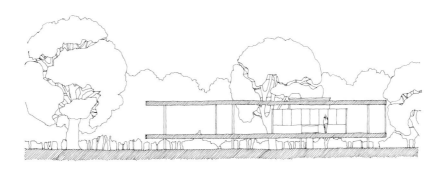

section

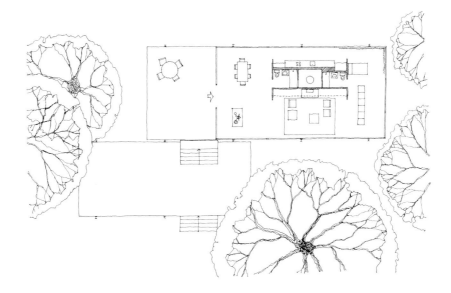

plan

It would be hard to find a building simpler in form. The Farnsworth House is made of materials – principally rolled steel sections and large sheets of plate glass – that became available for building only in the nineteenth and twentieth centuries but this small weekend house in rural Illinois has the elemental simplicity of a primitive shelter. Its underlying architectural idea is to accommodate life in the space between two identically sized rectangular horizontal planes – a platform floor and a flat roof – supported and held apart by eight steel columns. This simple idea manages to be novel (contemporary) and at the same time to make allusions to

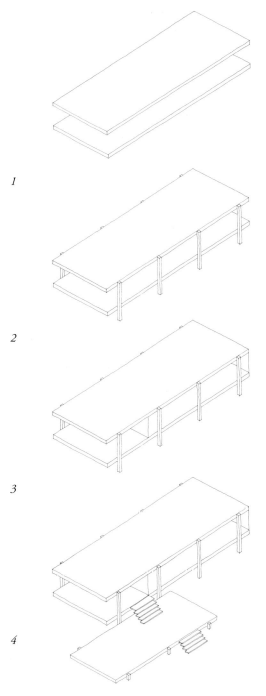

the past. The apparent simplicity of the house has many subtleties. The Farnsworth House is elegant, and the counterpoint of its white structure and disciplined geometry with the irregularity of its sylvan riverside setting is engaging and beautiful. The building is also replete with poetry that appeals to the intellect, deriving from the resonance of its form with ancient architectural precedents.

Identification of place and basic elements

Mies van der Rohe's brief was to make a house for his friend Dr Edith Farnsworth, to identify a place for her to enjoy at weekends and other recreational times. The house contains the usual accommodation: a hearth as a source of warmth and focus for general occupation and sociability; a bed for sleeping etc.; a kitchen; a dining table; two bathrooms; and various cupboards.

The form of the house is perhaps not usual. Its outer form consists of distinct and mostly unequivocal basic architectural elements. First of these, conceptually, is a pair of identically sized horizontal rectangular planes (*1*) – a floor raised above the ground as a platform and a flat roof directly above it. Conceptually (if not in their actual construction) these two planes are identical; it is as if one plane has been split into two to create a place in-between. These two planes define the living space of the house. They establish the special place of the human being, separate from and floating above the natural surroundings. In being rectangular these planes introduce into the setting a clear manifestation of the four horizontal directions intrinsic to the human form (see *Analysing Architecture*, pp. 140-144).

Maybe, in a world without gravity, Mies would have liked these two planes to have floated purely and simply in space; but of course they had to be kept up and firm, and so are welded between eight vertical and evenly spaced columns (*2*), four along each side. The planes and the columns are white – the 'pure' colour, and one that does not conflict with the changing colours of nature.

1

2

3

4

* *There was an intention also to enclose the 'portico' with mosquito excluding screens. These screens were in place when Dr Farnsworth occupied the house in the 1950s and '60s. (There is a photograph showing the screens in place in Blaser, 1972.)*

'I was in the (Farnsworth) house myself from morning till evening. I had never known till then what splendid colours nature can display.'

Mies van der Rohe, quoted in Blaser, 1972, p. 234.

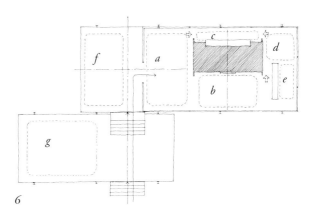

5 *(in the actual design the bathroom to the right is slightly different from as shown, to accommodate a deep cupboard in the kitchen; Vandenberg, 2003, p. 14 shows a preliminary plan apparently with an enclosed kitchen.)*

The third stage in the design, conceptually, is a glass wall separating an interior, physically but not visually, from the outside world (*3*). This glazed compartment does not fill the whole space between the floor and roof planes but leaves two sevenths of it open as an entrance porch or portico that may be used as a sitting terrace, sheltered from rain and shaded from sun.*

The next stage is a second platform, set against the house on the side facing the river (*4*). Its height is a little less than half that of the main floor. It creates a transitional level between the natural ground and the artificiality of the house. This platform too may be used as a sitting terrace, open to the sky. Flights of steps – series of small horizontal platforms that resonate with the general horizontality of the floor and roof – bridge the level changes.

Each of these stages in the composition of basic elements is made with a sense of practical needs: to lift the living space off the ground (the Fox River sometimes floods) and protect it from the rain and sun; to create an interior protected from wind and containing warmth; to provide outside sitting places; and to manage a hierarchical transition from outside to in. The disparate and particular functions the house has to accommodate – sleeping, cooking, eating, bathing… – have not as yet been taken into account. This is not a building where outward form follows the functions of occupation; there is a presumption they will fit between the rectangular planes and within the glass compartment.

The spatial organisation of the interior is best considered in plan. Mies provides for the more private functions by inserting a core (*5*) consisting of three cells – two bathrooms with a plant room in the middle. Along the north side of the core are ranged the kitchen fittings; on the south side is the hearth with cupboards above. Though the core itself is, to all intents and purposes, symmetrical, its asymmetrical position within the glass compartment is important in organising the interior space of the house. Its position nearer to the north glass wall than the south and slightly nearer the east wall than the west, creates four implied spaces of different sizes (*6*). The

6

largest space is the entrance space (*a*) which contains the dining table and may also be used as a study or guest bedroom. The lounge space (*b*) is by the hearth. The narrow north space (*c*) is the kitchen with implied thresholds at each end, from the entrance space and from the bedroom (*d*). Alongside the bedroom is a dressing space (*e*) screened from the lounge space by a high block of cupboards; these cupboards act as a free-standing wall and create an implied doorway between the lounge space and the bedroom. Outside the main doorway into the glass compartment is the sheltered sitting terrace (*f*). The approach crosses the lower terrace (*g*).

It is worth noting other interplays between symmetry and asymmetry in the house: the glass compartment is positioned symmetrically in relation to six of the columns; the steps rise from ground to platform to platform on the axis between the four 'portico' columns; the hearth is on the axis of the (almost) symmetrical core where it crosses the long axis of the house as a whole (*1*) emphasising its role as the symbolic heart of the house; the main doorway is positioned asymmetrically in its glass wall, giving preference to the lounge space over the kitchen.

The distinction of Mies's treatment of space in the Farnsworth House may be better understood by contrasting it with how the

'Many believe that the variable ground plan implies total freedom. That is a misunderstanding. It demands just as much discipline and intelligence from the architect as the conventional ground plan; it demands for example, that the enclosed elements, and they are always needed, be separated from the outside walls – as in the Farnsworth House. Only that way can free space be obtained.'

Mies van der Rohe, 1958.

'Architectural space becomes a defining rather than a confining space.' **Mies van der Rohe**, 1943.

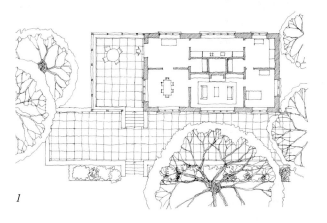

1

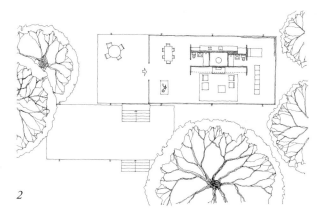

2

house might have been if designed in a more traditional way and built in masonry rather than steel. I have tried drawing such a plan (*1*). This version would have a pitched roof and its walls are supported on foundations in the ground. The core is in the same place, though some form of ventilation would be needed for these rooms. (In the actual Farnsworth House this is provided through the flat roof.) I have moved the dining space and the bedroom to the south side of the house overlooking the river. This has the effect of requiring the front door to be further from the steps, leading into a north facing entrance hall. The dressing room is consequently, and reasonably, now on the north side of the house, with its cupboards along one wall. I have also extended the lower terrace along the whole riverside front of the house and provided it with a shrubbery. The roof over the upper, sheltered, terrace is now supported on timber posts.

Comparing the masonry plan (*1*) with the actual plan (*2*) highlights significant aspects of Mies's treatment of space. Most immediately apparent is the enormous disparity between the areas of ground taken up with load-bearing structure. In the masonry version the roof is supported on thick walls all around the perimeter, and partly on some of the internal walls too. In the actual Farnsworth House this is reduced to eight slim I-section columns (plus four more short columns for the lower terrace). The consequences of this radically alter the nature of the house. Imagine how your experience of the two houses would be different. In the masonry version there is a sense of interior space being contained by walls rather than sandwiched between floor and roof and open to the surroundings. In the masonry house light enters and views out are through 'hole-in-wall' windows; whereas in the actual house the whole perimeter is glass. The Farnsworth is a house without walls, allowing uninterrupted views of the landscape all around. Inside, the masonry house is a sequence of box-like rooms defined by internal walls with doorways from each to the next; the actual house is open except for the core that contains the bathrooms, the cupboards that define and screen the dressing space, and the furniture; its only actual doors – between

the sitting terrace and the glass compartment – are glazed and trying to be part of the glass wall. This is an architectural language of openness, freedom of movement, light and visual contact with the surroundings. The house, which may seem from the outside like a display case for a life, refusing to allow it privacy except by drawing curtains, is intended also as a habitable garden pavilion, gazebo or belvedere – a sheltered place from which to watch and muse upon the landscape, the changing light and seasons, and the river flowing by. In the Farnsworth House the panorama beyond the glass fills the eye's field of view, constrained by the horizontals of the roof and floor, and subdivided only by the structural columns and slim vertical glazing bars.

'Nature too shall have its own life... we should attempt to bring nature, houses, and human beings together into a higher unity. If you view nature through the glass walls of the Farnsworth House, it gains a more profound significance than if viewed from outside.'

Mies van der Rohe, 1958, quoted in Neumeyer, 1991, p. 235.

'I discovered by working with glass models that the important thing is the play of reflections and not the effect of light and shadow as in ordinary buildings.'

Mies van der Rohe, 1922, quoted in Johnson, 1978, p. 187.

There is one significant way in which this last observation is not quite true; the panorama from inside the house is not unobstructed. The glass reflects. Immediately next to the Farnsworth House, as seen from inside, there are at least four or eight other Farnsworth House interiors – 'mirages', each seen, from various angles, 'through the looking glass' (*3*). Far from being a nuisance, this characteristic can be interpreted as part of the poetry of the house, projecting multiple images not only of the interior but also of the occupant out into the world, in a way comparable to that in which Palladio's Villa Rotonda (*Analysing Architecture*, 3rd edition, pp. 160-161) projects, by means of its axes, the presence of the person out into the landscape. Both buildings may be interpreted as 'temples' to the person, instruments for projecting the presence of the person out into the world. (Not having been to the Farnsworth House, I can only imagine what it might be like to be in its lit interior at night, with the reflections in the parallel glass walls stretching to infinity – a *mise en abyme*.)

Using things that are there (relationship to context)

The plan of the Farnsworth House is often published without context; it is a house that seems, in the abstract and pristine purity of its geometric form, to stand separate and aloof from the real world. But its design is sensitive to context. As with the Barcelona Pavilion, Mies located the house precisely (*4*, the positions of the trees are approximate). It is oriented east–west, with the sleeping space at the eastern end for the rising sun and the sitting terraces towards the west for the evening and sunset. The house is placed under the protection of a large existing maple tree, partly shading its southern face from the midday sun. Also, it sits (like a precious object, or at least the display case that contains a precious object) within the external 'room(s)' established by the trees and woods around; Mies created an orthogonal but 'free' plan within the house but in the context of the irregular free plan of the spaces amongst the trees.

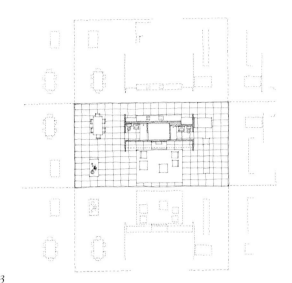

3

4

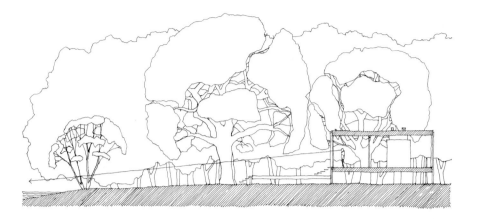

1

The house is placed neither too close nor too far from the river. It could have been positioned right on the bank with its feet in the water, the lower platform a landing stage for a boat; but then its relationship with the land would have been different. As it is, the house has a particular relationship with the river. From inside you see the river through a screen of trees (*1*). That this is significant is indicated by the recurrence of this idea in Mies's drawings for other houses. In the perspective Mies drew of his design for the Hubbe House of 1935 (which I have tried to replicate in the drawing alongside, *2*) he was keen to demonstrate the aesthetic and poetic relationship between the house and the river (a symbol of life's passing?). In this house, as in the Farnsworth, there is a zone that mediates between the house and the landscape. In the Hubbe House it is a paved area under the roof; in the Farnsworth it consists of the upper and lower terraces. This idea seems to relate to one from Japanese architecture. It is illustrated in Edward S. Morse's book *Japanese Homes and Their Surroundings* (*3* and *4*) which had been published in the USA in 1886 and had influenced American architects including Frank Lloyd Wright, whom Mies acknowledged as an influence on his

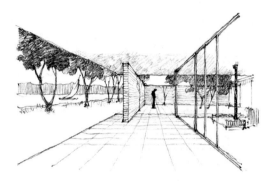

2 (Mies's perspective drawings tend not to depict buildings as objects but, by his choice of point of view, place you as viewer within the space of the house. The realisation that architecture is about human occupation of space is significant in Mies's work.)

own work. One of Morse's illustrations (*4*), which I have reversed for comparison with the drawing of the Hubbe House, shows a room with an open wall giving a view of a landscape. Interposed is a veranda or *engawa* ('*Yengawa*' in Morse's labelling of a similar section, *3*), which is typical of traditional Japanese architecture. This

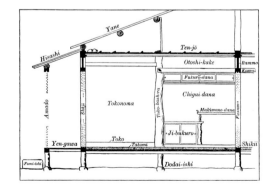

3

4

'What finally is beauty? Certainly nothing that can be calculated or measured. It is always something imponderable, something that lies between things.'

Mies van der Rohe, 1930.

engawa provides the occupant with a space that is neither inside nor out but in-between. Culturally, in Japan these were well used spaces, providing inhabitants with the opportunity to be in their house and part of the outside world at the same time. They suggest an attractive relationship, in which the person is neither excluded nor incarcerated by the house but protected and framed. Mies's design offered Dr Farnsworth the opportunity to sit in such a place, attached to her house but out in the world, warmed by the sun, cooled by the breeze, watching the river flowing by.

Geometry of making

As indicated in the quotation above, Mies was averse to using what I have called in *Analysing Architecture* 'Ideal Geometry' – the geometry of perfect circles, squares and proportional rectangles. His (moral) preference was for rigorous structural and constructional discipline (truth), which has its own innate geometry – 'The Geometry of Making' – rather than the arbitrary imposition of abstract mathematical shapes however perfect they might be. In the Farnsworth House you can search in vain for squares and proportional rectangles. Its geometry is based in the discipline of structural simplicity and the dimensions and nature of its materials, conditioned by a generous sense of human scale.

The drawing alongside (5) illustrates the underlying structural geometry of the house. Eight steel stanchions, four along each side, are deeply bedded, for stability and rigidity, into heavy concrete foundations sunk into the ground. Four long steel beams are welded to these stanchions, two at floor level, two for the roof. Between these are fixed, at equal spacing suited to the spanning capacity of the concrete planks or metal trays to be placed upon them, joists which support the substructure and surface finishes of the roof and the floor. (A drawing showing the make up of these substructures may be found in Vandenberg, 2003, p. 20.) Everything appears to be governed by sense alone.

'Where can we find greater structural clarity than in the wooden buildings of old? Where else can we find such unity of material, construction and form? Here the wisdom of whole generations is stored. What feeling for material and what power of expression there is in these buildings. What warmth and beauty they have! They seem to be echoes of old songs. And buildings of stone as well: what natural feeling they express! What clear understanding of the material! How surely it is joined! What sense they had of where stone could and could not be used! Where do we find such wealth of structure? Where more natural and healthy beauty? How easily they laid beamed ceilings on their old stone walls and with what sensitive feeling they cut doorways through them! What better examples could there be for young architects? Where else could they learn such simple and true crafts than from these unknown masters? We can also learn from brick. How sensible is this small handy shape, so useful for every purpose! What logic in its bonding, pattern and texture! What richness in the simplest wall surface! But what discipline this material imposes! Thus each material has its specific characteristics which we must understand if we want to use it. This is no less true of steel and concrete.'

Mies van der Rohe, 1938 (his inaugural address as Director of Architecture at the Armour Institute of Technology), quoted in Johnson, 1978, pp. 197-198.

5

1

The long quotation on the previous page indicates the inspiration and authority Mies found in traditional architecture, built by what he called 'unknown masters'. In *The Artless Word* (1991, pp. 117-118) Fritz Neumeyer reports that in December 1923 Mies delivered a lecture at the *Berlin Bund Deutscher Architekten* in which he illustrated various examples of traditional architecture (an Indian tent, a leaf hut, an Eskimo house, an Eskimo summer tent, a north German farmhouse) as exemplars for contemporary architects. Mies argued for their simplicity and directness, but using modern materials – steel, glass, concrete.

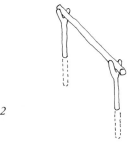

2

According to Neumeyer, at around the same time Mies had open on his desk a copy of a recently published book – *Das unbekannte Afrika* (*The Unknown Africa*) by Leo Frobenius (1923) – which illustrated traditional buildings (and other artefacts) from various regions of Africa. Alongside (*1*) I have drawn one of Frobenius's examples, a *Pfahlbauten* or pile-building from the southern Congo (Frobenius, 1923, Figure 127). The basic structural principle of this building is shown in *2*; it consists of upright forked sticks deeply bedded, for stability and rigidity, into the ground and supporting a cross pole. It is hard to think of a simpler form of structure more appropriate to the material being used; even the forks in the uprights are provided by the way trees branch. If the same directness of approach is transferred to stone it results in something like a trilithon, such as is found in Stonehenge (*3a*); here two massive stones are bedded into the ground with a lintel resting across them. The structural principle of the peristyle of a Greek temple (*3b*) is similar except that the uprights are not bedded into the ground but rely for their stability on the precision of their flat bases resting on a flat platform.

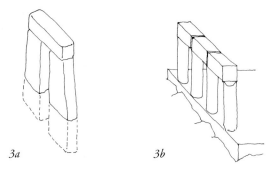

3a   *3b*

These examples suggest the ideal to which Mies was working in designing the Farnsworth House (*4*). The principle is the same; but steel is stronger than either timber or stone and 'wants to' span further (it also 'likes' cantilevers); and a weld, rather than forks or resting, seems the jointing method appropriate to the material.

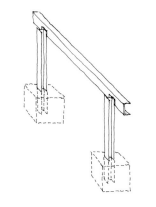

4

'In my very blood I have a sense of creation here, of a primal work of human creativity. It is full of mind and spirit, this perfectly fashioned movement in which we master the force of nature…. We have both withdrawn from nature and mastered it.'

Romano Guardini, 1923-25, p. 12. Guardini is writing about a sail boat on Lake Como. Mies acknowledged Guardini as an influence (Neumeyer, 1991).

'The building art is man's spatial dialogue with his environment and demonstrates how he asserts himself therein and how he masters it.' **Mies van der Rohe**, 1928.

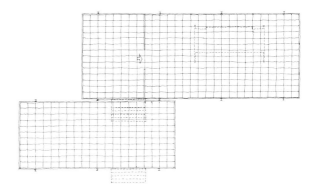

5

The geometry of making disciplines the proportions of the plan of the Farnsworth House too. As can be seen in *4* on page 68 and *6* on this page, the sizes of the rooms in a traditional Japanese house were determined by the unit of the tatami mat; rooms might be eight or six or even two tatami mats big. In the Farnsworth House it is the size of the travertine floor slab that determines the proportions of the plan, the spacing of the columns and the positions of the other elements. Each slab is 2'9" by 2' (a proportion of 11:8). The plan of the main portion of the house is 28 slabs long by 14 wide (a proportion of 2:1). The plan of the lower platform is 20 slabs long by 11 wide. The columns are 8 slabs apart with 2-slab cantilevers at each end. The steps occupy the middle four slabs between the 'portico' columns. The glass wall between the interior and the portico is positioned on a slab-joint line. The core is positioned in relation to the grid of slab-joint lines, which provides the governing framework for the design of the whole house. The house is disciplined by geometry, but it is not the abstract geometry of perfect squares or mathematical proportions. Its geometry is disciplined by the innate geometry of one of its own components, the module of the floor slab, lending the whole an almost genetic integrity.

Temples and cottages

Conditioned by nineteenth century Romantic poetry and twentieth century commercial advertising we perhaps tend to think that traditional architecture symbolises a submissive, or at least providential, relationship with nature. This is not the only interpretation. Traditional architecture, such as that mentioned opposite, may be interpreted as exemplifying human ingenuity in providing for needs using available resources. That is, traditional architecture may be interpreted as heroic – as a symbol of the human mind prevailing, by invention and the application of skill, over natural circumstances. The quotations above suggest that this was Mies's interpretation. It is in this way that the Farnsworth House can be seen as both a

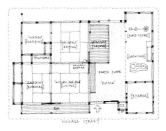

6 (notice too that in this traditional Japanese house the spaces to the left are the living spaces lifted on a platform above the ground. The floor of the utilitarian spaces to the right is the natural ground. Between the two is a step, on which shoes are left. As with the lower platform of the Farnsworth House, this step provides an intermediate level between the ground and the platform.)

'cottage' and a 'temple' (to use the terms discussed in *Analysing Architecture*, pp. 113-128).

In form, the house is clearly a 'temple'. It is regular. It does not impinge on the landscape. It is hermetic in its own form. Unlike a cottage or a country house it has no garden, no walled enclosure, not even a pathway that connects it to the ground and world beyond. It tries its very best to hover above the world rather than be part of it. (It is a cliché to suggest it is like a space craft that has just

' *"I have been having some shadowy doubts*
concerning the sanctity of the rectangle....
Of course it isn't Mies that vocalizes the rectangle
– he is the rectangle!" ' **Edith Farnsworth**, personal journal.

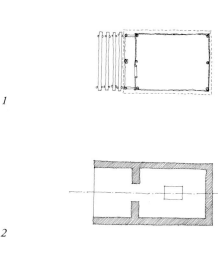

1

2

touched down.) Its materials are perfectly straight or flat, made not by manual skill but by machine. Its walls are all glass, but its interior is profoundly separate… like the intellect inside its skull.

It seems self-evident that Mies, whilst driven to try to achieve the same direct simplicity evident in cottages (and other traditional architecture), was equally fascinated by the poetic potential of the temple. His own architectural education, like that of his contemporaries, was rooted in neo-Classicism. Certainly the Farnsworth House has the underlying syntax of a temple – an enclosed room or *cella* with, through its doorway, a related porch, portico or *pronaos*. This is a syntax shared by the African pile-building illustrated by Frobenius (*1* and p. 70) and the ancient Greek temple's progenitor, the megaron (*2*). Even the Farnsworth House's right-angled approach (*3*) seems redolent of the approach to a Greek temple such as that of Poseidon at Sunium (below), as analysed by Rex Martienssen, a South African architect and academic (and follower of Mies), in his special issue of the *South African Architectural Record* (May 1942, three years before Mies was designing the Farnsworth House) entitled 'Space Construction in Greek Architecture'.

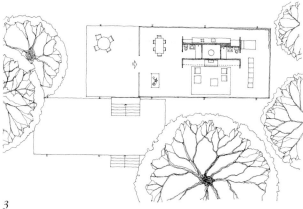

3

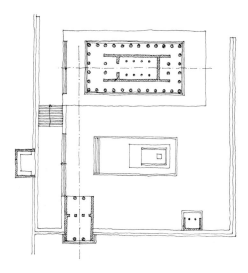

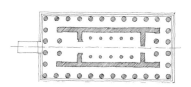

4 (an ancient Greek temple, like the Farnsworth House, helps to tie the surrounding landscape together by establishing a centre with the four cardinal directions of its four-sided orthogonal form projecting out into the world around.)

*'Through elevation on to the plinth and removal
from the common ground, the body becomes a
metaphor, symbol, emblem – a point of reference,
focus and thought.'*

Antony Gormley, 2009 (talking about 'One & Other', an art
work in which a succession of people would occupy the
vacant plinth in Trafalgar Square, London, each for
one hour over one hundred days).

Greek temples too are lent an almost genetic integrity by the application of a dimensional module deriving from one of their component parts; in their case the column and the space between columns (intercolumniation). The Farnsworth House seems to borrow ideas from the Greek temple in other ways too. Intriguingly, the proportions of the plan of its glazed interior are identical to those of another Greek temple, the temple of Aphaia at Aegina *(4 opposite)*. It has a column ratio of 12:6 (2:1, the same as the ratio of slab length to width in the Farnsworth House). The core of Mies's design also seems to be like a variation on the *cella* of the Greek temple, shifted off axis and with the *antae* or wall projections moved around to the sides where they help to define not porches but the kitchen and living spaces. In the Farnsworth House life occupies the space between the *cella* and the outer columns.

As suggested by Antony Gormley (above), a plinth or platform elevates, distinguishes and celebrates what is placed on it. In a Greek temple the celebrity was a god or goddess. In the Farnsworth House it was supposed to be, we might surmise, Dr Edith Farnsworth. But she lost faith in her architect (Farnsworth, personal journal) and seems to have had a 'love-hate' relationship with the house. It has been suggested in various places (including Vandenberg, 2003, p. 15) and mainly by apologists for Mies, that her aversion to the house stemmed from a failed intimate relationship with its architect. There may have been other reasons too, some to do with the fractiousness that developed between client and architect but perhaps also related to difficulties posed by the architecture of the house itself.

Dr Farnsworth's relationship with her house

In the BBC Radio 4 programme 'Start the Week' on Monday 24 November 2008, Malcolm Gladwell, the American writer, voiced an ancient way of interpreting the world, when he claimed that from the many houses we encounter each of us develops in our mind an idea of the quintessential, or Platonic, house – termed 'Platonic' because

it was a tenet of the philosophy of the ancient Greek philosopher Plato that the world could be seen as consisting of always imperfect variations on ideal essences – the ideal essence of 'dog', of 'tree', of 'human being', of the letter 'A'... even of abstract concepts such as 'how to live properly'. We carry this idea of the Platonic house around with us, perhaps amending it when we encounter something – an ingle-nook, a window seat, a walled vegetable garden... or a perfectly cubic room, a grand portico, an extensive formally laid out estate... – that we want to incorporate. Our Platonic houses are the evolved ideals, perhaps originating from extremely early experiences in our lives and developing through life and through education and discussion with peers, against which we each measure the (always in some way imperfect) actual houses we see, experience and live in. Even though Plato suggested that ideal essences exist independent of variations in human values and understandings in some transcendent realm, a more relativistic view (especially applicable to human artefacts rather than natural creatures) would accept that images of the ideal house might vary between cultures, social groups and between individuals with varying life experiences. But for whom and how might the Farnsworth House be deemed to approach a 'Platonic' ideal?

The Farnsworth House may have approached Mies van der Rohe's ideal conception but it seems to have been a mismatch with that of Dr Farnsworth and her reasonable desire to inhabit her own house in practical and physical comfort and security. Like any 'temple' worthy of the label, the Farnsworth House paid scant regard to the physical or psychological needs of its human inhabitant. Its practical failings are detailed in Vandenberg, 2003, and in Dr Farnsworth's personal journal written some years after the house was built. They include overheating in the sun of summer, with the large maple providing inadequate shading for the large glass walls, and the ventilation offered by two small hopper windows at the east end proving less than sufficient. In the depths of winter the heating system was not up to its task and condensation dripped down the

'In the past half century architecture has turned from enclosure to exposure: from the replacement of the wall by the window. Even in the dwelling-house, as Henry James was quick to note on his visit to the United States in 1905, all sense of intimacy and privacy was being forfeited by throwing one room into another, to create a kind of exposed public space for every moment and every function. This movement has perhaps now reached the natural terminus of every such arbitrary interpretation of human needs. In opening our buildings to the untempered glare of daylight and the outdoors, we have forgotten, at our peril and to our loss, the coordinate need for contrast, for quiet, for darkness, for privacy, for an inner retreat.... Today, the degredation of the inner life is symbolized by the fact that the only place sacred from intrusion is the private toilet.'*

Lewis Mumford, 1966, pp. 310-311.

* Henry James – *The American Scene*, Chapman & Hall, London, 1907, pp. 168-169 (Chapter IV, Section II).

glass walls. The hearth too proved to be more symbolic than practical, filling the interior with smoke and ash. Together with leaks in the flat roof, these failings were Dr Farnsworth's justification for not paying Mies his fees and formed the basis of court actions between client and architect in 1953 (see Vandenberg, 2003, p. 15 and Farnsworth, personal journal).

It is reported (Vandenberg, 2003) that, with the introduction of air conditioning and other improvements, these physical problems (apart from the periodic flooding of the river) were solved by the person who bought the house from Dr Farnsworth in 1971, Lord Peter Palumbo (though he sold the house at auction in 2003, and it is now run as a museum, historic property and occasional wedding venue). It seems however that the more significant problems with the house were psychological rather than practical; those that challenged expectations of how a house *should be* and made it difficult to inhabit.

The above quotation from Lewis Mumford's book *The City in History* is an expanded version of a similar paragraph, which included the comment about the 'private toilet', in his earlier book *The Culture of Cities* published in 1940, some half a decade before the Farnsworth House was designed. But this later amended and expanded version, from ten years after the house was built, acquires

'We agreed that we had never seen anything like it and that the two horizontal planes of the unfinished building, floating over the meadows, were unearthly beautiful under a sun that glowed like a wild rose.'

Edith Farnsworth, personal journal.

added conviction because the criticisms appear aimed directly at *its* openness 'to the untempered glare of daylight and the outdoors', at *its* failure to cater for 'the coordinate need for contrast, for quiet, for darkness, for privacy, for an inner retreat' and against 'the fact that (in it) the only place sacred from intrusion is the private toilet'. (In her entertaining personal journal, Dr Farnsworth recounts the story of her attempt to spend the night of December 31 1950 at the house, when it was nearly complete. Her single bare light bulb turned the glass house into a beacon, prompting her distant neighbours to take sympathy and insist she see the New Year in with them.) It is as if Mies had managed to achieve the Platonic ideal, not of Mumford's perfect house, but of the idea of a house against which he railed as some form of 'anti-house'.

While she lived there in the 1950s and 1960s, Dr Farnsworth apparently attempted to transform the house from Mies's concept into her own dwelling, from 'a propaganda issue into a home' (Farnsworth, personal journal). Vandenberg (2003, p. 15) passes on a report on a 1958 visit to the house by Adrian Gale (himself an architect who worked with Mies in the USA in the late 1950s and later became head of the Plymouth School of Architecture in the UK). He found it 'a sophisticated camp site rather than a weekend dreamhouse'. And when the future purchaser of the house, Peter Palumbo, visited Dr Farnsworth in 1971 he bemoaned the presence of the mosquito netting around the upper terrace (which had been part of the original design, but seemed in some way to dilute the house's purity of material and form) and found that Dr Farnsworth had attempted to provide the house with a traditional 'cottage' garden complete with roses and crazy paving (Vandenberg, 2003, p. 15 and Hughes, 2003).

And yet, despite its failings, the Farnsworth House remains an acknowledged masterwork of twentieth century, if not all-time, architecture.

So what is it that is happening when a building can be lauded as a great and seminal work of architecture and yet at the same time reviled as a failure, impractical and impossible to inhabit comfortably? Certainly the Farnsworth House is not the only instance in the history of architecture, particularly in the twentieth century: Le Corbusier's Villa Savoye of 1929 (see later analysis) suffered a comparable if more protracted fate, failing as a house and finally finding the meaning of its existence as a 'museum' house; and Zaha Hadid's celebrated 1994 Vitra Fire Station proved impossible to use as a fire station and latterly became a venue for cocktail parties and a museum of classic chairs.

Rather like the celebrated court case in which a 1920s Tennessee school teacher was prosecuted for teaching a Darwinian version of evolution, as portrayed in the film *Inherit the Wind* (Stanley Kramer, 1960), Farnsworth v. Mies in 1953 seems to have touched on philosophical issues concerning the nature of architecture and the duties of an architect. In her personal journal, Dr Farnsworth wrote disparagingly of Mies on the witness stand:

> '*You can't imagine what an exhibition of ignorance he put on! He didn't know anything about steel, its properties or its standard dimensions, nor about construction, or high school physics or just plain common sense. All he knows is that guff about his concept and in the Kendall County Courthouse that doesn't go down.*'

So perhaps in the end Dr Farnsworth hung herself and all those who do not quite understand what it is that architects do. For on what else can architecture ultimately depend except '*that guff…*'? It might have lessened Mies's discomfort on the witness stand if he had displayed to the court some knowledge of steel and construction, but that would not have changed the fundamental truth that such knowledge can never in itself generate the 'thought' (concept, idea) that 'good architecture', as Ludwig Wittgenstein observed, 'expresses' (see p. 2). At its essence architecture is not about knowing how the heating system works nor like Paul Newman in *The Towering Inferno* (John Guillermin, 1974) having an implausibly intimate knowledge of the electrical wiring of a skyscraper. At root, architecture, like some types of philosophy, is about generating ideas

and exploring propositions. But unlike in philosophy, in architecture this is done not through the medium of words but through form, construction and the organisation of space. Poets, novelists and playwrights are not expected to have intimate knowledge of desktop publishing software, industrial printing processes and book-binding because it is through these that their work will reach the shelf of a bookshop, a reader's armchair, or the stage in front of an audience. We accept that their stock in trade consists in ideas. The techniques of building, though their understanding may stimulate and support architectural ideas, are merely the means by which such ideas are realised. Like all great modes of human creativity – and architecture is arguably greater in its reach and effect than any other because its products frame just about everything we do (certainly including the shelving of books, reading in an armchair, and staging drama) – architecture depends fundamentally upon the ability of the human imagination to generate ideas to do with the organisation of space and the identification of place (see *Analysing Architecture*, third edition, 2009, pp. 25-34).

Even so… we are left in the Farnsworth House with a work of architecture that is, by some accounts, unfit for purpose.

In her personal journal Dr Farnsworth implicitly supplies what might offer another facet of this conundrum. She writes, with some irony and thinly veiled sarcasm, of the many architects who came to see the house even before it was complete:

> '*Architects came from various European countries…. Most of them were fulsome in their words of praise and wonderment at the miracle which was taking form in that rural spot; one or two of the German ones exclaimed, "Master!" and crawled across the terrace to the latter's feet where he sat on a low aluminium deckchair, impassively awaiting the throaty plaudits of the visitors, "Grossartig!", "Unglaublich!".*'

'Magnificent!', 'Unbelievable!'. It seems that Dr Farnsworth had come to see the house as a 'temple' not to herself but to its creator. However amusing and attractive that pricking of the pomposity

'Perhaps, as a man, he is not the clairvoyant primitive that I thought he was, but simply a colder and more cruel individual than anybody I have ever known.' **Edith Farnsworth**, personal journal.

*'**Schulze**: One sits in a vitreous prism of pure form and contemplates, in stillness, an ever-changing nature. Farnsworth is a shrine.*
***Freed**: Or a temple. Or a metaphor for a house, not a house in the psychological or physical sense.... A wonderful thing that house.'* **Franz Schulze**, 1989, p. 196.

of an evidently arrogant architect's ego might seem, as an explanation of how this house might be judged unimpeachably good and irretrievably bad at the same time it somehow misses the point. In 1971 Peter Palumbo, a respected and aesthetically acute man, paid large sums of good money to buy the house and put it into good repair. In 2003 the art critic Robert Hughes spent a night in the house and said in a BBC television programme about his experience that its *'very artificiality... makes you see its opposite... even more clearly. Without that house it's just trees; with the house it's a landscape, an idea about the world.'* It was clear from the programme that, although he knew he could not live in the house, Hughes respected it greatly as a work of architecture. And at the end of 2003 a very large amount of money was raised by various charitable bodies to save the house from being dismantled and moved elsewhere. What stronger evidence could there be that this is a building which is not merely respected but seriously loved?

So how can we make sense of the apparent conundrum? One approach is to distinguish idea and effect from purpose and expectation. The house is loved because it is elegant and a powerful example of how a work of architecture can act on us and intensify our perceptions of the world around. But this conflicts with our usual expectation of a house as a refuge. In his book *The Experience of Landscape* (1975), Jay Appleton argued that our aesthetic appreciation of our surroundings is conditioned by a primal need, as an aid to survival, to be able to survey our surroundings (to keep an eye out for threats) without being seen. The Farnsworth House allows its inhabitant to survey the land around, but as a 'display case' it does not provide a refuge, it rather draws attention. There is a mismatch between idea, effect, purpose and expectation.

Architectural ideas can have lives of their own; sometimes it takes time for them to find the meaning of their existence. This is a building that does not succeed as a refuge but which works well as a 'temple', whether to its inhabitant, to its architect, or to those weddings for which it is presently advertised.

Exploring variations

It is as interesting for architects to muse on how the work of others might be modified as it is for composers to write variations on musical themes by others or for philosophers to test other people's arguments. Such creative interaction with the work of other architects can be a source of ideas and develop an understanding of how architecture works more generally.

It would be impertinent, even irreverent, to suggest that the Farnsworth House, this seminal building, could be different in any way. Its fabric is elegant and distilled to its purest essence and, like a finely honed poem, cannot be improved, except to obviate its practical problems. (Periodic flooding remains a challenge for the building.) But architecture is not merely a matter of a building's fabric and the elimination of condensation and leaking roofs; it involves context and content too.

As illustrated above, one of the models from which the Farnsworth House derived (the 'theme' on which it is itself a variation) was the ancient Greek temple. The 'Platonic' Greek temple does not stand isolated in its landscape; it is protected in a sacred precinct (*temenos*) enclosed by a wall. The same is true of the shrines of Hindu temples in India, which are protected from the outside world by high walls around their sacred compounds; or of the traditional Tea Houses of Japan ensconced in their exquisite gardens. In *Doorway* (2007, pp. 18-19) I recounted the story of a recluse on a Scottish island, the core of whose existence was a battered caravan (his 'temple' and 'inner retreat'), who realised that he had to protect his solitude by the assertion of boundaries some distance away to deter intruders. Precedent suggests that sacred pavilions ('temples') need protection, sequestration from the world. Although the Farnsworth House has its own territory and is surrounded by trees, its peace and solitude for Dr Farnsworth were never sacrosanct: remember all those curious and intrusive architect visitors, and her failed attempt to spend New Year's Eve alone in the house; also, her decision to sell the

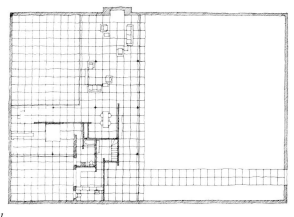

1

section

house in 1971 was prompted by the realignment of a nearby road, bringing it closer to the house and reducing her peace and privacy even more. While she lived in the house it seems Dr Farnsworth had to protect her solitude by cultivating a reputation for fierceness (Vandenberg, 2003, p. 24). Mies's architecture explored openness and a relationship with infinite space; a precinct wall would have radically altered (destroyed?) the intended architecture of the Farnsworth House, cutting it off from its uninterrupted relationship with its surroundings. The idea of a glass house in a secret walled garden is nevertheless intriguing. Mies himself designed a number of 'courtyard' houses in the 1930s. Above (*1*) is the plan of his House with Three Courts (1934).

The African house illustrated in Frobenius and on pages 70 and 72 provides refuge with its enclosed cell. This other traditional dwelling (*2*), in the Western Ghat mountains of Kerala, India, has an uninterrupted relationship with its surroundings. Its syntax is comparable to that of the Farnsworth House in that it comprises a roofed structure open to the landscape; the glass walls are not needed here because the climate is warm. This house too has a core, comprising two small rooms. Most of the life of the house is lived in the undivided space between the core and the structural columns, under the shelter of the roof and with a view of the landscape around. But the core plays a role that is different from that in the Farnsworth House. Here, rather than containing merely utilitarian functions of bathroom ('private toilet') and heating plant, the core consists of a storeroom and a *puja* room, which is the spiritual heart of the house. The *puja* room is a dark cell into which the inhabitant withdraws from the world for prayer and worship. It provides the house with its 'inner retreat', its refuge.

The content of a house consists in the life it accommodates as well as the disposition of its spaces, furniture and fittings. In this regard, the experience of the quintessential American hermit, Henry

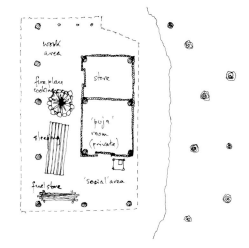

plan

2

David Thoreau, whose example the Farnsworth House certainly evokes, seems relevant. In the 1840s Thoreau decided to live alone in a small hut in woods by a lake, Walden Pond, near Concord, Massachusetts, to see if he could live simply. He wrote an account of his experience (Thoreau, 1854). His solitude was protected by the density of the surrounding woods as well as by his hut's isolation from the town. But crucially, and this was an important part of his 'experiment', he changed his mode of living. His hut contained nothing but a hearth at which to cook his food, a bed in which to sleep, a chest in which to store his few belongings and a table at which to sit and write; he also had an extra chair for any visitor with whom he could enjoy philosophical discussion. His hut was his refuge but he lived as much of his life as possible out in the woods and on the pond; and sometimes he sat on his threshold, enjoying being at home and in the world at the same time (see *Doorway*, pp. 93-94). He set a model of simple life away from the cares of business and society. The Farnsworth House, with its spare and pared down furniture,

*'Infinite space is the ideal that the Western soul
has always striven to find, and to see immediately
actualized, in its world around.'*
Oswald Spengler, (1918) 1932, p. 175.

invites a similar change in mode of living from its inhabitant. As a philosophical proposition, the house purports to require the occupant to live simply and meditatively, in communion with nature, in a quasi-religious relationship. If the occupant resists, the house, it seems, will not forgive. This may be interpreted as a dictatorial attitude on the part of the architect. It is didactic but no more dictatorial than the asceticism suggested by a monk's cell; and the situation of the Farnsworth House is more generous, aesthetically richer and more hedonistic than that.

In conclusion

For some buildings it seems as if the presence of the human being is merely incidental. One might cite Peter Eisenman's House VI and Eric Owen Moss's The Box (*Analysing Architecture*, Case Studies 9 and 10) and Frank Gehry's Bilbao Guggenheim Museum as three amongst many possible examples. It is as if in relation to such buildings the person may be *there* but is excluded from the architecture; left outside even when inside; expected to be content with admiring the visual complexity and intellectual ingenuity of the work as an onlooker rather than as a participant. This is an accusation that cannot be levelled at the Farnsworth House. Even though it might not work as a comfortable and commodious home, its essential and indispensable ingredient is the person. Without the person it is incomplete. Though it does look well in a photograph – its pure white geometry set against the dark green of the trees and floating above the greensward and floods – by all accounts, even that of the disillusioned Dr Farnsworth as well as of Robert Hughes, the house is most powerful when experienced, when it acts upon the person as an instrument by which the surrounding landscape is intensified.

Behind his arrogance and apparent coldness, behind the severe discipline of his tectonic language, it seems that Mies could achieve profound humanity in his work. The Farnsworth House *is* perhaps best described as a 'temple'. Possibly he did originally intend

it as a temple to a person for whom he felt affection but with whom he was to fall out. Certainly, as most architects would, he saw it as a temple to his own creative genius. But over and above either of these, maybe in ways that he himself could not verbalise, it turned out to be a temple to the human being. That is why the house is loved – because it provides something more than just an object to look at and admire. For its occupant, as an instrument and as a gift, it changes the world.

As the Farnsworth House's glass walls, steel columns, roof and travertine floor mediate between the contained person and the surrounding landscape, they together frame that person as a precious object, project that person's presence out into the landscape, and transform that person's perception of the world around… with its breezes shifting the branches of the trees, its changing light through dawn to noon to dusk to night, and with the annual cycle of the seasons, through floods, falling leaves, winter snows and burgeoning spring. Certainly this is not a house in which to live a quotidian life. It is a temple that, like a moral creed or a poem, sets down tenets for reflection and aesthetic contemplation.

Conclusion

Around the same time that the Farnsworth House was being built, Mies van der Rohe was experimenting with variations on the theme of the Farnsworth House. The principal example is an unbuilt project called the Fifty-by-fifty House (*1*); so called because of its dimensions in feet.

Most of the key ingredients of the Farnsworth House are present in this house too: the simple planar roof sheltering the accommodation; the glass wall; the grid of paving slabs, in this case square; the asymmetrically placed core for the private functions and plant room; the free plan; and the outside terrace intermediate between the human domain of the house and the landscape around. Here however the plan is a perfect square; the roof is supported on

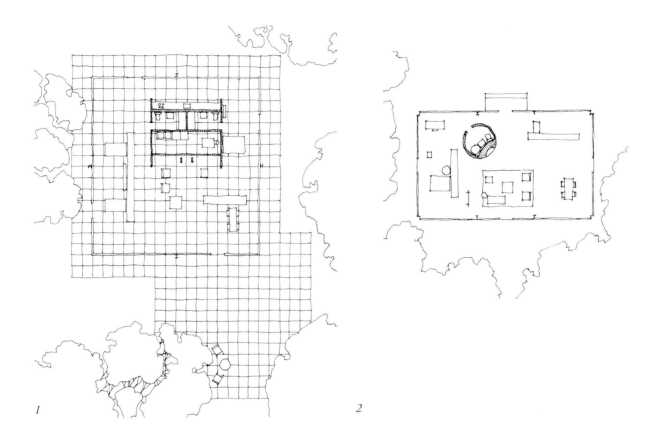

1   *2*

just four columns, one in the centre of each side; and neither the main floor nor the terrace are raised above the ground on platforms – they are distinguished from the surrounding grass only by their paved surface. As in the Farnsworth House there is a hearth, on the centre-line axis of the core, providing the focus of the living space. There are four doorways, arranged in a sort of radial symmetry, around the glass perimeter; two of these seem to relate to the bed spaces on each side; one leads out onto the terrace; whilst the remaining door seems the main entrance, leading into a lobby space and giving access to the kitchen. Otherwise the syntax of the spatial organisation is similar to that in the Farnsworth House.

The Fifty-by-fifty House illustrates that Mies was not, in the Farnsworth House, designing a one-off house but developing a language of architecture that could be used in a variety of circumstances, if not generally. This is a language prompted, or made possible, by the industrial development of materials such as plate glass and rolled steel sections. It is also a language that explores the arrangement of space free of the straightjacket of load-bearing walls, and rooms with doorways. The language depends, for its spatial freedom, on the use of flat roofs (pitched roofs have their own geometries that can compromise or dictate the layout of space beneath them); and on the grouping of private functions and other small enclosed spaces into cores detached from the outside walls (and thus depending on artificial ventilation).

Philip Johnson, acolyte of Mies van der Rohe, tried his own experiment with this language in the Glass House he designed and built for himself in 1949 (*2*), after the Farnsworth House had been designed but before it was built. In variation of Mies's language, it has doorways positioned symmetrically on each side; structural columns positioned inside the perimeter glass, except at the corners where they are exposed to the outside; and a circular core containing the bathroom.

References and other relevant publications, websites, broadcasts:

Jay Appleton – *The Experience of Landscape* (1975), Hull University Press/ John Wiley, London, 1986.

Werner Blaser – *Mies van der Rohe*, Thames and Hudson, London, 1972.

Peter Carter – *Mies van der Rohe at Work*, Phaidon, London, 1999.

Edith Farnsworth – Extract from personal journal, available at: www.farnsworthhouse.org/resource_center_references_2006.htm (accessed April 2009).

Edward R. Ford – *The Details of Modern Architecture*, MIT Press, Cambridge, MA, 1990.

Leo Frobenius – *Das unbekannte Afrika: aufhellung der schicksale eines Erdteils*, Oscar Beck, München, 1923.

Antony Gormley, quoted in Maev Kennedy – 'Antony Gormley wants you for fourth plinth', in *The Guardian*, 26 February 2009.

Romano Guardini, translated by Bromiley – *Letters from Lake Como: Explorations in Technology and the Human Race* (1923-25), William B. Eerdmans Publishing Company, Grand Rapids, Michigan, 1994.

Robert Hughes – 'Mies van der Rohe – Less is More', *Visions of Space* 4/7, BBC, 2003.

Philip Johnson – *Mies van der Rohe* (1947, 1953), Secker and Warburg, London, 1978.

Phyllis Lambert – *Mies in America*, Harry N. Abrams, New York, 2001.

Dirk Lohan – 'Farnsworth House, Plano, Illinois, 1945-50', *Global Architecture Detail*, ADA Edita, Tokyo, 1976.

R.D. Martienssen – *The Idea of Space in Greek Architecture* (1956), Witwatersrand University Press, Johannesburg, 1964.

R.D. Martienssen – 'Space Construction in Greek Architecture with Special Reference to Sanctuary Planning', in *South African Architectural Record*, Volume 27, Number 5, May 1942.

Lewis Mumford – *The City in History* (1961), Penguin Books, Harmondsworth, 1966.

Fritz Neumeyer – *The Artless Word: Mies van der Rohe on the Building Art*, MIT Press, Cambridge, MA, 1991.

Mies van der Rohe – 'The Preconditions of Architectural Work', lecture, February 1928, Staatliche Kunstbibliotek, translated and published in Neumeyer, 1991, p. 299.

Mies van der Rohe – 'Build Beautifully and Practically! Stop this Cold Functionality', in *Duisberger Generalanzeiger*, 49, January 26, 1930, translated and reprinted in Neumeyer, 1991, p. 307.

Mies van der Rohe – 'Museum for a Small City', in *Architectural Forum*, Volume 78, Number 5, 1943, pp. 84-85, reprinted in Neumeyer, 1991, p. 322.

Mies van der Rohe – 'Christian Norberg-Schulz: a Talk with Mies van der Rohe', in *Baukunst und Werkform*, Volume 11, Number 11, 1958, translated and reprinted in Neumeyer, 1991, pp. 338-339.

Franz Schulze – *The Farnsworth House* (a booklet that was available at the house), 1997.

Franz Schulze – *Mies van der Rohe: a Critical Biography*, University of Chicago Press, Chicago and London, 1985.

Franz Schulze – *Mies van der Rohe: Critical Essays*, Museum of Modern Art, New York, 1989.

David Spaeth – *Mies van der Rohe*, The Architectural Press, London, 1985.

Oswald Spengler, translated by Atkinson – *The Decline of the West* (1918, 1922), George Allen & Unwin, London, 1932.

Wolf Tegethoff – *Mies van der Rohe: the Villas and Country Houses*, MIT Press, Cambridge, Mass., 1985.

Henry David Thoreau – *Walden* (1854), Bantam, New York, 1981.

Simon Unwin – *Analysing Architecture*, Routledge, London, third edition, 2009.

Simon Unwin – *Doorway*, Routledge, London, 2007.

Maritz Vandenberg – *Farnsworth House: Mies van der Rohe*, Phaidon (Architecture in Detail Series), London, 2003.

LA CONGIUNTA

'Our profession is an old language and it has a grammar. And about this people don't know anything. So how is it they can do a building if they do not know the grammar? In the primary school you have a thing like an "A". Perhaps then you have "apple". A long time later you try to write a love letter. I think you have learned the language ten or eleven years until this moment. For me it's the same. It's very important that you give yourself time to learn this profession from the beginning.'

Peter Märkli, quoted in Beatrice Galilee
– 'Peter Märkli', in *Iconeye*, Number 059,
May 2008, available at:
www.iconeye.com/index.php?option=com_content&vie
w=article&id=3453:peter-m%C3%83%C2%A4rkli

LA CONGIUNTA

A gallery for the sculpture of Hans Josephsohn, Giornico, Switzerland
PETER MÄRKLI, 1992

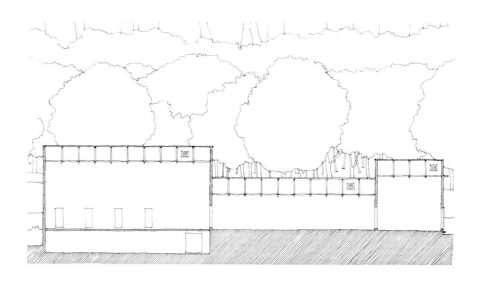

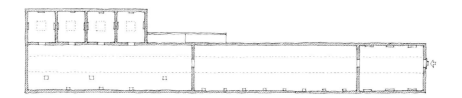

It might be argued that all 'temples' are female. This one certainly is. *La Congiunta* in Italian means 'the female relative', presumably a (or a potential) mother, suggesting a womb – a receptacle for a child conceived and brought to fruition through long gestation. Artists often refer to their works as their children. Peter Märkli's building is a receptacle for a collection of sculpture by Hans Josephsohn.

La Congiunta stands alone in a field amongst vineyards in a narrow valley close to the village of Giornico, in the Ticino district of Switzerland. It is a long, grey, windowless, concrete box. This austere building is a destination for pilgrimage. It was intended for those wishing to admire Josephsohn's sculpture. It has become a destination for pilgrims intrigued by Märkli's architecture.

The building has some of the key characteristics of pilgrim architecture. It stands apart. It is enigmatic. It is a shrine. Its interior offers a refuge, away from the world. The pilgrim has to commit time to travel there and has to make extra efforts to find the building and

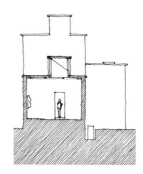

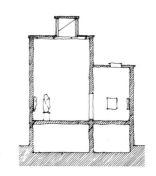

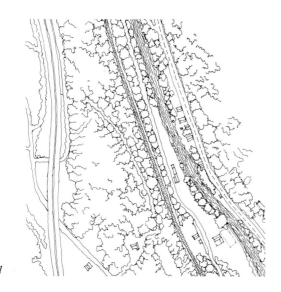

2   3   4

to gain entry. As if negotiating with a 'guardian of the doorway', visitors to *La Congiunta* must obtain a key from the owner of a local café; and to find the entrance to the building, which faces away from your approach, you must walk along the whole length of the building's blank walls. Like an old church it has no electricity, no services, no lavatory. But, also like an old church, it does have a 'crypt'; in this instance an undercroft used in connection with the local vine growing.

La Congiunta is a long building; its length echoes the length and narrowness of the steep-sided valley (*1*). Its long and narrow field lies next to the river, between the railway and the old road, the Via Cantonale. Including a lane that provides walking access to the building, four lines of movement – railway, lane, river and road – draw four almost parallel lines. (There is also an expressway, the E35, shown to the left of the drawing, which also generally follows the line of the valley heading north from Italy to the Gotthard

Tunnel.) The lines are divided and defined by layers of trees. The long and narrow *La Congiunta* fits into this grain. Approach is from the village just to the south. The building's entrance is at its northern end.

Basic, combined and modifying elements

La Congiunta is built of solid *in situ* concrete – concrete poured while liquid into moulds (formwork) erected on site and removed once the concrete has set (gone off). This is not a building that considers the comfort of people; it is a temple for sculptures that are indifferent to cold and damp. Internal daylight (there is no artificial light in the main part of the building) enters through clerestory strips – 'glazed' in translucent plastic which softens sunlight and prevents sharp shadows – running the full length of the building's three sections (*2-4*). This arrangement seems to have been influenced by Märkli's interest in the elemental quality of Romanesque church architecture (*5* and *6*). At the end of the building furthest from the entrance there are four side 'chapels', each with its own centred square rooflight. Josephsohn's enigmatic and apparently visceral work is disposed mainly on the walls, with three free-standing sculptures on pedestals in the last and highest of the building's three main chambers. Even on a bright sunny day the work is displayed in a soft even greyish light (slightly browner in the small side chapels). The interior is monochrome like a cave.

If the Farnsworth House denies the wall in favour of openness to the landscape, *La Congiunta* is a building that asserts the wall's archaic power to enclose and separate a place from everywhere else. It is a series of cells linked by doorways with a single entrance at one end. Apart from the light entering from above, there is very little more to this building. Its basic architectural elements are very few. Its floor is raised a couple of feet above the slight slope of the

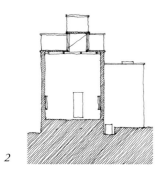

1

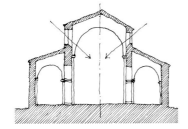

5

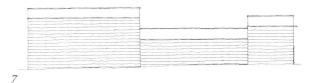

7

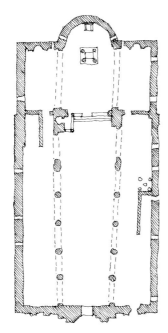

6 in lectures, Peter Märkli has analysed this Romanesque church to explain his interest in the potential of elemental architecture; its section, with the raised central roof allowing clerestory light into the nave, seems to have influenced that of La Congiunta, *though his spare structure of slim steel beams spanning between concrete parallel walls does not require the intermediate support of columns between 'nave' and 'aisles' in the Romanesque example*

ground outside but this is apparent only at the entrance. Whereas the Farnsworth House's floor floats supported on its columns above the ground, the walls of *La Congiunta* go down into the ground. As in the case of the Farnsworth House there are no made paths leading to the building; it stands like a ship in a sea of grass. There is a small step like a ledge at the entrance to help (make) you climb inside. The entrance doorway has a simple industrial metal door

fixed to the outside surface of the concrete wall. The roof projects slightly over the full width of the entrance wall, like a vestigial porch. Everything is as simple, minimal, reduced, condensed… as it can be. As you walk around the building to the entrance its sharp corners screen off the landscape of trees and distant mountains with a grey nothingness. And as you enter you are cut off from the landscape completely. Once inside the grey interior you can clang the door behind you or leave it open to retain a bright but distinctly separated glint of green and sunlight. Each of the doorways between the cells has a raised threshold which, like in a Hindu temple, makes you conscious of stepping from one into the next, from one frame into another. In *La Congiunta* the differences between the frames – the cells – is only subtle. The thresholds do not offer dramatic changes in states of being. The first cell (*2*) is short in length and medium in height; the second (*3*) is long but the lowest in height; the third (*4*) is the same length as the second but also the tallest of the three. The four side 'chapels' are almost square in plan and have a height between that of the first and second cells. One senses there is a harmonic proportioning discipline governing these dimensional relationships (see below).

Geometry of making

Apart from the plastic clerestory, the sheet metal roof and the slight steel roof structure, *La Congiunta* is a building of a single material, *in situ* concrete. In *Analysing Architecture* the 'geometry of making' is described in terms of the construction of materials such as bricks and sawn pieces of timber which are assembled by addition, i.e. by placing one piece of material on or attaching it to others. The geometry that governs *in situ* concrete is different. One might think that this initially fluid material would lend itself to freer shapes; but its form is determined by its mould, the formwork into which it is poured;

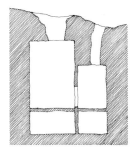

1 inside La Congiunta the outside world is no longer relevant; its interior is like a cave system; only at the entrance, as in a natural cave, is the outside apparent; the only other influence from outside is the light filtering through the roof

5

and this, whether made of timber or steel panels, is conditioned by its own geometry of making.

As money was gradually forthcoming for *La Congiunta*, different parts were built at different times. *In situ* concrete has to be constructed incrementally anyway. It is poured in 'lifts'. The combination of formwork and lifts leave 'joints' in the surface of the resultant concrete. These lines are apparent in the walls of *La Congiunta*. They give the building the appearance of being layered (*7* on previous page), like the strata in geological formations. They do not align exactly across the three sections of the building; each takes its datum from the top of its wall rather than from either the shared ground or floor level. This too suggests there is some proportioning discipline at play in this building, one that relates to the heights of

the blocks rather than to any module that might be suggested by the lines in the surface of the concrete.

Ideal geometry

The interior of *La Congiunta* may be like a cave system (*1*) but it is a cave system conceived by a human mind and constructed by human ingenuity; as such, it is rectangular. The cave-like quality of the interior is reinforced by the monolithic nature of the concrete walls, floor and thresholds, as if the spaces have been scoured out of solid rock. The human (intellectual) character of the rectangular spaces is enhanced, given measure, by the geometric proportional discipline that Märkli has imposed upon them.

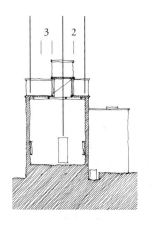

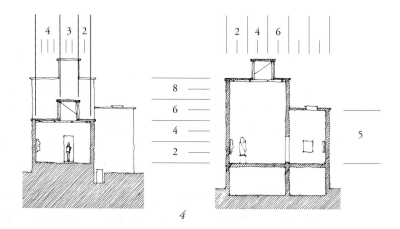

2

3

4

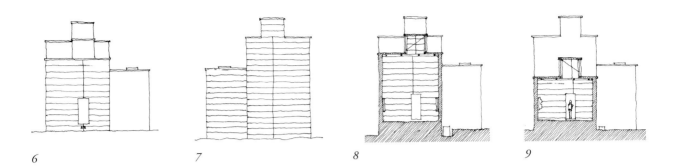

6   *7*   *8*   *9*

When looking for the underlying proportions of a building it is notoriously difficult to know whether you have found the right ones and it is very easy to persuade yourself that you have discovered a proportional relationship that is not actually there. In particular the thicknesses of walls and other parts of the building confuse matters, so do inaccuracies in construction. It is rarely certain whether measurements should be taken from the inside face of a wall, the outside face, or the wall's centre line. And there are always some differences between the 'platonic' accurate form of a building constructed by drawing on paper (or on a computer) and the building constructed in real materials. I apologise to the architect if in this case I have made mistakes or misrepresented his intentions. It is clear however that Märkli does use proportion in his design. I shall

not speculate as to whether he ascribes symbolic significance to the numbers on which his proportions are based or sees them primarily as imbuing his composition with a visual harmony equivalent to the aural harmony of music.

Some of the proportions apparent in *La Congiunta* are indicated in the drawings opposite (*2-4*). The tallest of the blocks, furthest from the entrance, appears to have proportions, measured externally, of eight units high by six units wide (*4*). The side 'chapels' add a further four of these units to the width and are five units high. The entrance and middle blocks are six and four units high respectively (*2* and *3*).

The position of the clerestory appears to be determined according to proportions measured internally (*3*). Here the width of

10

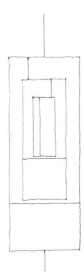

11

the space is divided into nine, with three ninths given to the clerestory, and two ninths and four ninths to the right and left 'aisles' respectively. The position of the doorways, with their shared axis, follows a different proportional rule. For these the width of the space seems divided into five (*2*), with the doorway axis on the two fifths line. These arrangements mean that the axis of the doorway is not (quite) aligned with that of the clerestory (*5*). And, obviously, neither the clerestory nor the line of doorways are aligned with the central axis of the cells themselves. Only the four side 'chapels' have centrally aligned doorways and rooflights. All the doorways are the same size and have a proportion of eight by three (*10* on previous page).

Märkli's architecture in *La Congiunta* refuses to acknowledge the geometric central axis of the three main cells of the building. This is evident in the asymmetrical positioning of the clerestory and the line of doorways. Märkli even refuses to allow the clerestory and doorways to share an axis of their own. There is a third element in the game Märkli plays with axes. This involves the positioning of the vertical 'joints' in the concrete, both internally and externally.

On the entrance elevation (*6* on previous page) the vertical line in the concrete is positioned to mark the doorway axis. On the elevation at the other end of the building (*7* on previous page) the line is positioned to mark the axis of the clerestory. Inside the building the lines in the concrete are positioned over the two doorways but neither marks the axial centre line. Over the doorway from the entrance gallery into the middle gallery (*8* on previous page) it is to the left. Over the doorway from the middle gallery into the tallest gallery (*9* on previous page) it is to the right. The vertical joint line in the wall at the end of the tallest gallery appears not to be on any axis. The result is that, as one looks down through the line of doorways the vertical lines in the adjacent concrete do not align (*11* on previous page); they oscillate first to the left, then to the right and then to the left again. As there is counterpoint in the music of the Barcelona Pavilion, so too is there a counterpoint of axes here.

Transition, hierarchy, heart

The effect of the general asymmetry of Märkli's design may be understood by comparing it with how the building might have been if designed around one central longitudinal axis (*2*) and with a progressive increase of ceiling height from the entrance inwards (*1*). When transformed in this way the building becomes more like a traditional Christian church. It acquires a staged progression from entrance to – if one moves one of the side 'chapels' to the end of the building – a 'sanctuary'. Discarding one of the side chapels and positioning the other two as 'transepts' would create the familiar, if elongated, cruciform plan of a Christian church. In this arrangement, the sculptures would probably be arranged like the sculptures in a church on both side walls of the cells and in the transept chapels. Maybe one special work would be positioned in the sanctuary, on the axis and visible in the distance through four doorways from *La Congiunta*'s threshold, providing a focus and terminus to the route similar to the altar in a church.

Even though the allusions to church architecture are clear, in the building as Märkli designed it (*4*) the hierarchy is not so definite and hierarchical. It avoids a single culmination in a 'sanctuary'. In the building as built each of the four side 'chapels' has equivalent significance. Also, the asymmetry of the route from the entrance, though powerful because of the axial alignment of the doorways, gives the space a bias to one side, with a route (a pathway) to the right hand side and space for the exhibits to the left (*5*). This bias is then, in the final cell, counterbalanced by the doorways into the side 'chapels'. Of course, as you look at the sculptures, you deviate from the axis established by the building. But at each doorway you are brought back to it before stepping over the threshold into the next frame. This is not a building that takes you to a spiritual goal but one that takes you further into a psychological world divorced from the natural world outside.

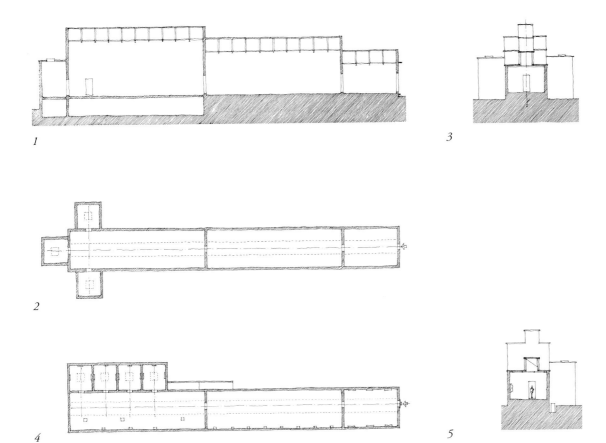

1

3

2

4

5

Conclusion, and a comment on flat roofs

I am sure that more proportional relationships could be found in this building than have been identified in this analysis. The instances identified are sufficient to indicate how Märkli's mind was working when drawing its plans and elevations, and also to hint at how such games may be played in architecture. A difficulty lies in deciding when such games change from playing an effective part in one's experience of a building into an architect's private indulgence. Experience of an aligned series of doorways is always powerful. When they culminate in a focal point – an altar, an object or a monarch on a throne – an additional power is brought into play. But it remains a moot point whether more subtle proportional refinements contribute to the aesthetic appreciation of a building or merely help architects make decisions about dimensions that might otherwise seem arbitrary.

Märkli's use of number-based proportion contrasts with Mies van der Rohe's refusal to do so. Mies's refusal was an aspect of his rejection of Beaux Arts architectural principles. Märkli's use of them derives from a belief in principles of visual and spatial harmony, stretching back to ancient architecture, that transcend geometries of making. Both architects however used flat roofs; both avoided the awkward diagonal introduced by the gable or hip of a pitched roof. It is intriguing to muse on why, and whether there are differences in Märkli's reasoning from that of Mies.

Mies argued that freedom in spatial planning required a flat roof, but it is clear that he also like the geometrical purity of two horizontal planes (as in the Farnsworth House) without the visual disruption caused by a diagonal. He might have suggested that the flat roof offered an improvement to the Greek temple, reducing it to base and entablature and omitting the pediment.

Märkli's reasoning seems different. In *La Congiunta* he is not interested in a free plan. Its main body of three cells is defined by two long parallel walls onto which it would be easy, as in his example of the Romanesque church, to construct a pitched roof. Märkli's use of the flat roof seems to derive more from his interest in geometric proportion. Numbers may be applied to rectangles – as formed by horizontal ground, two vertical walls and a horizontal roof line – easily and can be composed readily through drawing. When diagonals are introduced such proportions become confused.

The power of Märkli's building lies in its starkness, the alien severity of its rectangular concrete faces set in the rich greenery, blue skies, distant mountains, bright sun and dark shadows of southern Switzerland. It lies too in the way that entering it takes you away from that rich landscape into a monochrome grey, evenly lit series of 'caves' inhabited by enigmatic, but apparently tortured, sculpture. Such effects are timeless, and are reinforced by *La Congiunta*'s elemental simplicity.

References and other relevant publications, websites, broadcasts:

YouTube video clip at: www.youtube.com/watch?v=iHC2av_O6Lg

Claudia Kugel – 'Raw Intensity', in *Architectural Review*, Volume 203, Number 1212, February 1998, pp. 70-71.

Peter Märkli – *Architecture Fest: a Lecture by Peter Märkli* (DVD), with an introduction by Florian Beigel, 30 November 2006, London Metropolitan University and Architecture Research Unit, 2007.

Peter Märkli – *La Congiunta: House for Sculptures*, available at: www.archiweb.cz/buildings.php?type=arch&action=show&id=282 (June 2009).

Peter Märkli, quoted in Beatrice Galilee – 'Peter Märkli', in *Iconeye*, Number 059, May 2008, available at: www.iconeye.com/index.php?option=com_content&view=article&id=3453:peter-m%C3%83%C2%A4rkli (June 2009)

Mohsen Mostafavi, editor – *Approximations: The Architecture of Peter Märkli*, AA Publications, London, 2002.

Martin Steinmann and Beat Wismer, translated by Bachmann-Clarke – 'A World Without Windows', in *Passages*, Number 30, Summer 2001, pp. 51-53, available at: www3.pro-helvetia.ch/download/pass/en/pass30_en.pdf (June 2009).

Ellis Woodman – 'Beyond Babel: the Work of Swiss Architect Peter Märkli', in *Building Design*, 27 July 2007.

LE CABANON

'J'ai un château sur la Côte d'Azur qui a 3,66 mètres par 3,66 mètres. C'est pour ma femme, c'est extravagant de confort, de gentillesse.'

'I have a castle on the Riviera of 3.66m by 3.66m. It is for my wife, has outstanding comfort and is out of the ordinary.'

Le Corbusier, 1950s.

LE CABANON

An architect's vacation cabin at Cap Martin, on the south coast of France
LE CORBUSIER, 1952

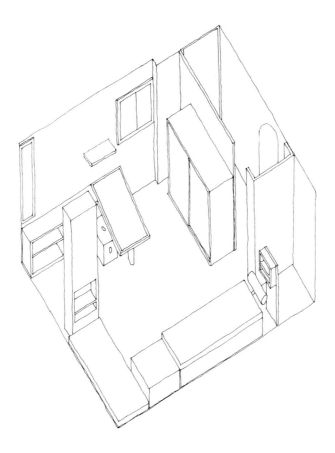

The idea of a refuge from the world, the monk's cell, even the garden shed as a place of escape for a pipe and meditation, has an ancient and venerable heritage. The cell – an enclosed (small) volume of space, separated by its walls and roof from everywhere else, is one of the fundamental and most powerful elements of architecture. Its power derives from its phenomenological effects. Stepping from the open air into a cell, and closing the door, you are transported into a radically different situation, one that can take a moment to adjust to; inside may be quiet, dark, still, and perhaps be infused with the perfume of timber. There are obvious metaphors with the womb, and with the skull – the interior of one's own head. Going into a small cell has a psychological effect. Inside, you can relax, take a breath, think, reflect, perhaps pray. At the beginning of her book *The Private Life of the Brain* (2002) Susan Greenfield writes of the powerful effect just a few words can have on our emotional state. Our experience of architecture can have emotional effects too. Antonio Damasio refers to them at the beginning of his book, *The Feeling of What Happens* (2000):

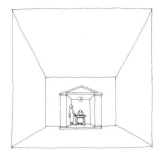

1

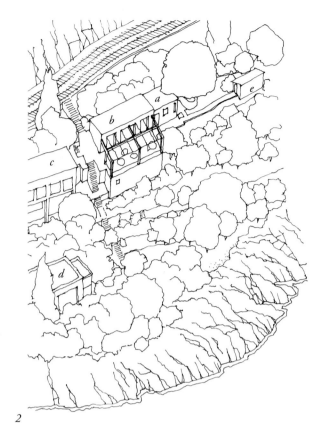

2

'*I have always been intrigued by the specific moment when, as we sit waiting in the audience, the door to the stage opens and a performer steps into the light; or, to take the other perspective, the moment when a performer who waits in semi-darkness sees the same door open, revealing the lights, the stage, and the audience. I realized some years ago that the moving quality of this moment, whichever point of view one takes, comes from its embodiment of an instance of birth, of passage through a threshold that separates a protected but limiting shelter from the possibility and risk of a world beyond and ahead.*'

The cell, the shed, the refuge… offers the third perspective: the possibility of passing through a threshold in the opposite direction, of a return to a metaphorical womb.

In the Bible there is the story of Elisha, who, having been recognised by the woman of Shunem as 'an holy man of God' has a room made for him where he can stay whenever he visits. The woman pleads wirh her husband:

> '*Let us make a little chamber, I pray thee, on the wall; and let us set for him there a bed, and a table, and a stool, and a candlestick.*'
> 2 Kings, 4, 10.

These four elements became the basic requirements for a monk's cell: the bed for rest; the chair, table and lamp for intellectual work – the study of the Scriptures, the revelation of truths about the workings of the world, i.e. God's design.

Elisha repaid the husband's kindness by prophesying that the woman would become pregnant. The early nineteenth century English visionary poet and artist William Blake made a drawing (*1*, which is my sketch of Blake's composition) showing Elisha, in his room, telling the woman that she will give birth to a son. The bed, strangely, is absent. But the table and chair are there. The lamp hangs from the ceiling, like a light bulb over a cartoon character's head, shining the light of revelation out into the world.

Blake's interpretation of 'on the wall' is questionable. He shows Elisha's room against the wall of a cavernous rectangular interior space, which suggests Blake saw the light of imagination illuminating its own world, i.e. the world as constructed (made sense of, architected, philosophically explained…) by itself. Le Corbusier built *Le Cabanon* – his 'Elisha's Cell', the only residence he ever built for himself – against the outside wall of a restaurant owned by friends – *Étoile de Mer* (Star of the Sea) – on the south coast of France, at Roquebrune Cap Martin (*2*). He said he built it for his wife.

Intrigue

The clutch of buildings which includes *Le Cabanon* is like the setting for a Greek tragedy. There is not space here to tell all the stories with their ramifications, some of which are unclear, but they have the classic ingredients of pride, jealousy, sexual intrigue, misfortune, murder, and possible suicide.

In the above drawing *a* is *Le Cabanon* and *b* the restaurant to which it is attached and linked by an internal connecting doorway; *e* is a small *atelier* that Le Corbusier added later, a refuge from his refuge; and *c* is a block of apartments built by Le Corbusier in the 1950s. The most interesting building in the group is *d*. This is the Villa E.1027 designed in the mid-1920s by the Irish architect Eileen

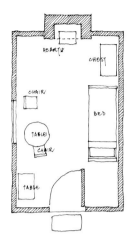

3

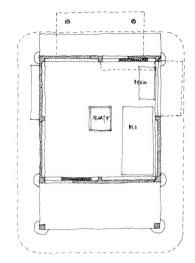

4

Gray for her lover Jean Badovici. (See later analysis. The enigmatic name of the villa is a coded form of their initials.) Le Corbusier admired this villa, and was invited to stay there in the mid-1930s. Some accounts imply he felt professional envy that he had not designed it himself. When Gray left Badovici, Le Corbusier was invited back, this time to paint murals in the house. Gray subsequently complained it was as if the house had been raped. The house's history did not finish there. In the Second World War it was occupied by Italian and German troops, and damaged by gunfire. After the war, the next owner was murdered by vagrants he had taken in. In 1965 Le Corbusier drowned off Cap Martin, having previously suggested to a friend that to die swimming out to sea would be a good way to go.

Contents

Through history there have been many examples of cells that frame the existence of great intellects. They belong to all cultures and times. The cabin at Walden Pond (*3*), built by Henry David Thoreau, belongs to the 1830s. It was here that the American writer and philosopher experimented with living the simple life in contact with nature. The Ten Foot Square House (*4*) was built in the beginning of the thirteenth century by the Japanese writer Kami no Chomei; he described it in *Hōjōki*.

Both Thoreau's cabin and Kami no Chomei's Ten Foot Square House were inspired by a desire to reduce life to its barest essentials and thereby to find a spiritual purity associated with simplicity. Both houses have the same basic ingredients as Elisha's '*little chamber*'

– bed, chair, table, lamp – plus, because they were in climates with cold winters, a hearth for a fire. Kami no Chomei probably sat at his desk on a rush mat rather than a chair; Thoreau had one extra chair for a guest so he could enjoy philosophical conversation. He also had a chest for storage.

Le Cabanon has a similar inventory (*5*): a bed (or two); a fixed table for work, with a couple of box-like stools; and a cupboard for storage; but no hearth. Le Corbusier added a small sink for washing his hands, which is fixed to the hidden side of the tall element at the left of the drawing, and a lavatory, in the small cubicle on the right of the drawing. You enter *Le Cabanon* along a short passageway from

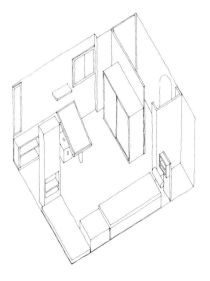

5

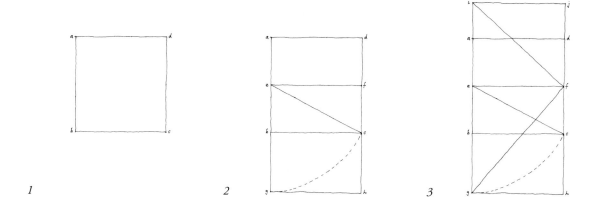

1   2   3

the doorway. The doorway into the restaurant next door is from this short passage too and, with its high threshold and curved sill and head, looks like a doorway on board ship. The cabin's main door slides sideways; it has a secondary mesh door to keep out mosquitoes. *Le Cabanon* has three shuttered windows and two ventilation slots, also shuttered, one of which is in the lavatory cubicle. The window shutters are hinged down the middle; one half has a painting by Le Corbusier, the other is a mirror, which in both cases can be adjusted to reflect light and the view into the interior of the cabin.

Geometry

Whatever the intrigue surrounding the clutch of buildings of which *Le Cabanon* is part, the interior of this shed is a 'temple' (a shrine) to a particular kind of geometry. In 1948, just four years before he built *Le Cabanon*, Le Corbusier wrote a book call *The Modulor*. It was an account of a project which he claimed to have been working on for forty five years. It was a project to find a mathematical basis for aesthetics, one that tied the human form into its world. He wrote:

'Mathematics is the majestic structure conceived by man to grant him comprehension of the universe. It holds both the absolute and the infinite, the understandable and the forever elusive. It has walls before which one may pace up and down without result; sometimes there is a door: one opens it – enters – one is in another realm, the realm of the gods, the room which holds the key to the great systems.'

Le Corbusier (1948), 1954, p. 71.

It is difficult to know where mathematics *is*. It is something only our minds apply to the world, and yet it seems to be 'out there', logical, predictable, pure, reliable. As far back as the sixteenth century the British mathematician John Dee suggested mathematics

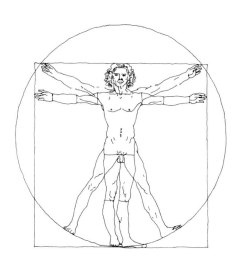

7

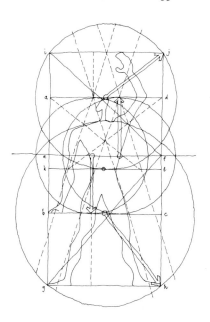

8

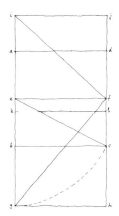
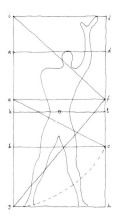
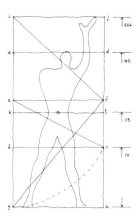

4   5   6

occupied a place in-between the natural and the supernatural. In the above quotation Le Corbusier first says it is 'conceived by man' and later that it 'holds the key to the great systems', suggesting that mathematics is a human creation but also lies at the heart of natural creation. The uncertainty about exactly where mathematics resides – in the human mind or in the natural world – adds to its mystique. Its logic, perfection and incorruptibility lend it an apparently unassailable authority. John Dee – who identified architecture as one of the 'Sciences Mathematicall' – and Le Corbusier agreed that there is a vital relationship between mathematics and the creative activity of architecture, that geometry and number is the medium through which architecture is generated.

In *The Modulor* Le Corbusier laid out a mathematical system for dimensions in architecture. It was based on the square (*1*). From this he generated a Golden Section rectangle (*2*). Then, drawing a line at right angles to line *g-f* from point *f*, he found point *i* (*3*). This he found to make a double square, so he drew the line to divide them (*4*). The resultant figure he found agreed with the basic underlying proportions of the human figure (*5*): the navel is on the mid line of the two squares; the top of the head at the top line of the original square; and the upreaching hand touches the top line of the upper of the two squares. In this way Le Corbusier claimed to have found a system for dimensions derived from the human frame. This exercise was similar in intent to that carried out by Renaissance artists and architects, such as Leonardo da Vinci (*7*), interpreting the descriptions of the relationships between the human form and geometry in the third of *The Ten Books of Architecture* by the first century BC Roman architect Vitruvius. But Le Corbusier claimed his system was better, more accurate and more subtle (*8*); that it related to actual human postures – sitting, leaning, reaching etc.; and that it generated dimensions for useful parts of architecture – seats, sills, tables etc. – rather than merely abstract proportions.

Having developed his abstract geometric figure, Le Corbusier had to find its (give it some) real dimensions (*6*). After various attempts he came up with a series of dimensions based on 113 centimetres as the height of the navel and 70 centimetres for the height of the base line of the original square. Using the principles of the Fibonacci sequence he developed this into a series: 4, 6, 10, 16, 27, 43, 70, 113, 183, 296, with each number being added to the previous to produce the next. This series he called the 'Red Series', which gives a (rather generous) value of 183 centimetres for the height of the top of the head. Next he doubled 113 and generated another series from the number 226, the height of the upreaching hand: 13, 20, 33, 53, 86, 140, 226, 366, 592. This he called the 'Blue Series'. These two series of numbers generated a diagram that has become as iconic as it seems enigmatic. Le Corbusier had it cast into the concrete walls of some of his buildings (*9*), giving the system added precision by expressing the dimensions in millimetres.

9

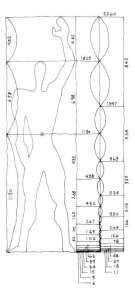

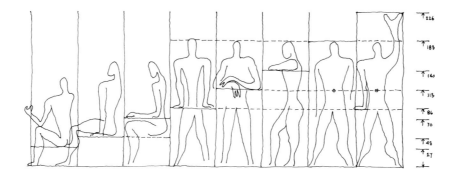

1

The next step in the process was to select various of the dimensions generated geometrically and authorised by their relation to the stature of the human body, and apply them to architectural elements related to particular human postures (*1*). In this way Le Corbusier determined the height of a low seat, a normal seat, an arm rest, a work surface, a window sill, and a high leaning surface. While the dimension 226 centimetres seems to offer a reasonable ceiling height, that of 183 centimetres is more problematic, being too low for the head of a doorway if it also marked the height of a (rather tall but not abnormally so) person. Le Corbusier's aim was to produce a scale of dimensions, related to the human form but regulated by mathematics, that would lend visual and spatial harmony to architecture; a harmony equivalent to that available in music, itself reducible to geometric proportions. In his book *The Modulor* Le Corbusier gives some examples of furniture layouts governed by this scale of dimensions (*2*).

This is the scale of dimensions according to which Le Corbusier designed the interior of *Le Cabanon* (*3*). The ceiling height is, as the system dictates, 226 centimetres. The overall dimensions of the plan were declared by Le Corbusier himself as being 3.66 metres by 3.66 metres. These are sequential numbers from his Blue Series.

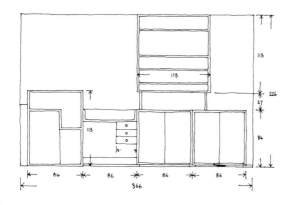

2

The interior is arranged according to four rectangles, each nominally 140 centimetres by 226 centimetres, arranged in a spiral around a 70 centimetre by 70 centimetre square (dotted in *3*) which is represented by a moveable low table on castors. These dimensions are nominal because, as in all applications of geometry to architecture, difficulties arise with the thickness of the fabric. Should the dimension be taken from one face of a wall or the other, or from its centre line? In *Le Cabanon* the overall dimension of 3.66 metres does not accord with the overall external dimensions nor the internal; it includes the thickness of one external wall in each direction.

The spiral of rectangles divide the interior into zones for different purposes. Two, in the darker part of the cabin, are allocated to sleeping; a third to dressing; and the fourth to work. The wash basin is in the work area. The entrance passage and lavatory occupy an additional area, outside the square but (of course) dimensioned according to the Modulor. The spiral of rectangles also seems to determine the positions of other elements, such as the doorway into the restaurant and the tall unit to which the wash basin is attached.

All other components are regulated by the dimensioning system of the Modulor. Windows, work surfaces, shelves, cupboards… all have dimensions dictated by either the Red or Blue Series. Even the stools, which are like simple packing crates, have dimensions selected from the series. As a counterpoint to the prevailing orthogonal layout of the interior, the work table is a parallelogram in plan rather than a rectangle, with its angles apparently determined also by the Modulor framework. In practical terms, its angle allows a little more space for the dressing area. In the version of the plan of *Le Cabanon* published in Le Corbusier's *Œuvre Complète*, this work table is positioned at right angles to the wall but with one edge angled to orient the person sitting at it towards the adjacent window.

The dimensions of the Modulor are used vertically too (*4*). The ceiling is stepped to allow access to storage in the roof space. The higher part is 43 centimetres higher than the main part at 226

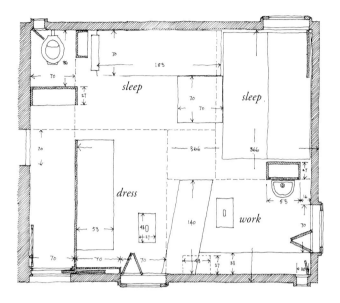

3

centimetres above the floor. Even the plywood panelling on the walls, holding in the glass fibre insulation, follows the dimensions set by the Modulor. The main doorway is the one element, as suggested by the problem identified in *1*, not to obey the Modulor, or at least not accept the same datum (the floor) as the other elements. At 183 centimetres its height would be too low, so its head is at 226 above the ground level outside instead. The doorway into the restaurant does however have a head height of 183 centimetres and a high threshold at 20 centimetres. The combination, as well as making it feel that you are on board ship, makes you take care entering and leaving the cabin by this doorway – a device used in sacred places for thousands of years to instil due reverence when entering a shrine.

Conclusion

The shrine-like nature of the cabin's interior is reinforced also by the entrance passage which creates a chicane, or simple labyrinth entrance, such as those used in ancient times to contain spirits inside their temples. *Le Cabanon* is not a sociable building. There is no veranda, no place for sitting and chatting, the windows are small and have high sills. The sociability of eating takes place elsewhere, next door. The austerity of its interior may be relieved by colourful paintings but this is a place apart, a place for concentration.

Robin Evans, amongst others, has pointed out that the Modulor system of dimensions is based on a geometrical inaccuracy (see Evans, 1995). The figure shown in the diagrams on the previous two pages may appear to work when constructed graphically but they do not work when checked by calculation. Evans provides a diagram showing the innaccuracies. Le Corbusier himself acknowledged the problems but did not seem worried. Maybe he realised that all such systems are contrived, and depend for their efficacy on internal consistency rather than external authority. What mattered to him

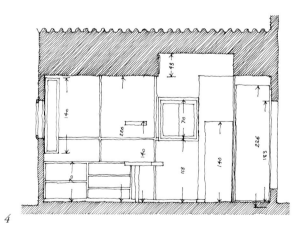

4

was that he had conjured for himself a game with its own rules, one that he could play over and over again with different permutations, one in which it was sometimes appropriate to ignore the rules.

Le Cabanon provided Le Corbusier with a refuge in the landscape and a prospect across the Mediterranean Sea. Appleton (1975) has shown this is a common theme in our relationship with the world. But perhaps the distinctive power of *Le Cabanon* lies in its establishment of a small box of space in which the rules of Le Corbusier's mathematical game hold sway. It is like a carefully constructed mathematical solution, or a honed philosophical argument, true to itself within the confines of its own medium. In this the cabin fulfils the requirements set down by George MacDonald in his essay on 'The Fantastic Imagination' (1893), which I referred to at the outset of the present collection of case studies.

In his *Œuvre Complète*, Le Corbusier refers to the Modulor as '*révélatrice*' ('one who reveals', feminine, maybe 'muse'). Elsewhere he referred to it as 'that ingenious slave' (*Modulor 2*, p. 257) illustrating his tendency to give his system of dimensions a personality, as if it were alive and ready at hand to help in the challenges of design. It is tempting to think that when he said that *Le Cabanon* was made for his 'wife' he was being disingenuous. With its single beds and the austerity of a monk's cell, it is hardly the sort of room that one would make for a lover or life companion. This is a cabin in which to be alone, voyaging on an ocean of reflective creativity. Perhaps he meant he had built it as a shrine to his intellectual mathematical 'wife', his muse and ingenious slave, the Modulor.

References and other relevant publications, websites, broadcasts:

Jay Appleton – *The Experience of Landscape* (1975), Hull University Press, Hull, 1986.

Caroline Constant – *Eileen Gray*, Phaidon, London, 2000.

Bruno Chiambretto – *Le Cabanon*, available at: http://www.lablog.org.uk/2006/02/20/le-cabanon/, February 20, 2006 (July 2009).

Le Corbusier, translated by de Francia and Bostock – *The Modulor* (1948), Faber and Faber, London, 1954.

Le Corbusier – *Œuvre Complète, Volume 5 - 1946-52* (1953), Les Editions d'Architecture, Zurich, 1995, pp. 62-63.

Le Corbusier, translated by de Francia and Bostock – *The Modulor 2 (Let the user speak next)* (1955), Faber and Faber, London, 1958.

William Curtis – *Le Corbusier: Idea and Forms*, Phaidon, London, 1986.

Antonio Damasio – *The Feeling of What Happens: Body, Emotion and the Making of Consciousness*, Vintage, London, 2000.

John Dee – *Mathematicall Praeface to the Elements of Geometrie of Euclid of Megara* (1570), Kessinger Publishing, Whitefish, MT, 1999.

Robin Evans – 'Comic Lines', in *The Projective Cast: Architecture and its Three Geometries*, MIT Press, Cambridge, MA, 1995.

Susan Greenfield – *The Private Life of the Brain*, Penguin, London, 2002.

Sarah Menin and Flora Samuel – *Nature and Space: Aalto and Le Corbusier*, Routledge, London, 2003.

Shane O'Toole – 'Eileen Gray: E-1027, Roquebrune Cap Martin', in *Archiseek*, available at: http://www.irish-architecture.com/tesserae/000007.html (July 2009).

Flora Samuel – *Le Corbusier in Detail*, Architectural Press, London, 2007.

ESHERICK HOUSE

'A child in the dark, gripped with fear, comforts himself by singing under his breath… Lost, he takes shelter, or orients himself with his little song as best he can. The song is like a rough sketch of a calming and stabilizing, calm and stable, center in the heart of chaos… it jumps from chaos to the beginnings of order in chaos and is in danger of breaking apart at any moment.

Now we are at home. But home does not pre-exist: it was necessary to draw a circle around that uncertain and fragile center, to organize a limited space… The forces of chaos are kept outside as much as possible, and the interior space protects the germinal forces of a task to fulfill or a deed to do.'

Gilles Deleuze and Félix Guattari, translated by Massumi – '1837: Of the Refrain', in *A Thousand Plateaus: Capitalism and Schizophrenia* (1980), Continuum, New York, 1987, p. 343.

ESHERICK HOUSE

A house in Chestnut Hill, Philadelphia, Pennsylvania
LOUIS KAHN, 1959-61

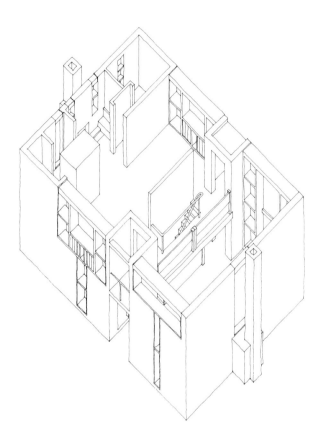

The Esherick House has one bedroom, a dining room and a double-height living room. Alongside these there are the usual ancillary spaces: lobby, cloakroom, boiler room and kitchen downstairs; shower room and dressing room upstairs. The stair divides the double-height living room from the two storey part of the house. The stair's landing creates a gallery looking down into the living room. There is a chimney stack at each end of the house: one serving a hearth in the living room; the other the boiler and a hearth in what was intended (apparently) as a television space off the main bedroom upstairs (though this was changed into a bathroom).

Parallel walls; inhabited walls; transition, hierarchy, heart

The Esherick House has a clear spatial organisation based in some of Louis Kahn's ideas about structuring space. In particular the house is arranged in zones of two different types of space: the main living spaces and the ancillary spaces – the 'served' and the 'servant' spaces.

The plan of the Esherick House is divided into two by three parallel 'walls' (see the simplified plan of the house, 5, on following pages), two of which are 'inhabited' by servant spaces. The spaces

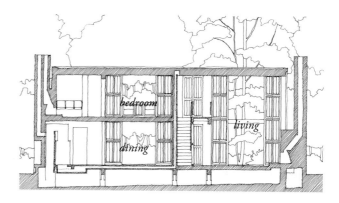

1 section

between these walls contain the main served living spaces. The thicker of the inhabited walls accommodates the cloakroom, boiler room and kitchen downstairs (*5* and *3*), and the shower room and dressing room upstairs (*5* and *2*). Assembling all the wet areas – the cloakroom, kitchen and shower room – all in one zone simplifies the provision of services and drainage.

The thinner inhabited wall (*5*, *2* and *3*) accommodates the stair and two recessed porches with doorways: from the public street (to the north, at the bottom of the plan); and out to the garden (on the south of the house, at the top of the plan). At the front of the house – the elevation facing the public road – the doorway is in the side of the porch and leads into the lobby. This arrangement creates a hierarchical transitional sequence from the outside to the inside of the living room (*3*). In the other porch the doorway leads straight out into the garden from under the gallery. Upstairs (*2*), these porches become small Juliet balconies, both accessed from the gallery.

The third of the parallel walls is a plain, vertical and rectangular wall with a single window at its centre. Though simple, this wall (the most basic of architectural elements), which frames the hearth of the living room – the heart of the house – is the culmination of the plan's arrangement (the house's hierarchy of spaces). The rest of the house faces towards this wall with its hearth and window.

The house is bookended by the two chimney stacks. The simplified section (*4*) illustrates the integrated relationship of the three main served spaces, modulated by the perforated (permeable) inhabited wall containing the stair and gallery. The television space, with its hearth, is like a traditional ingle-nook off the bedroom (*2*).

The ends of the main served spaces are smaller inhabited walls. These contain the glazing (windows) but are also constructed with deep enough reveals to contain cupboards and bookstacks. The ground floor of the north (public) elevation has narrow windows to preserve privacy (*3*). The south elevation to the garden is more open. All may be modified by opening or closing timber shutters in various permutations.

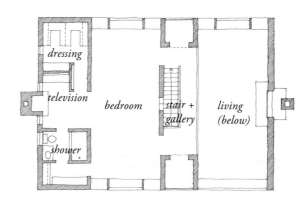

2 upstairs

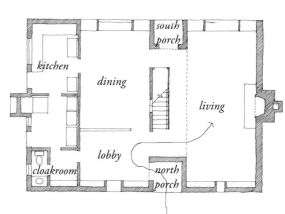

3 downstairs

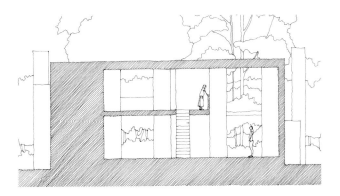

4 simplified section

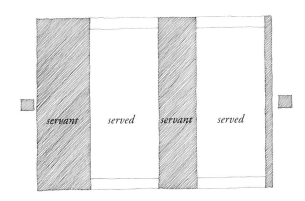

5 simplified plan – parallel walls

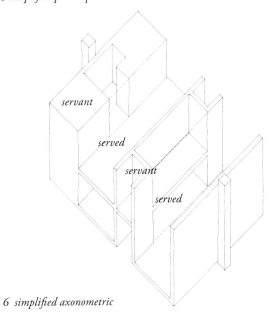

6 simplified axonometric

Ideal geometry

Simple but subtle in its spatial arrangement, the Esherick House is designed on an intricate matrix of ideal geometry.

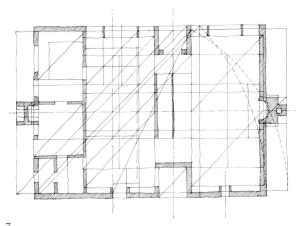

7

This geometric matrix governs the positions and relationships between just about every part of the house. It is based upon squares, √2 rectangles, and Golden Section rectangles.

The external walls of the house form a √2 rectangle (8).

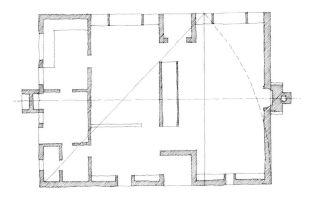

8 √2 rectangle

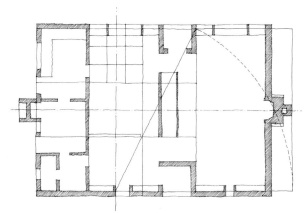

1 Golden Section rectangle

The extent of the living room chimney stack seems governed by a Golden Section rectangle (*1*) delimited by the external face of the kitchen end wall but the internal faces of the long walls. One side of the square from which this Golden Section rectangle is constructed determines the position of the living room side of the thinner inhabited wall (containing the porches, stairway and gallery).

If this square is divided into three in both directions (*2*), the lines appear to determine the positions of, for example: the lowest step of the stairway; the internal extent of the thicker inhabited wall; the position of the wall dividing lobby and dining room; and the positions of various window jambs and mullions. Other positions seem determined by centre lines or by further division of these squares into three.

To complicate matters, the plan of the house seems to contain another matrix of different sized squares (*3*). The proportional relationship between the smaller and the larger squares might be √2. The thinner inhabited wall is one of these smaller squares thick, and the two main living zones of the house are each two of these squares wide. These smaller squares also determine the sizes of the porches, though they determine different faces of the innermost walls in each case, and the uppermost step of the stairway.

If one overlays these different geometries: the squares, the √2 rectangles, and the Golden Section rectangles one gets a complex 'cat's cradle' of lines determining the various parts of the house. In *4* I have added the diagonals of various squares and centre lines apparent in the plan.

It is this complex overlay of different geometries that constitute an architectural equivalent of what Deleuze and Guattari, to repeat from the quotation at the beginning of this analysis, might call 'the refrain' – the song a person hums to fend off uncertainty:

'A child in the dark, gripped with fear, comforts himself by singing under his breath… Lost, he takes shelter, or orients himself with his little song as best he can. The song is like a rough sketch of a calming and stabilizing, calm and stable, center in the heart of

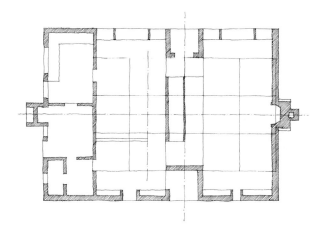

2 division into thirds

3 another layer of squares

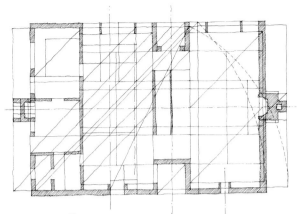

4 the 'cat's cradle'

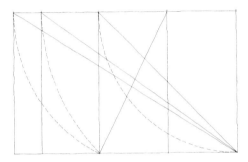

5 square, √2 rectangle, Golden Section rectangle...

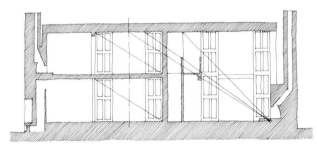

6 emanating from the hearth in the living room...

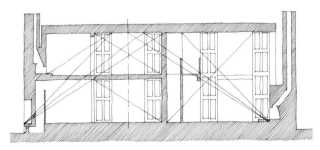

7 and from a false hearth on the outside of the other chimney stack

chaos... it jumps from chaos to the beginnings of order in chaos and is in danger of breaking apart at any moment. Now we are at home. But home does not pre-exist: it was necessary to draw a circle around that uncertain and fragile center, to organize a limited space... The forces of chaos are kept outside as much as possible, and the interior space protects the germinal forces of a task to fulfill or a deed to do.'

The geometry of the Esherick House is neither simple nor resolved. The house may appear 'a calm and stable center' but its intricate geometry suggests that 'the forces of chaos' have not been entirely 'kept out'; it is in danger of 'breaking apart at any moment'.

Ideal geometry determines the section of the house too. One may construct the three figures that underlie the organisation of this house – the square, the √2 rectangle and the Golden Section rectangle – from the same point (5). In the Esherick House all of these may be drawn from its focus, the hearth in the living room (6). The square determines the side of the stairway and the centre line of the porches. The √2 rectangle determines the position of one of the mullions in the dining room and bedroom windows. The Golden Section rectangle determines the centre line of those windows. In addition, the sections of both the dining room and the bedroom are Golden Section rectangles.

If one turns the construction of the three figures around, one finds that they similarly focus on another 'hearth', a false hearth cut into the outside of the base of the chimney stack at the other end of the house.

Conclusion: a comment on the poetics of the Esherick House

This analysis begins to hint that the design of the house is based on more than ideal geometry. The fact that some of that geometry has its origin in the hearths (real and false) reinforces the identity of the house as a home.

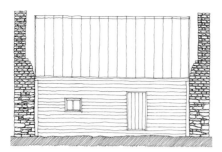

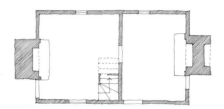

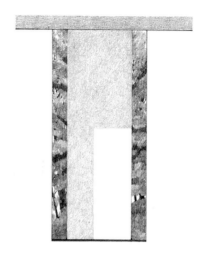

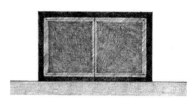

1 a settler house with chimney stacks at each end

The chimney stacks are, as always, external manifestations of this identity, symbols of home. Their arrangement in the Esherick House is redolent of that in settler houses. It is even the case that in some remains of settler houses a hearth is left outside by the removal of an extension. Such hearths, and remnant chimney stacks, are like the ghosts of the houses they once warmed.

Finally, above the hearth in the living room there is that window (one of the most celebrated features of this house). This is the window cut through the wall towards which the rest of the house faces. It gives a view from the living room and gallery to the chimney stack outside, with glimpses of the trees beyond. It frames a picture like an abstract work of art on the wall. The play of light on the surface of the chimney stack changes through the day and night. This window is reminiscent of the Japanese device of framing a tree or a portion of the landscape (as in Sverre Fehn's Villa Busk, see later analysis). In the Esherick House it reinforces an air of spirituality. Just as the chancel arch in a church gives a view into another world, this window gives a view into the beyond or perhaps the other country where ghosts from the past live.

References and other relevant publications, websites, broadcasts:

Klaus-Peter Gast – *Louis I. Kahn: The Idea of Order*, Birkäuser, Basel, 1998, pp. 44-51.

Klaus-Peter Gast – *Louis I. Kahn: Complete Works*, Deutsche Verlags-Anstalt, Munich, 2001, pp. 96-101.

Heinz Ronner, Sharad Jhaveri and **Alessandro Vasella** – *Louis I. Kahn: Complete Work 1935-74*, Institute for the History and Theory of Architecture, Swiss Federal Institute of Technology, Zurich, 1977, pp. 133-135.

Joseph Rykwert – *Louis Kahn*, Harry N. Abrams, New York, pp. 50-57.

MAISON À BORDEAUX

'Every morning their supervisor…
instructs them in "nonsense"
– meaningless, enigmatic jokes and
slogans that will sow uncertainty
in the crowds.'

Rem Koolhaas – *Delirious New York* (1978),
Monacelli Press, New York, 1994, p. 46.

MAISON À BORDEAUX

A house for a man confined to a wheelchair
REM KOOLHAAS, 1998

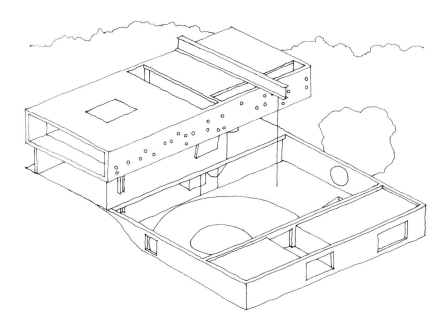

This house stands just at the top of a wooded hill in the south-eastern outskirts of Bordeaux. It has views across the city and the valley of the river Garonne. The house was designed for a client confined to a wheelchair after a car accident. It incorporates a hydraulic platform, capable of moving between the levels of the house and large enough for the wheelchair-bound client to use as a work space. The platform moves up and down alongside a tall bookstack.

Stratification

It may not look like it but, appropriate to its hilltop site, the *Maison à Bordeaux* is arranged like a medieval castle. It has an entry courtyard like a bailey, off which there is some secondary accommodation for

guests and the housekeeper. Along the courtyard's south-western side stands a three-storey range of accommodation for the client and his family.

The levels – stratification – of a castle are an important part of its architecture. Because of the need for defence, the walls of its bailey isolate the courtyard from the outside world. The principal buildings were founded on solid rock, with dungeons in caves beneath. The main living rooms were usually a floor above ground level. And the battlements had extensive views across the landscape so that approaching enemies could be spotted. The walls had loopholes for bowmen to fire arrows at attackers.

The arrangements are similar but not identical in Koolhaas's design. The general principle he follows is to question and subvert the orthodox or obvious. This is an acknowledged route to novelty.

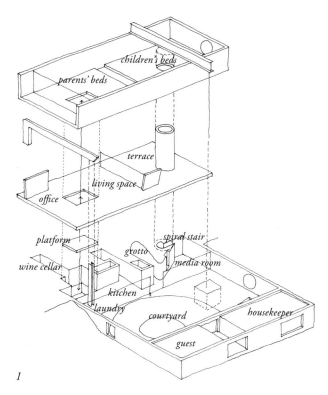

1

4

The three levels of the house are pulled apart in the above drawing (*1*). Though simplified (some of the internal divisions of the upper floors have been removed), it shows that the spatial character of each level is different. These differences can be compared to the stratification of a medieval castle (*3*).

The nature of caves and dungeons excavated out of rock is that they do not have to follow the 'geometry of making' that conditions built structure. Spatially their form may be freer. This happens in the lowest floor of the *Maison à Bordeaux*. Here there are: a *cave* or wine cellar; a store; a curvy staircase in cave-like grotto; and a spiral stair (just like a tower stair in a castle). It is as if these spaces are excavated from the ground of the hill. Attached to them are a washroom and a room for the technology of the house, and in front, separated from

the courtyard by a glass wall (some clear, some translucent), are a laundry, kitchen and a media room for the children of the house. The main doorway enters at the narrowest part of the plan. The door is an electrically operated panel of metal opened by means of a large illuminated joystick alongside in the courtyard.

The moving platform comes down to this lowest level. It is only when it is at this level that it is possible to enter the wine cellar. The person who controls the platform controls access to the wine.

The upper two floors invert the arrangement found in a castle. In a castle (*3*) a hall with thick walls and small windows supports an open roof from which the surrounding landscape may be surveyed. In the *Maison à Bordeaux* it is the first level that is open to the surroundings. As in the castle it is the main living floor for the family but, protected only by glass screens and curtains to shade the sun, it has open views to the woods and across the valley to Bordeaux.

Koolhaas uses the slope of the hillside; the living level is a storey above the courtyard but level with the grassy top of the hill. This floor, open to the landscape, is sheltered and shaded by the floor above. It is an arrangement reminiscent of that suggested by Le Corbusier in 'Five Points Towards a New Architecture' (1927). He argued that buildings did not need to take up ground space; by the use of columns ('pilotis') ground and space could be allowed to flow continuously under them (*4*). He argued for roof gardens too.

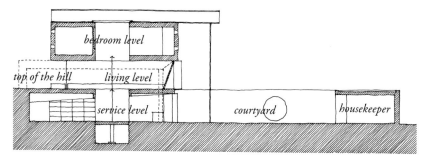

2

3

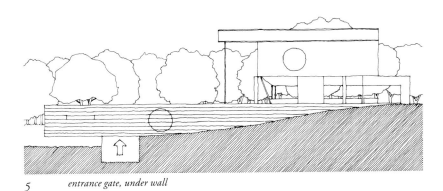

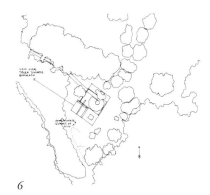

5   *entrance gate, under wall*   6

In the *Maison à Bordeaux* Koolhaas does not provide a roof garden. The uppermost floor contains the bedrooms. In comparison with the medieval castle, this is the level with the thick (concrete) walls and the small windows ('loopholes'). As will be seen in the plans on the following pages, this floor is divided into two, with half for the children's rooms and half for the parents. The moving platform gives access to the parents' half while the children's half is reached by the spiral stair contained in its cylindrical drum. The two halves are separated by a slot – a 'divide' between the generations. The parents' rooms have a veranda facing the morning sun.

The accommodation on the top floor is contained in a concrete box that appears to float above the open middle level. At its western end there is a large circular panel – centrally pivoted – echoing a similar circular panel in the courtyard wall. The first is operated by a winding handle; the latter swivels freely. The upper opens a view towards Bordeaux; the lower, like a so-called 'moon' door in a Chinese garden, frames a flickering view of the trees outside.

Transition, hierarchy, heart

The section (*2*) shows the various levels of the house. The entrance into the courtyard cannot be seen. The gateway is under rather than through the wall (*5* and *6*), and the driveway is steep. This gateway marks the threshold between the outside world and the controlled world of the house. Everything inside is precise and geometrical – determined, designed, by a mind; everything outside is irregular and natural. In this the house is similar to a neo-classical house from the eighteenth century.

In *Doorway* (Routledge, 2007, p. 98) I analysed an eighteenth century neo-classical house in Scotland designed by William Adam, called The House of Dun. It was common in such houses to manage the route of approach to influence visitors' perceptions of the world in which the owner lived. Even though the house faced the south – the sun – and the main road, the approach to the main entrance

was manoeuvred around to the north elevation (*7* and *8*). This was so a visitor would approach the main doorway in shade, rise onto the main living floor – the *piano nobile* – and then emerge into the sunny Saloon with a view over the sunlit garden, giving the impression that the owner and his family lived in a world sunnier and better appointed than the ordinary outside world.

Something similar happens in the *Maison à Bordeaux*. Having entered the courtyard by climbing the steep driveway, you are on the northern side of the three-storey block of accommodation. As in the neo-classical house the menial accommodation – kitchen, storerooms, wine cellar etc. – is on the lowest level. Entering, you rise to the open middle level – the *piano nobile* – into the sunshine and with the view. As in the neo-classical house, it is as if you have

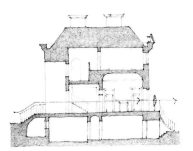

7

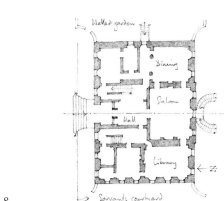

8

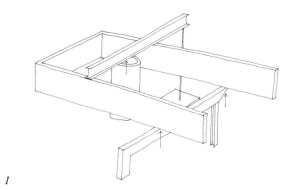

1

been invited to enter into the better appointed world inhabited by the owner. Architecture is the instrument for manipulating our perception of the world in this way. It is by means of architecture that an architect can orchestrate experience, eliciting different emotional responses, and changing how we ascribe meaning to our surroundings.

Space and structure

I have mentioned that the design of the *Maison à Bordeaux* is influenced by Le Corbusier's idea of a ground floor open to its surroundings. In analysing the Farnsworth House I also wondered if Mies van der Rohe would have liked to make his floor and roof planes float without visible means of support. In the *Maison à Bordeaux* Rem Koolhaas has almost done this. If he is emulating Le Corbusier's open floor, he has done so without the *pilotis*.

There is a film about the house – *Koolhaas houselife* (Bêka and Lemoîne, 2008) – which follows the housekeeper in her daily chores. One section of the film – 'it's going to fall' – is devoted to her puzzlement at how the concrete box of the uppermost floor is supported. Koolhaas, in collaboration with his engineer Cecil Balmond, uses architectural sleight of hand to make it appear as if the concrete box has no structural support. It seems only to be held down – prevented from floating away like a balloon – by a rod attached to a large steel I-beam across its roof, and anchored into the ground of the courtyard.

The way this is done is best illustrated in a drawing (*1*). The concrete box is actually supported in three places: by the cylinder of the spiral staircase; and by an L-shaped piece of structure that is propped by a steel stanchion rising from the kitchen area below. The stair cylinder supports the large I-beam across the roof, from which the concrete box 'hangs'. The anchoring rod does little; perhaps stabilising the box against rocking. The sleight of hand in making the building appear to be without support works in various ways.

At the open middle level the cylinder of the spiral stair is clad in highly polished mirror-like stainless steel. This reflects the landscape around reducing the cylinder's appearance as a structural column. The L-shaped structure is stepped out into the grassy plateau at the top of the hill, and therefore appears detached from the house itself. The only clearly visible piece of structure within the house is the stanchion rising through the lower two floors, and this appears on the main living floor to be part of the bookstack that stands alongside the moving platform. All these devices conspire to make it appear as if the building has no support.

Modifying elements: time and mutability

It takes time to explore this building. And it is a building that changes with time; it changes with the time of day and the seasons. These are characteristics shared with most buildings. But the *Maison à Bordeaux* is also a building that can be changed, quite radically. If you look closely at the various photographs of it published in journals, books and on the Internet, you will see variations; sometimes a wall is one place, sometimes in another; lights hang from the ceilings in different locations; parts of the building shift.

Many parts of the house may be moved so that it can be set up in different ways for different situations and conditions. In addition to the two circular panels already mentioned, and of course the platform that moves between the three floors, the principle movable elements of the house are the glass walls, curtains and lights of the main living level. Using tracks in the floor and ceiling these may be arranged to provide appropriate shelter from wind and rain, and shade from the sun. For example: a large portion of the south wall can slide along into the open terrace to shelter it from south-easterly breezes; a smaller portion of solid wall can slide in the other direction, onto a track outside the floor plate of the house, to open the office space to the grassy plateau on the top of the hill; long curtains can also be arranged in a variety of places to shade

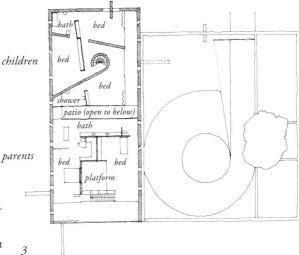

children

parents

3

different parts of the interior from the southern French sun at different times of day.

The mutability of the house means it may be used in different ways in different circumstances and respond to the variations of the seasons. In some of the published plans the terrace at the western end of the house is termed the 'summer dining room' with the interior space over the kitchen labelled as the 'winter dining room'.

Ideal geometry

The three floor plans are drawn alongside (*1* – courtyard level; *2* – open middle level, living space; *3* – uppermost, bedroom level). On the lowest level you can see the driveway entering the courtyard under the wall and curving around towards the front door. There is a bridge over the gateway, like the wall walk of a castle, leading to the door of the housekeeper's flat. You can also see the 'free' 'excavated' form of the wine cellar, store, stairs and media room. You can see too how the moving platform controls access to the wine cellar. The dot within the dashed square in the courtyard is the rod 'holding down' the large I-beam across the roof.

In the middle floor you can see the lack of structure and the tracks (dashed) of the movable curtains and walls. You can see where the large section of south wall can slide over the open west-facing terrace to shelter the 'summer dining room', and how the small solid piece of wall can slide aside to open the office to the sunny hill top. The bookstack alongside the moving platform is aligned with the L-shaped structure and steel stanchion (I-shaped on plan).

The platform rises to the top floor where the parents' area is open plan and separated from the children's zone by the 'chasm' – labelled 'patio (open to below)' in the plan (*3*). The children's zone is divided by diagonal walls and reached by the medieval castle spiral stair near its centre. The children's zone has a long narrow patio where 'arrows' may be fired through the 'loopholes'. The parents have their open veranda facing the morning sun.

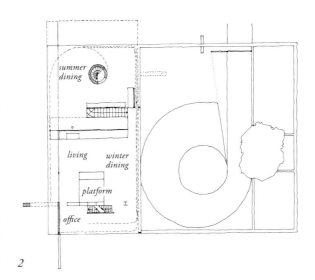

2

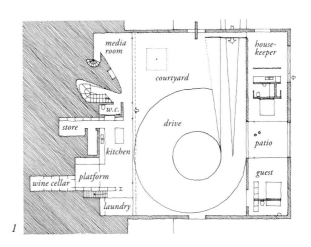

1

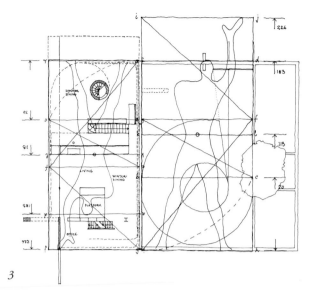

3

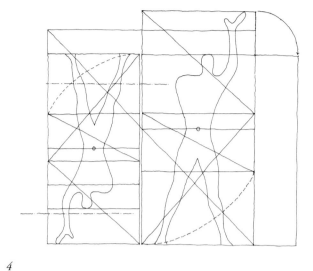

4

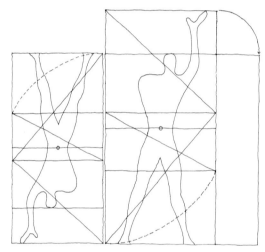

2

A glance at the plans suggests they are ordered according to some underlying geometry.

The courtyard is a Golden Section rectangle and the open middle floor is a double square (*1*). We have seen this combination in a previous analysis – *Le Cabanon* by Le Corbusier. Rem Koolhaas has often expressed his respect for Le Corbusier. This analysis is based on no more than a hunch… but if we reconstruct the geometric framework of the Modulor onto the Golden Section rectangle and the double square of the *Maison à Bordeaux* (*2*), and then superimpose them on the middle floor plan (*3*), we see that a number of significant parts of the building fit. This works particularly if we invert the figure in the double square of the living accommodation. In the courtyard the curve of the driveway fits neatly into the part of the Golden Section rectangle left once half the original square is taken away. The 'navel' line seems to determine the position of the stair up from the 'grotto' and the 'chasm' between the parents' and children's zones on the uppermost floor. The dimension of the 'upstretched hand', if rotated through ninety degrees gives the width of the housekeeper's flat and guest room.

In the double square, the console against the glass wall between the living space and the terrace (between the 'winter' and 'summer' dining rooms) is positioned on the mid line. The head of 'Modulor man', perhaps significantly, occurs on the moving platform. And even the upstretched hand seems to push the office's movable wall outwards.

Projecting a square from the combined bases of the double square and the Golden Section rectangle gives the overhang of the uppermost floor (*4*). And the positions of the L-shaped structure and the large I-beam across the roof seem determined by centrelines between significant lines in the Modulor diagram. One suspects

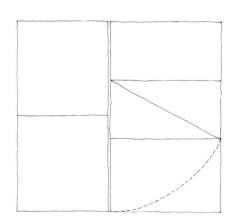

1

116

that other major elements in the design are also determined by the underlying geometric framework provided by Le Corbusier's system of aesthetic proportions.

Conclusion: a note on the 'paranoid critical method'

If you Google 'funniest joke' you get directed to a Wikipedia article on a piece of research conducted by Richard Wiseman of the University of Hertfordshire in 2002. The joke voted for as funniest was:

'A couple of Mississippi hunters are out in the woods when one of them falls to the ground. He doesn't seem to be breathing, his eyes are rolled back in his head. The other guy whips out his cell phone and calls the emergency services. He gasps to the operator: "My friend is dead! What can I do?" The operator, in a calm soothing voice says: "Just take it easy. I can help. First, let's make sure he's dead." There is a silence, then a shot is heard. The guy's voice comes back on the line. He says: "OK, now what?" ' '

Joke theory suggests that the effect of a punchline depends in part on surprise and contradiction; it upsets expectation and you smile because you feel you should have seen it coming though you are simultaneously aware that it conflicts with the obvious. Even anti-jokes work in this way. The punchline 'To get to the other side' in response to the question 'Why did the chicken cross the road?' works (perhaps once) because you expected it to be cleverer and funnier, and you smile because it is so obvious.

Countering Mies van der Rohe's dictum 'Less is more', Robert Venturi wrote in 1966, 'Less is a bore'. Architects can work like joke writers, by upsetting expectation and challenging or contradicting orthodoxies, by resonating with irony and the contrary rather than attempting to find resolution.

Like religion humour deals with uncertainty, the inability to subject everything to consistent logical explanation. Unlike religion, humour celebrates, plays with and exploits uncertainty, incongruity, complexity and contradiction.

Much of architecture is without humour. A large part of its literature over the past two centuries or so has argued about how to identify the 'right' way to design, to eliminate vagaries and to find the simple, direct and appropriate way to do architecture. In the nineteenth century when, due to extensive travel to other cultures, European architects experimented with architectures from other times and other parts of the world – ancient Greek, medieval Gothic, Chinese, pre-industrial vernacular… critics such as John Ruskin suggested that, behind all these multifarious variant styles there must be a 'true' architecture. Aspiring to the holy grail of 'truth' in architecture, architects worried about the right architecture for their own cultures, their own countries, the particular tasks in hand, the materials they had available, even the weather. The search for 'truth' in architecture resulted in the emergence of 'modernism' in which the styles of the past and other cultures (condemned as cosmetic and by Le Corbusier in his 1923 book *Towards a New Architecture* as 'a lie') were rejected in favour of an unornamented elemental architecture.

Frank Lloyd Wright, in a 1910 passage that would have influenced European architects such as Mies van der Rohe, wrote:

'The true basis for any serious study of the art of Architecture still lies in those indigenous structures; more humble buildings everywhere… It is the traits of these many folk-structures that are of the soil. Natural. Though often slight, their virtue is intimately related to environment and to the heart-life of the people. Functions are usually truthfully conceived and rendered invariably with natural feeling.' Wright (1910), (p. 85).

Wright promoted concepts such as 'truth', 'natural', 'heart-life' and 'simplicity'. By contrast, Rem Koolhaas has promoted an architecture of make-believe, artificiality, confusion and complexity… suggesting these are more in tune with the times. In his writing he has tended to quote Salvador Dali rather than Wright:

'I believe that the moment is at hand when by a paranoid and active advance of the mind, it will be possible to systematize confusion

1 Dali's 'diagram of the inner workings of the Paranoid Critical Method: limp, unprovable conjectures generated through the deliberate simulation of paranoic thought processes, supported (made critical) by the "crutches" of Cartesian rationality.' Koolhaas (1978), p. 236.

and thus help to discredit completely the world of reality.' Salvador Dali (*La Femme Visible*, 1930), quoted in Rem Koolhaas (1978), 1994, p. 235.

This passage sums up the 'paranoid critical method' for dealing with the world. Koolhaas's attitude also echoes that of Robert Venturi who published, in 1966, a book entitled *Complexity and Contradiction in Architecture*. This book questioned the fundamental precepts of the 'modern' attitude to design. It contains the riposte to Mies van der Rohe – 'Less is a bore'. It also presented Venturi's creed:

'I like complexity and contradiction in architecture. I do not like the incoherence or arbitrariness of incompetent architecture nor the precious intricacies of picturesqueness or expressionism. Instead, I speak of a complex and contradictory architecture based on the richness and ambiguity of modern experience, including that experience which is inherent in art. Everywhere, except in architecture, complexity and contradiction have been acknowledged, from Gödel's proof of ultimate inconsistency in mathematics to T.S. Eliot's analysis of "difficult" poetry and Joseph Albers' definition of the paradoxical quality of painting.' Venturi, 1966, p. 22.

Rem Koolhaas's *Maison à Bordeaux* is a 'complex and contradictory' building informed by a desire to upset expectation, to 'sow uncertainty'. It does so by means of its mutability, its sleight of hand and its hints at a make-believe world made possible only by the artifical art of architecture.

References and other relevant publications, websites, broadcasts:

Le Corbusier – 'Five Points Towards a New Architecture' (1926), translated in Ulrich Conrads – *Programmes and Manifestoes on 20th-Century Architecture*, Lund Humphries, London, 1970.

Ila Bêka and Louise Lemoîne – *Koolhaas houselife* (film and book), Bêkafilms and Les Pneumatiques, Bordeaux, 2008.

Salvador Dali – *La Femme Visible* (1930), quoted in Koolhaas (1978), p. 235.

Robert Gargiani, translated by Piccolo – *Rem Koolhaas/OMA: The Construction of* Merveilles, EPFL Press distributed by Routledge, Abingdon, 2008.

Rem Koolhaas – *Delirious New York* (1978), Monacelli Press, New York, 1994.

Le Corbusier, translated by Etchells – *Towards a New Architecture* (1923), John Rodker, London, 1927.

Robert Venturi – *Complexity and Contradiction in Architecture*, Museum of Modern Art, New York, 1966.

Frank Lloyd Wright – from *Ausgeführte Bauten und Entwürfe* (1910), reprinted as 'The Sovereignty of the Individual' in Kaufmann and Raeburn, editors – *Frank Lloyd Wright: Writings and Buildings*, Meridian, New York, 1960, pp. 84-106.

IL DANTEUM

*'Nel mezzo del cammin di nostra vita
mi ritrovai per una selva oscura,
che la diritta via era smarrita.'*

Dante – 'Commedia', 1300.

*'Halfway along the path of [our] life
I found myself in a dark wood,
[which was] the right (direct, straight) way was lost.'*

Dante – 'The Divine Comedy', 1300, literal translation of the
first three lines.

IL DANTEUM

An unbuilt memorial to Dante Alghieri
GIUSEPPE TERRAGNI, 1938

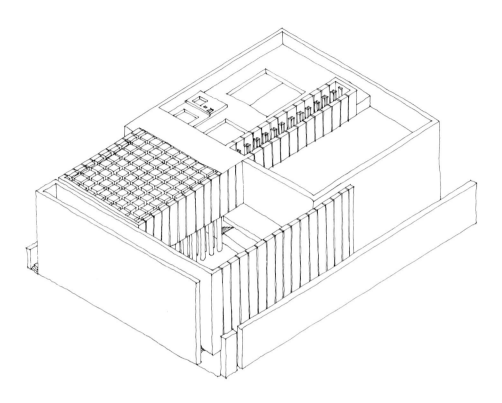

Il Danteum is an exercise in the imposition of ideal geometry on form and space. Though it was designed for a specific site on the *Via dei Fori Imperiali* in Rome, in the midst of the ruins of ancient Rome not far from the Colosseum, it is a work of architecture that exists in that special and strange transcendent world of mathematics (see the quotation from John Dee on page 154 of *Analysing Architecture*), and would have done even if it had been built.

Il Danteum was commissioned from Giuseppe Terragni by Benvenuto Mussolini, Italian Fascist dictator of the 1930s, as a memorial to Italy's greatest ever poet Dante Alghieri, author of the *Commedia*, known in English as *The Divine Comedy* (written around AD1300). This long poem is a description of its narrator's journey through the various levels of hell and heaven – *Inferno*, *Purgatorio* and *Paradiso* – guided in parts by the spirit of the Roman poet Virgil. Terragni's design is a built representation of the levels of hell and heaven.

Apart from a library on its lowest level *Il Danteum* has no spaces that might be called functional. The building would have been something like an art installation in which the visitor would be taken through a series of spaces, equivalent to sections of Dante's poem. There were proposals too to ornament the spaces with free-standing and wall-mounted relief sculptures representing souls in torment. At the culmination of the route through the building, in a section called *Impero* (Empire – a dead end on the top floor of the building) there was to be a depiction of the Imperial Eagle. Mussolini intended this building to be a political statement, a monument not only to Dante but to Italy and to Fascism. Terragni, who designed *Il Danteum* with its *Impero* as a dead end, died in 1943 during the

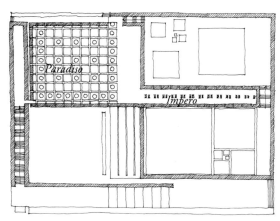

1 top level

Second World War, the outbreak of which in 1939 stopped his building being realised.

Ideal geometry and basic elements

In designing *Il Danteum* Terragni used a limited palette of basic architectural elements: wall; column; platform; roof. There are stairs and roof lights but only one doorway (which is not the main entrance) and, appropriately for a built representation of hell, no windows. Some of the walls, with regularly spaced long vertical slits, seem to have been caught in the process of metamorphosing into columns. (Maybe these too are tormented souls.) Everything is arranged orthogonally; this is a world where the right angle rules.

The geometrical organisation of *Il Danteum* is complex and many layered. The plan overall is based on a √2 rectangle (*4*). This includes an entrance space screened from the *Via dei Fori Imperiali* by a high wall. The main body of the building is based on a number of overlapping Golden Section rectangles of varying sizes (*5*). And the subsidiary spaces are proportioned according to a bewildering array of smaller Golden Section rectangles (*6*) and √2 rectangles

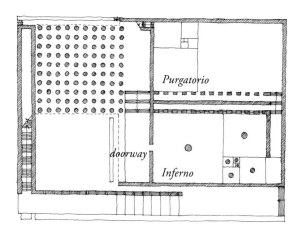

2 intermediate level

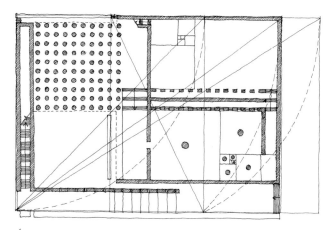

4

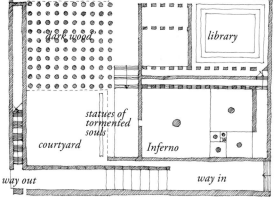

3 entrance level

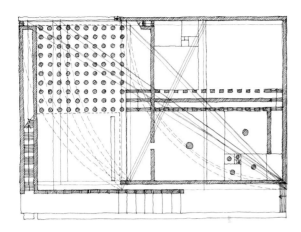

5

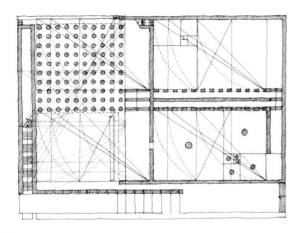

6

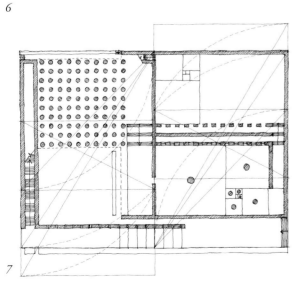

7

9 the section is organised according to Golden Section and √2 rectangles too

(*7*). The *Inferno* and *Purgatorio* spaces are overtly divided, by varying floor and ceiling surfaces, according to the classic diagram of the Golden Section rectangle (*8*). In the case of the *Inferno*, each of the squares on which the Golden Section rectangles are based has a column fixed at its centre. The *Purgatorio* has square openings to the sky that conform to the same geometry. It is as if the whole building is tightly bound (imprisoned) in a matrix of incontrovertible mathematics. Maybe for Terragni, this was hell.

(Thomas Schumacher, in his book *Danteum*, offers a slightly different interpretation of the underlying geometry of Terragni's design.)

The path through *Il Danteum*; transition, hierarchy, heart

The mathematical structure of *Il Danteum* reflects the mathematical structure of Dante's poem. Schumacher has noted:

> '*The poem is divided into three canticles of thirty three cantos each, plus one extra in the first, the Inferno, making a total of one hundred*

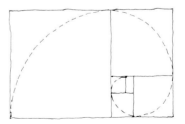

8

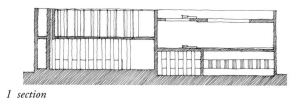

1 section

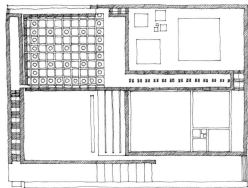

2 top level

cantos. Each canto is composed of three-line tercets; the first and third lines rhyme, the second line rhymes with the beginning of the next tercet, establishing a kind of overlap, reflected in the overlapping motif of the Danteum design.' Schumacher, 1993, p. 91.

Terragni's building is the architectural equivalent of 'programme' music, i.e. music with a story to tell. The parts of *Il Danteum* relate to the canticles of the *Commedia*. The journey, for visitors in Mussolini's Rome, would have started on the *Via dei Fori Imperiali* (then the *Via dell Impero*). First they would have slipped out of the public realm behind the screen wall, and found themselves passing through a simple narrow labyrinthine entrance into the generous sunlit courtyard. There they would have been welcomed by the statues of the souls in torment on their plinth. The entrance sequence was designed to take the visitor out of the real everyday world and into an other world, sterile and governed by geometry. Entering would have elicited a sense of trepidation and dislocation.

The journey according to Dante's poem would not have begun until the next stage, when the visitor would walk from the courtyard into the shade of the hall of a hundred columns – a representation of the 'dark wood' in which Dante finds himself at the beginning of his poem (see the quotation at the beginning of this analysis) and of the poem's one hundred cantos. Terragni's architecture, although 'modern' in its lack of ornament, is replete with references to ancient architectures. The labyrinth entrance may be a reference to that at the Necromanteion in western Greece (*5*, see *Analysing Architecture*, 3rd edition, page 214). The columned hall is reminiscent of both the Egyptian hypostyle hall and of the Greek Telesterion (hall of the mysteries) at Eleusis (*6* and *7*, see *Analysing Architecture*, 3rd edition, page 175). The columned hall was lit through narrow gaps in the floor of Paradise above, divided into squares each supported by one of the 'canto' columns. It would have made a geometric version of sunlight filtering through a dense canopy of leaves.

From the columned hall visitors would have been able to go down to the library to consult the collection of editions of Dante,

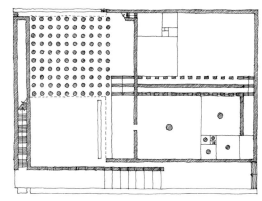

3 intermediate level

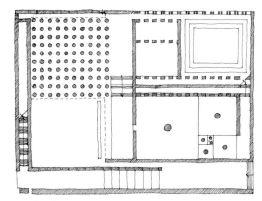

4 entrance level

124

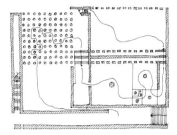

9 spiral route

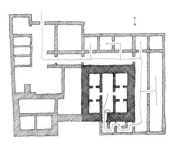

5 Necromanteion

or, following the route of the poem, up stairs to a platform behind the tormented souls. Here they would encounter the one doorway in the building – Terragni's representation of the gateway into Hell over which, in Dante's poem, was written '*Lasciate ogni speranza, voi che entrate*' ('Abandon all hope, you who enter'). With a frisson of uncertainty visitors would have stepped across the threshold into the *Inferno*, finding it a dark space with columns arranged according to the Golden Section. These free-standing columns are reminiscent of those found in the pillar crypts of ancient Egypt and Crete (see the Case Study on the Royal Villa, Knossos, *8*, in *Analysing Architecture*, 3rd edition). Applying the timeless reading of columns as vicarious representatives of ancestors, the *Inferno* columns may also be read as souls locked for eternity in Hell and like Lot's wife who was turned to a pillar of salt when she disobeyed the injunction not to look back at the destruction of Sodom and Gomorrah.

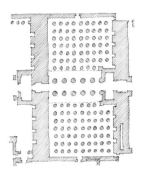

6 hypostyle hall

The escape from the Inferno is not clear. One whole wall is perforated with identical openings with short flights of steps up. All but one, the last, meets a blank wall. The last, in the corner, leads up more steps to a space different in character. The *Purgatorio* would have been lit with sunlight flooding in through square openings in its ceiling, framing heaven and casting square shadows slowly tracking, like the beam of sunlight from the oculus of the Pantheon, across the wall and floor. This space too was composed according to the Golden Section, but here the spiral is inverted and the floor, rather than descending as in the *Inferno*, rises in squares to form a small geometric 'mountain' – a weak symbol of the possibility of salvation.

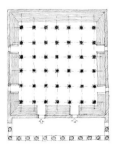

7 Telesterion

The exit from the *Purgatorio* is again in the corner. It leads up more stairs (the general route through *Il Danteum* is a spiral (*9*) rising to the *Paradiso*. This is a space defined by glass. The columns and the roof they support, divided again into squares, are all of glass. It would have made an ethereal space. By reflection and refraction the glass columns would have transformed other people into shimmering spirits.

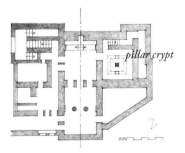

pillar crypt

8 Royal Villa, Knossos

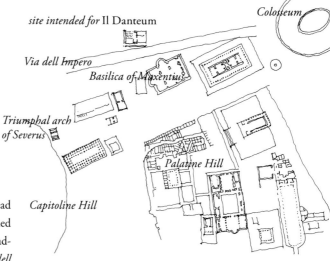

site intended for Il Danteum

Colosseum

Via dell Impero

Basilica of Maxentius

Triumphal arch
of Severus

Palatine Hill

Capitoline Hill

1 ancient Rome

After the *Paradiso*, visitors could have gone down the dead end of the *Impero* to admire the Eagle. They would the have returned through paradise to exit the building through a small opening leading to a long stair between two high walls back down to the *Via dell Impero* and the views across to the reminders of the glories of ancient Rome in the ruins of the forum, the pine trees and houses of the Caesars on the Palatine Hill and the Colosseum just along the road (*1*). The client intended this building as a political statement.

Conclusion: a note on identification of place

The defining factor in architecture is that it identifies place. It is easiest to think of place in terms of function, practical purpose: a place to light a fire; a place to cook; a place to sleep; a place of refuge protected by walls, door and roof from enemies and inclement weather; a place to play football. Like the Barcelona Pavilion, *Il Danteum* has no practical purpose (other than the library in its basement). Both show that architecture can transcend practical purpose, and that place may be characterised by subtle factors such as dislocation, transportation, abstraction… – the creation of strange 'other' worlds. In the case of *Il Danteum* it involves narrative too and the eliciting of emotional response. *Il Danteum* would have been a place to follow a well-known story and to be prompted into feelings of trepidation, uncertainty, depression… perplexity, elevation, aspiration… enlightenment, wonder, amusement… respect (or satire, for the political authorities of the day)… and finally escape back to the ordinary and everyday but with a transformed perception of the world.

References and other relevant publications, websites, broadcasts:

Giorgio Ciucci – *Giuseppe Terragni: Opera Completa*, Electa, Milan, 1996.

Peter Eisenman – *The Formal Basis of Modern Architecture*, Lars Müller, Baden, 2006.

Peter Eisenman – *Giuseppe Terragni: Transformations, Decompositions, Critiques*, The Monacelli Press, New York, 2003.

Thomas L. Schumacher – *Surface & Symbol: Giuseppe Terragni and the Architecture of Italian Rationalism*, Princeton Architectural Press, New York, 1991.

Thomas L. Schumacher – *The Danteum*, Triangle Architectural Publishing, London and Princeton Architectural Press, New York, 1993.

Bruno Zevi, translated by Beltrandi – *Giuseppe Terragni* (1968), Triangle Architectural Publishing, London, 1989.

FALLINGWATER

'We start with the ground… The ground already has form. Why not begin to give at once by accepting that? Why not give by accepting the gifts of nature?… Is the ground sunny or the shaded slope of some hill, high or low, bare or wooded, triangular or square? Has the site features, trees, rocks, stream, or a visible trend of some kind? Has it some fault or special virtue, or several? In any and every case the character of the site is the beginning of the building that aspires to architecture.'

Frank Lloyd Wright – *The Future of Architecture* (1953), 1970, pp. 321-322.

FALLINGWATER

The house hanging over a waterfall
FRANK LLOYD WRIGHT, 1963-66

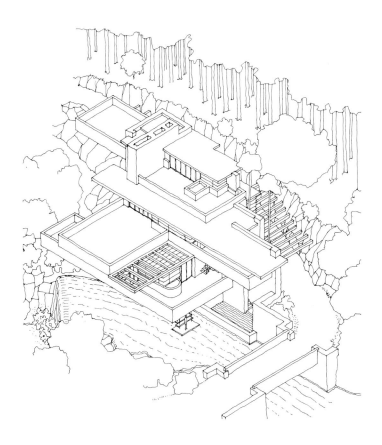

There is a story told that when Frank Lloyd Wright was given the commission for Fallingwater by Edgar Kaufmann he drew nothing for nine months (see McCarter, 2002). Then he invited the client to see the design for his new weekend house, and proceeded to complete sketch design drawings, from which the built house hardly deviated, in the two hours while Kaufmann was driving to see him. If this is true, it is evidence that Wright had a clear architectural idea for how the house should be composed, and that what he did, while his client was driving to see him, was apply that idea as a mediator between the site and the brief for a weekend house.

Wright's architectural idea, expressed in words, was to mark a place for a fire on the rocks beside a waterfall and to let a house, composed of rectangular horizontal planes, grow from that hearth over the water. This idea was the basis for a negotiation, played out on the paper on Wright's drawing board, between the conditions presented by the site and the desires associated with a place to live. This is what an architect does: comes up with an idea by which the desires contained in a design brief might be reconciled with their conditions, physical and otherwise. The idea emerges neither from the brief nor from the site but from the architect's imagination.

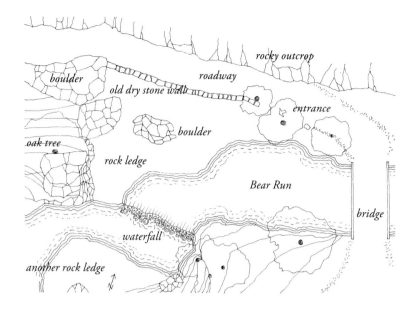

1 site

Identification of place; using things that are there

In architecture, the first decision is to choose a site. Sometimes while wandering through the countryside one encounters places – a clearing in the woods, a ledge of rock alongside a stream, a recess in a cliff face with a view of the sea – that seem to invite one to settle, if only for a moment. Whereas most parts of the countryside – pathways, open moors, beaches – tend to keep one moving, such settling places seem to invite one to stop. Maybe they do this because they offer a sense of protection, enclosure, a refuge; maybe they are light, warmed by the sunshine; maybe they offer a viewpoint, from which to enjoy a prospect. Recognising and inter-relating with such places is a fundamental act of architecture. Identification of place is the conceptual seed from which architecture grows.

The site on which Fallingwater was built (*1*) must have seemed such a place to Frank Lloyd Wright. In the sense that one can make sense of it as a place to be, untouched except by the mind, it is a work of architecture in itself. (Architecture as identification of place does not necessarily entail building.) With its bridge, water, trees and rocks it is also reminiscent of a Japanese garden. (Throughout his career Wright was interested in and influenced by Japanese architecture and garden design. See Nute, 2002.)

This place in the woods of south-west Pennsylvania has some key elements: first there is an almost horizontal slab of rock (labelled '*rock ledge*' in *1*); across this slab of rock flows the river – Bear Run – which falls from its edge as a waterfall; the river flows from under a bridge that leads onto an old roadway; the roadway runs along a

rocky outcrop with an old dry stone wall between it and the rock ledge; on and immediately to the west of the rock ledge there are large boulders; the sun shines into this clearing surrounded by trees on the sloping sides of the river valley. One of the boulders stands like an altar near the centre of gravity of the rock ledge. Two trees stand as sentinels marking an entrance onto the rock ledge from the roadway. On the opposite bank of the river there is another rock ledge – a place from which to admire the waterfall with the site of Fallingwater as its backdrop. Not only is this site like a Japanese garden, it is a theatre too, with a stage – the rock ledge – ready for a performance.

Wright began his architectural performance with a camp fire on the top of the 'altar' boulder, making it into a hearth (*2*). This was the germ of the seed from which the rest of the house grew in this particular place. The boulder provided the foundation for the focus of the house and for the chimney stack that would be its structural support and symbolic centre. Around this hearth Wright constructed artificial versions of the natural rock ledge – adding strata to the geology of the site – concrete slabs cantilevered out over the river. These slabs provide the horizontal surfaces for the living accommodation and the outdoor terraces of the house. From the main living floor a suspended stair descends to a small platform just above the level of the water. Wright retained the two sentinel trees; the entrance into the house is between them. The old dry stone wall at the back of the site is replaced with a series of fragmented but parallel walls. The last of these, rising the slope of the roadway, butts up against a boulder. In these ways the house is tied into its site.

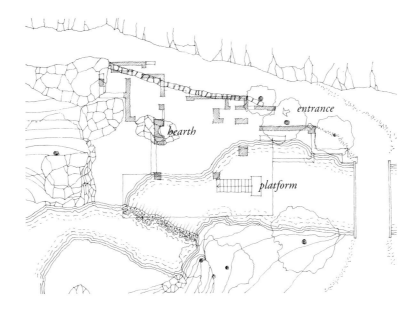

2

Geometry; temples and cottages

As is generally the case in Wright's designs, the composition of Fallingwater in plan is governed by a regular grid, in this case 5 foot by 5 foot. Wright takes the orientation of the grid from that of the bridge, which is approximately 15 degrees west of north (*3*). As part of the project the original wooden bridge was reconstructed 15 feet wide.

A grid is powerful in mathematics and geography because points may be plotted on it and given coordinates – X and Y – i.e.

identified by a precise location that can be defined by means of numbers (see *Analysing Architecture*, pages 154-155). The grid is a device for making sense of space and irregularity.

In architecture a grid has more powers. It helps an architect make decisions about the location of elements. By its regularity it lends design a graphic integrity (maybe comparable to the rhythmic integrity lent to a piece of music by its beat). On a site like this one by Bear Run it imposes an orthogonal layer that is abstract and quintessentially human (intellectual) upon the irregular (natural) topography. It *measures* the world for the architect. It begins the

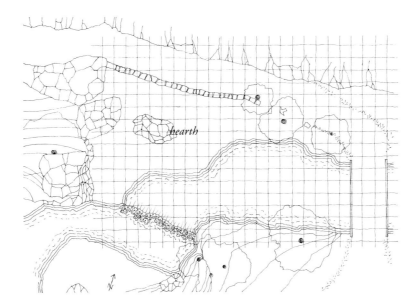

3

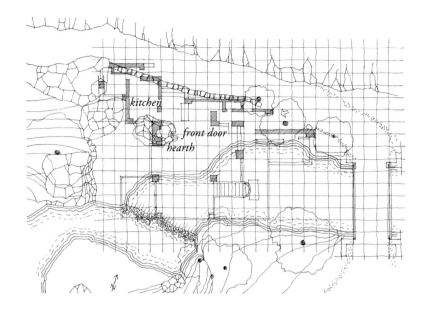

1

process of adding a different kind of architecture to that which a mind recognises as already present in the natural layout of a site. It adds a geometry that can be attuned to both the geometry of making and to the ideal geometry of squares and rectangles proportioned according to simple and special ratios. If the ruler, or scale rule, is the architect's equivalent of a magician's wand (because both the rule and wand are instruments of power) then the grid is a prime agent of the rule; it helps an architect perform magic.

There are many, perhaps infinite, ways in which a grid might be used in laying out a plan. When great tracts of the flat lands of North America were laid out as real estate they were merely divided into simple rectangles (until the curvature of the earth disrupted this simple strategy). The Greek architect and city planner Hippodamus, when he laid out the city of Miletus (*2*, on the west coast of modern Turkey), imposed a regular grid on the irregular topography of a promontory, with the result that straight alleys pass up and down the hilly terrain. Something similar happens in Manhattan, New York. Wright however plays a different game. At Fallingwater the grid is there only as a ghost. Wright uses it selectively, to give his design discipline. You can see from the drawing above (1) that the hearth on its boulder occupies two of the squares in width but, according to the published drawings, not quite a full square in its depth. Some of the walls have one face on a grid line, others have the other; yet others are centred on a grid line. The entrance sequence occupies a zone two squares wide and the front door of the house, with its three steps down, is one square wide. The extent of the terraces on this level are determined by grid lines, except the western most end seems

to come on a half grid line. The stairs down to the water platform occupy one square's width. The kitchen is three squares wide, and its doorway is positioned with its centre on a grid line.

Another aspect of the way in which Wright uses the grid in this instance is that although it imposes discipline, he allows that discipline to interact with (rather than ignore) the topography. Hence the grid begins with the altar boulder and accommodates the hearth

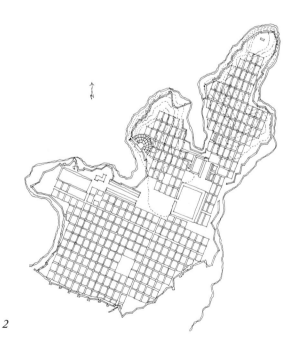

2

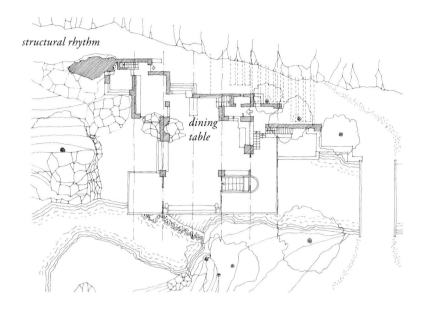

structural rhythm

dining table

3

with its chimney stack. The staggered walls of the house along the roadway, whilst obeying the orthogonal grid, also relate to the line of the old dry stone wall. The lines of the external walls step in right angles linking the house to its bridge, formalising the natural line of the river bank. The cantilevered terraces stretch out to the very brink of the waterfall. The stairs descend to the middle of the river. This is intellectual sense and discipline in interplay with natural features. The architect is responding to opportunities at the same time as imposing order. The result is a plan in which human-determined walls and natural features are in complex harmony (3); neither one nor the other prevails. The person – the inhabitant of this house – lives and moves within and around this subtle frame.

The south elevation of Fallingwater (4) shows that the house has another rhythm to it, that of the structure. Hidden in the shadows under the lowest slab there are some buttresses helping to support its outrageous cantilever (5). These buttresses are spaced at two and a half grid squares apart, i.e. 12 foot 6 inches. One centre line comes under the hearth (3), treating the 'altar' boulder as a structural support for the chimney stack; the next is under the open space of the living area coinciding with that of the built-in dining table; a third lines up with the top of the stairs down to the water; and a fourth with the wall alongside the entrance. This structural rhythm, to continue the musical analogy, counterpoints that of the spatial grid of 5 foot squares. The result is a complex interplay of ideal geometry and natural topography. In the Villa Rotonda for example (see *Analysing Architecture*, pages 160-161) the ideal geometry of the building is, apart from its orientation, independent of the setting. In Stoneywell Cottage (*Analysing Architecture*, page 72) the building's

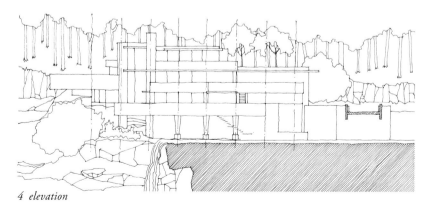

4 elevation

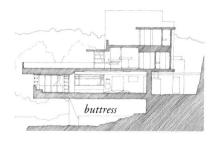

buttress

5 section

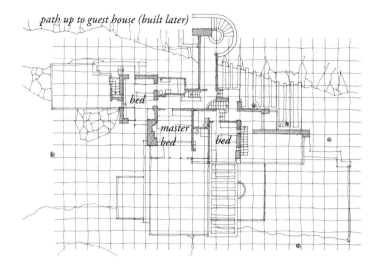

1 upper floor

form is strongly influenced by its setting, though there is an interplay between the irregular topography and the building's geometry of making. These two buildings represent the 'temple' and the 'cottage' type in terms of the different attitudes to setting they manifest. The distinction is not so easy to decide in the case of Fallingwater; it is both 'temple' and 'cottage', or neither.

The 5-foot square grid disciplines the upper floors too (*1* and *2*). Each floor plan is far from identical. Wright changes the layout radically on each level, though he does follow some rules, in addition to adhering to the discipline of the orthogonal grid. For example: the chimney stack rises vertically through all floors, a datum and reference point for each; attached to the chimney stack is a 'tower' containing the kitchen on the living level, a bedroom

on the middle level, and the study on the top level; the rooms on all levels open to the south and sun; all have external terraces; all are screened from the roadway by the staggered and fragmented parallel walls. Otherwise, within these rules, the form of the house varies at each level like a formalised, geometrically regular, version of a geological rock formation.

Conclusion: some notes on influences

If the composition of Fallingwater is simplified into its component planes (*3*) it is easy to see its relation to 1920s Neo-Plastic ideas as expressed, for example, in Theo van Doesburg's spatial studies (see page 36) or Gerrit Rietveld's Schröder House in Utrecht, Nether-

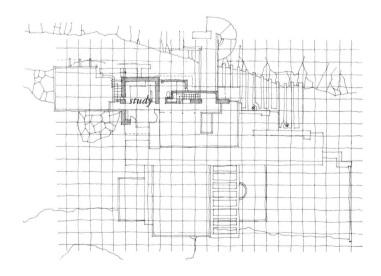

2 top floor

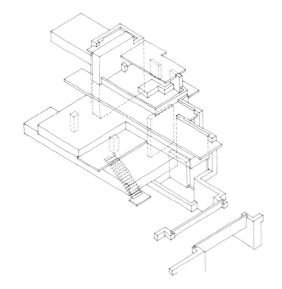

3

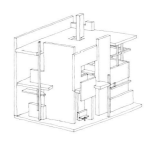

4

lands (*4*). Fallingwater is less abstract than van Doesburg's studies. It is more tied into the world. Its planes to the south emphasise the horizontal strata of the rocks and of human movement; they open to the sun. Fallingwater is also more thoroughly three-dimensional than the Schröder House; in the latter the planes seem like scales attached to a box, whereas in Wright's design the planes stretch right through the building, vertically as well as horizontally, and out into the landscape. The Neo-Plasticists were influenced by the publication of a portfolio of Wright's designs in Berlin in 1911 (available on the Internet at the University of Utah's Marriot Library – www.lib.utah. edu/portal/site/marriottlibrary/) which included his designs for the Prairie Houses such as the Ward Willits House (1901, *5*) so it could be argued that in Fallingwater Wright was influenced by a European development of his own earlier architectural ideas.

The projecting planes of Fallingwater are clearly a development from those of the Ward Willits House, though those of the later house are more complex and site related. The idea of the central hearth has poetic connotations – emphasising the idea of home. It also refers to traditional architecture, maybe even that of Wales (*6*), from which Wright claimed ancestry.

But perhaps the most significant influences in Fallingwater are those Wright acquired from Japan. As Kevin Nute has shown (Nute, 1993) these influenced Wright's architecture throughout his career; and Wright lived in Tokyo from 1916 to 1922. It is from Japan that Wright acquired the idea of in-between space (discussed in the analysis of Mies van der Rohe's Farnsworth House) as exemplified in the terraces and overhanging roofs of the Prairie Houses and of Fallingwater. It was in Japan that Wright saw subtle interplay between the regularity of human constructions and the irregularity of natural forms. This is evident in the relationship between Fallingwater and its site, as discussed earlier in this analysis, and in the way that the irregular top of the 'altar' boulder, which is the hearth of the living

5

6

1

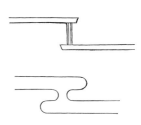

2 'thin mist shelves', similar to the way in which mist is depicted in traditional Japanese painting

space, penetrates through the floor like an island through the surface of water. This device is reminiscent of Japanese Zen rock gardens and of the introduction of gnarled pieces of timber into otherwise regular Japanese rooms (*1*, from Morse, 1886). Japanese designers also played with compositions of horizontal planes, as in the so-called *usu kasumi dana* or 'thin mist shelves' and small garden bridges (*2* and *3*, also from Morse). Fallingwater is a bridge that stretches across Bear Run but does not touch the other side. Perhaps Wright also thought of it as early morning mist caught between the sides of the narrow valley. Certainly he was striving to achieve the sensitivity to human aesthetic sensibility and wit, and their relation to nature, evident in traditional Japanese architecture (*4*).

Traditionally Japanese architects and garden designers were interested in creating pleasing compositions that could be viewed either through the rectangular openings of buildings or from particular viewpoints. At Fallingwater Wright had steps specially cut to provide a way down to the rock ledge on the other side of Bear Run. The classic photographs of the house are taken from this point. It was as if Wright was standing back to admire his own work in its setting, and offering others an opportunity to do so too.

3

References and other relevant publications, websites, broadcasts:

There is a computer-generated video of Fallingwater at:
http://www.youtube.com/watch?v=9CVKU3ErrGM

William J.R. Curtis – 'The Architectural System of Frank Lloyd Wright', in *Modern Architecture Since 1900*, Phaidon, Oxford, 1987.

Grant Hildebrand – *The Wright Space: Pattern and Meaning in Frank Lloyd Wright's Houses*, University of Washington Press, Seattle, 1991.

Donald Hoffmann – *Frank Lloyd Wright: Architecture and Nature*, Dover, New York, 1986.

Donald Hoffmann – *Frank Lloyd Wright's Fallingwater: the House and its History* (1978), Dover, New York, 1993.

Donald Hoffmann – *Understanding Frank Lloyd Wright's Architecture*, Dover, New York, 1995.

Edgar Kaufmann and **Ben Raeburn** – *Frank Lloyd Wright: Writings and Buildings*, Meridian, New York, 1960.

Edgar Kaufmann – *Fallingwater*, Abbeville Press, New York, 1986.

Robert McCarter – *Fallingwater: Frank Lloyd Wright*, Phaidon (Architecture in Detail Series), London, 2002.

Edward S. Morse – *Japanese Homes and Their Surroundings* (1886), Dover, New York, 1961.

Kevin Nute – *Frank Lloyd Wright and Japan*, Routledge, London, 1993.

Frank Lloyd Wright – *An Autobiography* (The Frank Lloyd Wright Foundation, 1932, 1943, 1977), Quartet Books, London, 1977.

Frank Lloyd Wright – *The Future of Architecture* (1953), Meridian, New York, 1970.

Bruno Zevi – *The Modern Language of Architecture*, University of Washington Press, Seattle, 1978.

4

VILLA SAVOYE

'That house looks as though it hated the ground, with vast vanity trying to rise superior to it regardless of nature, depending on a detachment called "classical" for such human values and association of ideas could give to it.'

Frank Lloyd Wright – *The Future of Architecture* (1953), 1970, p. 322.

VILLA SAVOYE

A house in the Poissy suburb of Paris, France
LE CORBUSIER, 1929

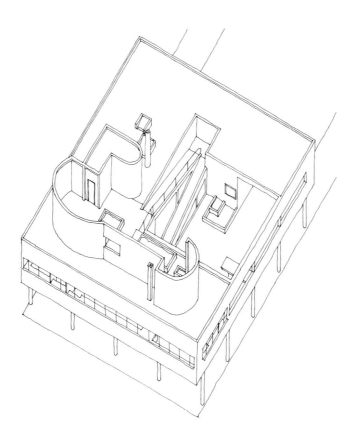

In the quotation opposite, which occupies the space of one of the ellipses in the quotation at the beginning of the analysis of Fallingwater, Frank Lloyd Wright was not specifically referring to Le Corbusier's Villa Savoye but to the American 'Colonial' house. Wright wanted to cultivate the idea of an American architecture rooted in American ground in contrast to an architecture imposed by colonial powers. It was a matter of asserting independence and identity. Even so, it is tempting to suggest that Wright was also taking a side swipe at his main rival for the title of 'greatest architect of the twentieth century' – Le Corbusier, whose Villa Savoye, in contrast to Fallingwater's strong relationship to its topography, stands aloof from the ground on columns, which Le Corbusier called 'pilotis'.

The difference between the two architects' attitudes to the ground – as exemplified in Wright's Fallingwater and Le Corbusier's Villa Savoye – neatly highlights one of the timeless quandaries of architecture: should architecture be something that human beings impose on the world, or should it be responsive to what the world offers? It is not of course a quandary that requires a definitive answer. Architecture has been produced according to both attitudes. I discussed this in the chapter on 'Temples and Cottages' in *Analysing Architecture*. The Villa Savoye does have a fireplace but it is far from being a dominant core element, founded on a natural boulder, as it is in Fallingwater. It is, by contrast, a small brick box with a concrete lit and a tube-like flue. Differences such as these suggest, symbolise, or may be interpreted as representing different views

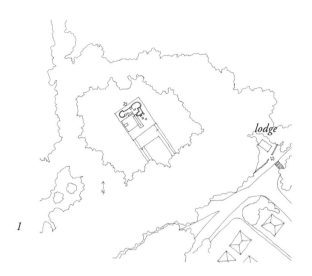

1

lodge

2

about our relationship with the world. Architecture is philosophical. It makes propositions about how to make sense of, and how to relate to, the world. Sometimes such propositions are instilled in buildings unthinkingly, as in most traditional architecture when things are done in the ways they always have been. Sometimes architects are conscious of the philosophical dimensions and potential of what they do, and contrive their propositions as political or social arguments. We are perhaps used to thinking of philosophy as something that is done with words; architects (whether formally trained and professionally accredited or not) do it with space and matter.

For Frank Lloyd Wright in Fallingwater the challenge of architecture lay in finding a symbiotic relationship with the landscape, exploiting the rocks and waterfalls that were already there. For Le Corbusier in the Villa Savoye it lay in transcending, rising above the land to make a place apart.

Identification of place

Nowadays the Villa Savoye stands in a field isolated from the wider landscape by a ring of trees that also screen adjacent buildings (*1*). When it was built the house stood in open meadow land on the top of a gentle hill and visible from all around.

In 1911, eighteen years before the Villa Savoye was built, Le Corbusier had travelled to Turkey, Greece and Italy. The trip was his equivalent of the Grand Tour undertaken by wealthy British gentlemen in the eighteenth and nineteenth centuries. Great buildings – Hagia Sophia in Istanbul, the Parthenon in Athens, the Pantheon in Rome and the remains of Pompeii… – made a deep impression on him and gave him ideas for his own work. He recorded what he saw in a series of personal notebooks (see Le Corbusier, 1987, 2002).

Although the setting of the Villa Savoye is less dramatic and less craggy, and although its appearance was starkly original for its time, it seems clear that Le Corbusier was influenced in its design by his encounters with and interpretations of Greek temples.

In the sketchbook Le Corbusier used in Athens there is a drawing of the Acropolis showing the Parthenon (the main temple) and the Propylaea (the gateway) with the small temple of Nike Apteros which stands like a sentinel at the entrance to the temenos (sacred enclosure). My copy of Le Corbusier's drawing is above (*2*). Redrawing it, what he seems to have wanted to record was: the regular geometry of the buildings against the irregularity of the craggy rock and scrubby vegetation; the bright whiteness of the marble temples against the sky and the play of sunlight and shadows in and amongst their geometric masses; and the grandeur of a world above the ordinary – the world of the gods, superior beings.

In *Vers Une Architecture* (1923; *Towards a New Architecture*, 1927) Le Corbusier illustrated the Parthenon again in a chapter entitled 'Architecture: Pure Creation of the Mind'. He wrote of the temple's Doric order:

> *'We must realize clearly that Doric architecture did not grow in the fields with the asphodels, and that it is a pure creation of the mind.'* (p. 209)

In the same chapter he included another of the drawings from his sketchbook (which I have redrawn at *3*). It shows the Parthenon on the Acropolis silhouetted against a distant view of the sea. This drawing is less about recording a particular scene and more about recording the realisation of an idea. As suggested in the quotation on Doric architecture, the idea was that architecture was a medium in which the human mind could break free of, transcend, its natural conditions – to rise into the realm of the gods. This drawing shows

3

5

the temple as a representation of the human intellect, towering over the world.

The Villa Savoye stands like a temple in its temenos. It even has its little temple of Nike Apteros, the gardener's lodge which Le Corbusier positioned alongside the entrance onto the site (*1*). In Volume 1, 1910-29, of his *Œuvre Compléte* there is a drawing (redrawn at *4*) illustrating the image of the house in Le Corbusier's mind. Its caption reads '*La villa est entourée d'une ceinture de futaies*' ('The villa is surrounded by a belt of mature trees'). Though the Villa Savoye does not have the benefit of the same majestic setting as the Parthenon, there is a clear link between the way in which Le Corbusier imagined his design and his memory of the Greek temple in its landscape. The villa stands on a hill. It is a pure geometric form set in irregular nature and lit by the sun. It has columns, and establishes a 'place above the world'. The villa is not a replica of a Greek temple but a reinterpretation of ideas that may be traced back to the Greek temple. The building identifies not only a place to live but also the place of the human intellect, separated from and surveying the world around.

Stratification

The Villa Savoye, like the Parthenon on its Acropolis, is an architecture of levels. *Acropolis* means 'high city', the sacred precinct above the ordinary everyday city. There are hierarchical levels in the architecture of the temple too (*5*). The superstructure of the temple is lifted off the ground by a platform, the stylobate; this was the level of the priests. On the stylobate stand the columns which support the entablature, the beams spanning from column to column. The upper part of the entablature is divided by the triglyphs (thought to represent the ends of beams as they would have appeared in ancient timber temples) into panels containing deep relief sculpture – the metopes. The Parthenon metopes depict battles between lapiths and centaurs (heroes versus creatures that were half man half horse), between civilisation and barbarism. Around the inner wall of the Parthenon there was also a carved frieze depicting the soldiers lost in a battle against the Persians in the fifth century BC. With its lapiths and soldiers the entablature was the level of the heroes. At the ends of the temple above the entablature were the pediments.

4

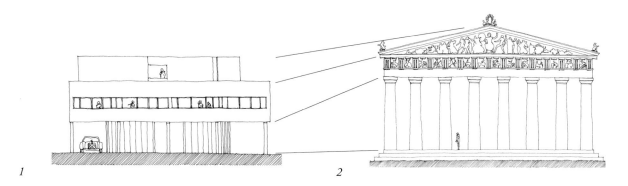

1   2

These contained sculptures of the gods. This then was the highest in the hierarchy represented by the levels of the temple.

The Villa Savoye has a comparable stratification (*1*). It has no stylobate, only the gravel drive out of which the columns rise. This is the level of the motor car and the entrance. Above that, supported on the columns like an entablature, is the box containing the main living areas. With its long horizontal window like the row of metopes on the temple, this is the level of the residents (heroes?). Above that is the roof garden/solarium, the equivalent of the temple's pediment. This is the level at which the residents are closest to the sky and the sun; the level at which they become like gods.

Le Corbusier sketched the section of the house. (I have redrawn his sketch at *3*.) He shows the house with four levels: the solarium; the level of inhabitation; the pilotis level which belongs to the motor car; and a fourth level below ground, the cellar. Between these he draws a squiggle representing a spiral stair that stretches from underground to the roof garden. He also draws a ramp from the ground level to the first floor. If one accepts that like the Greek temple the Villa Savoye is a layering of different states of being, then this section includes the level of the cave. The house may be interpreted as a representation of the ascent of human beings from darkness to light, from the primitive to sophisticated civilisation, from (to borrow a phrase from Friedrich Nietzsche's *Thus Sprake Zarathustra*, 1883-85) 'animal to superman'.

Le Corbusier was of course not the only architect in history to explore the idea that architecture, as a product of the intellect, transcends the natural world, and that architecture can layer, vertically, different states of being. Andrea Palladio expressed the same in his Villa Rotonda (*4*) which, in a way similar to the Villa Savoye, stands on top of a mounded hill (outside Vicenza in north Italy) surveying the countryside all around. The lowest layer of this house was for the servants (the underclass) and menial activities. The main floor was for those who thought of themselves as superior, noble. And the dome represented the heavens above.

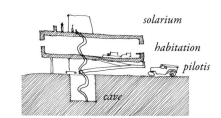

solarium

habitation

pilotis

cave

3

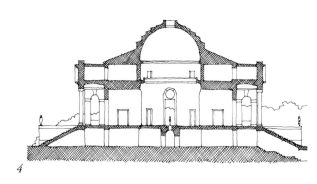

4

Ideal geometry

Intriguingly, the entrance elevation of the Villa Savoye fits quite neatly into that of the Parthenon (*5*). Both are based on two √2 rectangles placed side by side. In the Parthenon, a Golden Rectangle the same height determines the positions of the two central columns (*6*). In the Villa Savoye the sides of the panel in which the doorway is set are determined in the same way (*7*). And just as the overall height of the Parthenon above the stylobate seems determined by a Golden

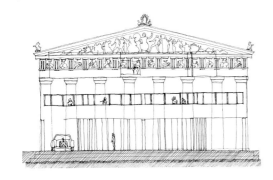

5

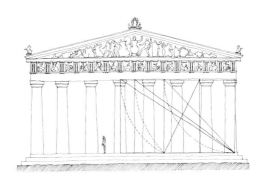

6

Rectangle drawn between the centre lines of the outermost columns (*8*), so the overall height of the Villa Savoye seems determined by a Golden Rectangle drawn between four of the five columns (*9*).

The plans (*10* and *11*) are clearly organised according to the four by four square grid of columns, though as shown in *Analysing*

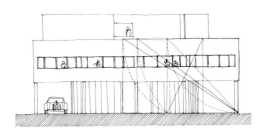

7

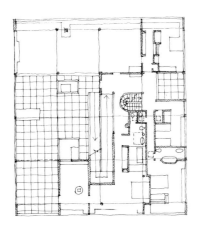

11 middle floor

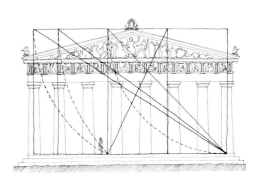

8

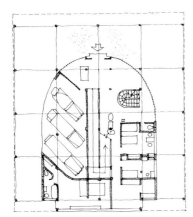

10 ground floor

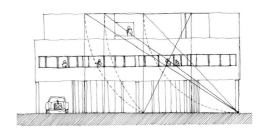

9

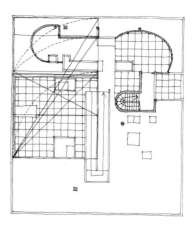

1 roof (solarium)

Architecture (page 181) the columns deviate from the discipline of the grid for practical reasons around the ramp at the centre of the plan. The north-south dimension of the middle floor is however slightly longer. The overhang is determined by a √2 rectangle (*2*). On the ground floor the position of the start of the ramp seems to be determined by the square inside a Golden Rectangle drawn between one end of the building and the other (*3*). And the size of the courtyard on the middle floor, together with the positions of various of the screen walls on the roof, seem determined also by a √2 rectangle and a Golden Rectangle (*1*). This brief analysis does not exhaust the various ways in which Le Corbusier ordered the Villa Savoye according to ideal geometry. The use of ideal geometry is one aspect of the way in which the building was considered to represent the transcendent potential of the human intellect.

Modifying elements: light and time

For Le Corbusier the two principal modifying elements of architecture were light and time. He had appreciated the contribution to architecture of both these elements in the ancient buildings he visited during his 1911 travels. He wrote about light in the houses of Pompeii:

> 'The Pompeian did not cut up his wall-spaces; he was devoted to wall-spaces and loved light. Light is intense when it falls between walls which reflect it. The ancients built walls, walls which stretch out and meet to amplify the wall. In this way they created volumes, which are the basis of architectural and sensorial feeling. The light bursts on you, by a definite intention, at one end and illuminates the walls. The impression of light is extended outside by cylinders (I hardly like to say columns, it is a worn-out word), peristyles of pillars. The floor stretches everywhere it can, uniformly and without irregularity... There are no other architectural elements internally: light, and its reflection in a great flood by the walls and floor, which is really a horizontal wall.' (1927, pp. 185-186)

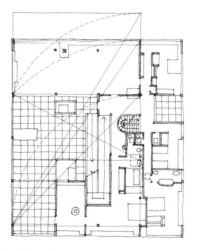

2 middle floor (living)

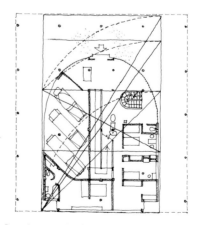

3 ground floor (entrance)

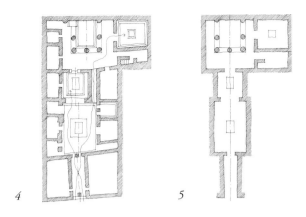

4   5

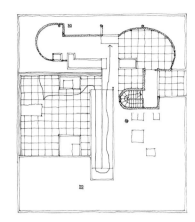

6 roof

He wrote about the axis as extent in time rather than the means of balancing a visual composition:

'An axis is perhaps the first human manifestation; it is the means of every human act. The toddling child moves along an axis, the man striving in the tempest of life traces for himself an axis. The axis is the regulator of architecture. To establish order is to begin to work. Architecture is based on axes.' (1927, p. 187)

And again he used an example from Pompeii, the House of the Tragic Poet (*4*), the plan of which he sketched:

'The axis here is not an arid thing of theory; it links together the main volumes which are clearly stated and differentiated one from another.' (1927, p. 189)

If the House of the Tragic Poet had been built strictly according to a straight axis its main spaces would have been arranged something like as shown in *5*. The actuality is more complex and subtle. Le Corbusier suggests it is richer because is incorporates the axis of movement of the person rather than obeying the mindless authority of a geometric rule. In *4* the loosely related axes of the main spaces are shown alongside a couple of possible routes through the house.

The Villa Savoye is the House of the Tragic Poet, though the axis of movement runs from ground to roof rather than from front to back. The villa has, like the Pompeian house, a geometric axis around which a route meanders (*8, 7, 6*). Like the Pompeian house the route has a beginning and an end. Like in the Pompeian house there are different possible routes around the axis. In the Villa Savoye the main axis is represented by the ramp at the centre of the plan. This is the datum to which the route always returns.

Le Corbusier's realisation that architecture involved experience of time came also from his admiration of the Parthenon on the Acropolis. In ancient Athens this composition of buildings was built

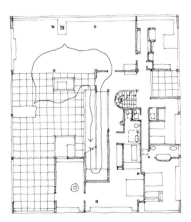

7 middle

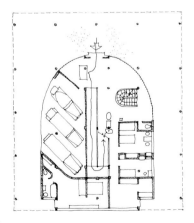

8 ground

145

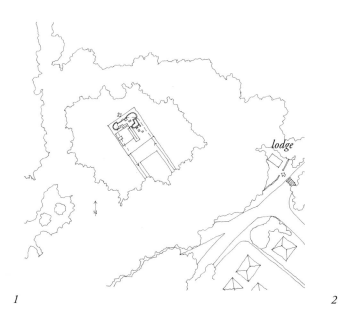

1

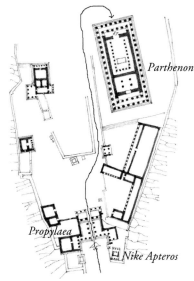

2   *Agora*

around a processional route that passed through the Agora at the base of the hill, up a ramped route to the Propylaea (gateway), through into the Temenos (sacred precinct) and alongside the Parthenon (the main temple) to reach its doorway at the far end (*2*). The arrangement at the Villa Savoye, if not so grand, is similar (*1*). As you go through the gateway you pass the lodge that stands alongside like the small temple of Nike Apteros on the Acropolis. The trees with their trunks like columns stand in place of the Propylaea. The path leads into the 'sacred precinct' of the Villa Savoye – the meadow encircled by its belt of trees. Then you pass alongside and under the 'temple' – the house itself – to reach the doorway at the far end.

Le Corbusier designed the Villa Savoye to show that he was a Pompeian too in his love of light. He described another house in Pompeii, the Casa del Noce:

> *'Again the little vestibule which frees your mind from the street. And then you are in the Atrium; four columns in the middle (four* cylinders) *shoot up towards the shade of the roof, giving a feeling of force and a witness of potent methods; but at the far end is the brilliance of the garden seen through the peristyle which spreads out this light with a large gesture, distributes it and accentuates it, stretching widely from left to right, making a great space.'* (1927, p. 183)

Something similar happens in the House of the Tragic Poet (*3*). The house takes you from the street into a narrow shaded passage. This leads to the Atrium which is lit from the sky. In the distance, at the end of the house is the Piscina (a pool) again lit from the sky, seen through the Peristyle (columns, cylinders).

In the Villa Savoye (*4*) the building takes you in under its shade into a hallway with a low ceiling. The ramp takes you up to the first floor. The route becomes progressively lighter as you rise alongside the glazed wall to the first floor courtyard on your left. When you reach the saloon you are in the realm of sunlight. The courtyard is open to the sky. The route continues up to the roof where, in the solarium, you can submit yourself to the sun.

The sequence is comparable to that already mentioned (in the analysis of Koolhaas's *Maison à Bordeaux*) found in country houses of the eighteenth century, where visitors were taken from outside into shade and then into sunshine to give a good impression of the place in which the host lived (*4*).

Conclusion: the role of ideas

It is arguable that the essential characteristic of the movement in architecture of which Le Corbusier was a leading protagonist – usually called Modernism – was a rejection of the established ways of doing things. It was about having new ideas, reinventing architecture. Le Corbusier made the point himself in *Towards a New Architecture* (page 179) contrasting what he thought should happen in architectural design with what was happening in one of the most esteemed French schools of architecture of the time:

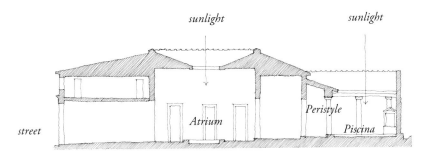

sunlight   *sunlight*

street   Atrium   Peristyle   Piscina

3

'To make a plan is to determine and fix ideas. It is to have had ideas. It is so to order these ideas that they become intelligible, capable of execution and communicable. It is essential therefore to exhibit precise intention, and to have had ideas in order to be able to furnish oneself with an intention. A plan is to some extent a summary like an analytical contents table. In a form so condensed that it seems as clear as crystal and like a geometric figure, it contains an enormous quantity of ideas and the impulse of intention. In a great public institution, the École des Beaux Arts, the principles of good planning have been studied, and then as time has gone by, dogmas have been established, and recipes and tricks. A method of teaching useful enough at the beginning has become a dangerous practice.'

Stated in these terms Modernism was a negative or contradictory movement. It rejected established ways in favour of freedom. And with that freedom architects were presented with the challenge of generating new ideas.

The Villa Savoye is a symbol of that freedom. It is so unlike a 'house'. In his book *Précisions* (page 136) Le Corbusier wrote:

'The visitor moves about the house, wondering how it all works, finding it hard to understand the reasons for what he sees and feels; he finds nothing of what is generally known as a "house". He senses that he is in something else, something quite different. And I do not think he finds it uninteresting.'

The villa also shows Le Corbusier's ability to generate ideas. But he did not design in a vacuum. He did not sit with a blank sheet of paper and think 'I must come up with an original idea'. In the challenging spirit of Modernism he did it by taking established ideas and reinterpreting them, sometimes coming up with novel combinations, sometimes turning them on their head.

His 'Five Points Towards a New Architecture', published in 1926, are a case in point. Le Corbusier did various drawings to illustrate that a new architecture could be generated by the use of: 1. pilotis; 2. flat roofs with gardens; 3. free plans; 4. free façades; and 5. the horizontal strip window. (The Villa Savoye, built a couple of years later, follows these broadly, though neither its plan nor its façades could really be said to be 'free'.) Always they are presented as contradictions of the orthodox ways of doing things. I have redrawn one of these sets of drawings on the next page. The new way of doing things is presented as having the benefits of 'economy, hygiene and freedom of movement' instead of 'unhealthiness, inefficiency and waste', but it is achieved by contradiction. Orthodox houses have solid ground floors on substantial foundations: Le Corbusier

sunlight   *sunlight*

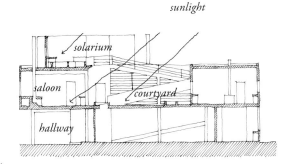

solarium

saloon   *courtyard*

hallway

4

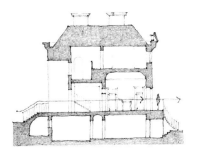

5

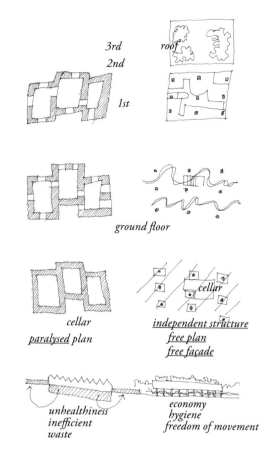

gets rid of the ground floor. Orthodox houses do not have gardens on their roofs: Le Corbusier plants trees on the roof. Orthodox houses have small or vertical windows: Le Corbusier demands long horizontal strip windows. Orthodox houses have ordered elevations and plans divided into rooms: Le Corbusier suggests free elevations and free plans. The resulting ideas are seductive (perhaps because of their novelty).

Even more seductive for architects than the actual 'Five Points' was the notion that architecture should be reinvented, over and over again, and that orthodoxy should henceforth be anathema. The seductiveness of this idea is one of the reasons why the present book is as it is.

References and other relevant publications, websites, broadcasts:

Geoffrey H. Baker – *Le Corbusier: an Analysis of Form*, Van Nostrand Reinhold, London, 1984.

Le Corbusier – 'Five Points Towards a New Architecture' (1926), translated in Ulrich Conrads – *Programmes and Manifestoes on 20th-Century Architecture*, Lund Humphries, London, 1970.

Le Corbusier – *Œuvre Complète 1910-1929*, Les Éditions d'Architecture, Zurich, 1964.

Le Corbusier – *Œuvre Complète 1929-1934*, Les Éditions d'Architecture, Zurich, 1964.

Le Corbusier, translated by Aujame – *Precisions on the Present State of Architecture and Urbanism* (1930), MIT Press, Cambridge MA, 1991.

Le Corbusier, translated by Etchells – *Towards a New Architecture* (1923), John Rodker, London, 1927.

Le Corbusier, edited by Gresleri, translated by Munson and Shore – *Voyage d'Orient: Carnets*, Electa, Milan, 1987 (in Italian), 2002 (in English).

William J.R. Curtis – *Le Corbusier: Ideas and Forms*, Phaidon, London, 1986.

Sarah Menin and Flora Samuel – Nature and Space: Aalto and Le Corbusier, Routledge, London, 2003.

Guillemette Morel-Journel – *Le Corbusier's Villa Savoye*, Éditions du Patrimoine, Paris, 2000.

Flora Samuel – *Le Corbusier in Detail*, Architectural Press, Oxford, 2007.

KEMPSEY GUEST STUDIO

*'I also learned something about the
beauty of simple space, and about
containment, security, prospect, refuge
and materiality.'*

Glenn Murcutt, quoted in Beck and Cooper
– *Glenn Murcutt: A Singular Architectural
Practice*, 2002, p. 14.

KEMPSEY GUEST STUDIO

A converted shed in New South Wales, Australia
GLENN MURCUTT, 1992

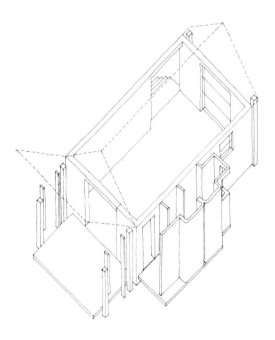

In the 1970s the Australian-based architect Glenn Murcutt designed a house in open countryside near the small town of Kempsey in New South Wales. He designed it for a lady called Marie Short. In the 1980s he acquired the house for his own use and extended it. In the 1990s he converted a traditionally built timber shed, south of the main house, into accommodation for guests. This small apartment is the Kempsey (or Murcutt) Guest Studio.

Those reading this in the north should remember that in the southern hemisphere at noon the sun shines from the north.

Using things that are there

A consequence of using something that is already there is that some of the fundamental factors in relating to context are already determined or are there to be played with, exploited, modified, counterpointed. An architect can have a creative 'dialogue' with things that are there already.

In the case of the Kempsey Guest Studio, what was there was a small, rectangular, traditionally built, timber shed. A shed – a simple rectangular cell or aedicule – is one of the basic *combined elements* of architecture (*Analysing Architecture*, 3rd edition, pages 39-42), consisting at the very least of a floor, walls, roof and doorway (and perhaps a window). Its power is simple but very strong. It identifies a place by framing it within a structure that shelters it from the sky and separates it from everywhere else. Even a tiny shed creates a human world within and in relation to its natural surroundings. It imposes its geometry on nature's irregularity, and projects that geometry outwards into the world. The shed is the basis of the temple.

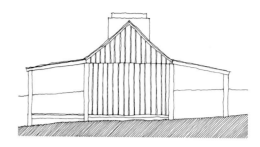

1

I have not found much information on what this shed was like before it was made into the Kempsey Guest Studio, but it was obviously the sort of building that is constructed for practical purposes, using materials readily available, and without what are called 'architectural pretensions' – that is, without ornamentation, ideal geometrical proportions or sophisticated poetic ideas. This was a shed built to shade, shelter, protect…, to secure farm equipment, fertilisers or produce. It was no doubt built in as straightforward a way as possible to achieve the strength and practicalities required.

All over the world buildings have been constructed in this way and with this attitude. They often exhibit regionally identifiable characteristics related to the ways in which available materials can be used and to climatic challenges, using construction techniques and details that have evolved by builders learning from predecessors. Sheds are rarely complex spatially, but in the case of houses these regional characteristics may also include the ways in which use and the organisation of space relates to culture, to domestic customs, practical requirements, and to mores, aspirations and beliefs.

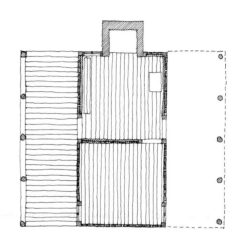

2

Geometry of making

Because of their lack of pretension and their conservative attitude, the builders of such traditional, regional, architecture usually 'obeyed', as best they might, the geometry of making (*Analysing Architecture*, 3rd edition, pages 148-150). Their concern would most likely have been to build for use rather than show, particularly when erecting a humble shed. Such directness of effort and use of materials has its attractions. It suggests a quality that has sometimes been called the architectural equivalent of 'truth' (though that is a slippery concept).

The shed at Kempsey was no doubt built by a European settler on the land, a farmer. The drawings alongside are the section (*1*) and plan (*2*) of a small house also built for a European settler in the outback of south-east Australia. Its construction is similar to that of

the original Kempsey shed, though the latter had no veranda, nor a hearth and chimney stack.

This small house illustrates the ways in which the geometry of making disciplines construction. It is rectangular because that is the easiest, 'no nonsense', way to build. It has parallel sides, with the roof spanning from one to the other. The floor and walls are rectangular because the planks of wood are themselves long thin rectangles. The structure of the roof is composed of rafters laid parallel to each other about 2ft (600mm) apart, supporting battens, laid at right angles to the rafters, onto which the rectangular sheets of corrugated metal roofing are fixed. The only place where a geometry other than that of making comes into play is in the triangular gable of the roof, the geometry of which is determined by a desire (need) to shed rain water. The life of this small house took place, literally, within the geometrical frame of this structure disciplined by the geometry of making.

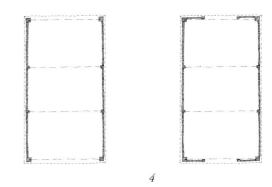

3   *4*

The Kempsey Guest Studio began with a similar, though even simpler, frame disciplined by the geometry of making. There is a reference in Françoise Fromonot's 1995 book on the work of Murcutt to his having 'closed off its ends' (p. 148), so the plan of the shed may have been something like this (*3*), completely open at each end, or maybe with the walls returning at the corners to form wide doorways in each end (*4*). The dash-dot lines dividing the plan into three indicate the positions of the simple triangular trusses supporting the roof; themselves supported by posts. The walls are vertical planks.

In its renovated state the shed's timber floor is supported off the ground on short posts. I do not know whether the shed was originally built with a timber floor. With or without, its character and use would have been different. Without a floor it would have been more suited to be a shelter for wheeled farm equipment, allowing a tractor to be driven in and out. With a floor it may have been used for shearing sheep in the shade and out of the dust, and for storing wool. The floor would have been supported off the ground on posts both to keep it out of the rain in occasional wet weather and, more importantly, to reduce attack from termites. Murcutt himself reports that, when he first saw it, the shed had, in the past, been converted into 'a rural worker's flat and tractor shed… At Christmas, (it) was the local dance hall. Some of the floor was propped in the 1930s and 40s' (Beck and Cooper, 2002, p. 144).

Six-directions-plus-centre; transition, hierarchy, heart

The shed sits south of the main house (*5*), amongst a loose clump of trees and under a particularly large one, probably planted to give it some shade. It is oriented roughly north-south. This orientation makes the shed into a compass, with each of the four sides of its rectangular plan facing one of the cardinal points – North, South, East and West (*6*). Each of these directions has its own characteristics and potential, related to the passage of the sun and to elements in

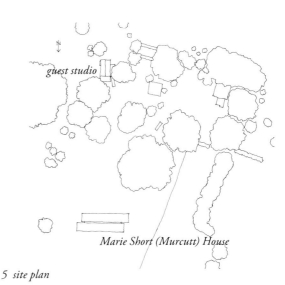

guest studio

Marie Short (Murcutt) House

5 site plan

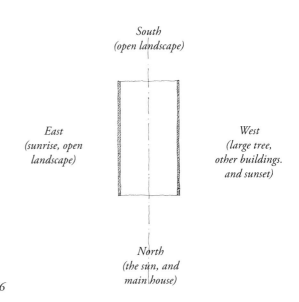

*South
(open landscape)*

*East
(sunrise, open
landscape)*

*West
(large tree,
other buildings.
and sunset)*

*North
(the sun, and
main house)*

6

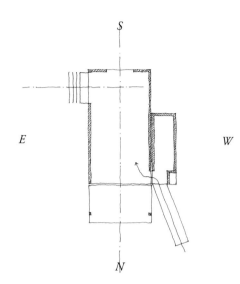

1

the surrounding landscape. Murcutt's refurbishment responds to and exploits these differences (*1*).

To the North, he extends the shed onto a veranda for sitting in shade or sun. This veranda creates one of those special types of space (place) found in architectures across the world – an in-between space where you are neither inside nor outside, where you are both 'at home' and 'in the world' at the same time. It makes the shed like a megaron (*Analysing Architecture*, page 85). In the case of the Guest Studio this veranda also faces the main house some distance away and on slightly higher ground, and catches the evening sun from the West. This is a type of space particularly attuned to the landscape and climatic challenges of Australia. as illustrated by the traditional house with its verandas shown on page 152.

To the South, the shed is given a large window which gives views of open sunlit landscape.

2

To the East, and in the South and most private corner, Murcutt opens a broad doorway facing the sunrise. Here the roof overhangs slightly and there are steps down onto the earth. This is a place for breakfast.

The West of the shed faces other buildings and the large shade tree. On this side Murcutt attaches a pod containing a shower, lavatory and hand basin. This pod allows the main space of the shed to remain free and open. Gas cylinders and the water heater are also attached to this service pod. Differentiating the purpose 'entrance' from that of the veranda, he makes part of the pod into a small porch giving access to a corner doorway into the main room. This is the most protected corner of the building. Murcutt made the studio accessible for people in wheelchairs, so this porch is approached by a ramp, angled to align with the line of approach. Together, the approach path through the trees, the ramp passing by the veranda as it lifts you gently onto the higher plane of the shed's floor, the porch which draws you in, and the threshold of the doorway create a transition sequence taking you from the open air into the private interior.

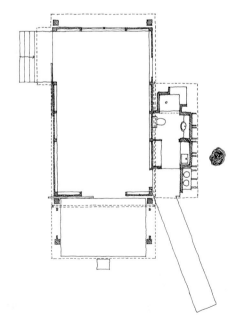

3

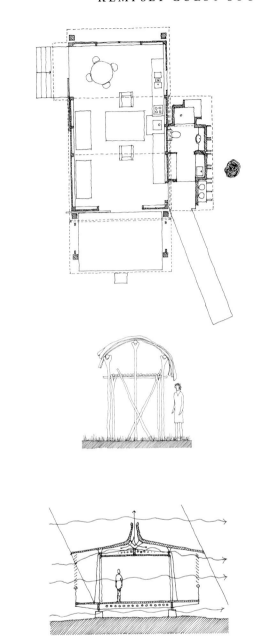

4

5

6

The plan of the shed is shown in more detail in *3*. The pod, is divided into four sections, each with its own function: the porch, a washing place and coat store, a lavatory and hand basin area, and a shower. Screened from the main house by the rest of the pod, this shower has a large corner window, with its sill just above waist height, that can be opened to the outdoors. The plan of the pod is irregular in shape, as if its space had been excavated from the general space outside the shed, like a cave. Its irregular plan is however sheltered (shaded) under a simple rectangular corrugated metal roof canted up away from the main part of the studio (*2*), with a gutter between the two roofs.

Internally, the layout is suggested by the structure of the roof; the two trusses, dotted in *4*, divide the space into three: an entrance zone; a sitting zone in front of a stove placed centrally on the West wall; and a dining (breakfast) zone related to the broad doorway facing East. The kitchen equipment and work surface is placed like furniture along the West wall, with a window over the sink. Two beds, which can be rearranged, stand alongside the East wall. It can be seen in the plan that the veranda adds a fourth zone, equivalent in dimensions to each of the internal three. The veranda too is shaded by a simple rectangular corrugated metal roof similarly canted up away from the main part of the studio. Whereas the middle zone inside would be the heart of this small dwelling in the winter, the veranda is the heart in the summer. It is provided with insect screens. The cant of its roof shades it from the noon-day summer sun whilst admitting the lower angled winter sun.

Modifying elements

In south-east Australia the summers can be very hot but winter nights can be cold. Murcutt's Guest Studio is designed to work without air conditioning and has a stove for winter heating. Aborigine Australians do not build many buildings. Some tribes build sleeping shelters, sometimes called 'mosquito huts', of sticks and large sheets of bark stripped from trees (*5*). These small structures demonstrate the basic principles of designing shelters in the hot Australian climate. The platform lifts the sleeping place off the ground, into the air and away from snakes and other animals. The roof provides shade but is open at the ends for ventilation. In 1942, the architect Jean Prouvé followed the same principles in his design for a tropical house (*6*), though his structure was steel and he allowed the hot air that would gather inside the house to escape through a vent in the roof. He also provided verandas to shade the walls.

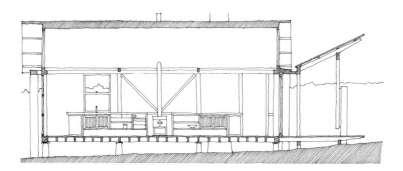

1

Murcutt follows similar principles in the design of his Guest Studio too (*1*). Though the building can be closed to keep in warmth when necessary, in the summer the windows in the South elevation and the doorway onto the veranda can be opened fully to allow free ventilation. The studio stands on posts or stumps so that air can flow under it too. The roof of the veranda and the glazed gable of the North elevation are arranged so that the sun at noon in the summer is kept out whilst in the winter, when its angle is lower, the sun and its warmth can reach deep into the interior (2).

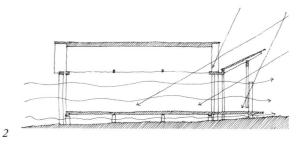

2

Conclusion: prospect and refuge

In the short quotation at the beginning of this analysis, Murcutt mentions prospect and refuge. This is a concept identified in a book by Jay Appleton, published first in the mid-1970s, called *The Experience of Landscape*. In brief, Appleton argues that our aesthetic evaluation of the landscape is influenced if not governed by our sense of advantage we feel (over possible threats) when enjoying a protected refuge with a wide view of the land around.

'Prospect and refuge' is a concept fundamental to architecture. It is evident in Murcutt's Guest Studio. Even a small shed establishes a centre, a home in the wide world, a datum against which one may know where one is. We make such centres with our beach camps when we spend a day on the beach. More permanent centres have to be built in more substantial ways, but still they change the generality of the open landscape by establishing somewhere specific – a place. Such places hold psychological emotional power as well as providing physical comfort. We gravitate towards them. We occupy them. We enjoy the containment and security they offer. We also enjoy sitting at their mouths, anchored but able to take refuge if necessary, surveying the prospect of the world around. To establish a place is the fundamental power of architecture.

References and other relevant publications, websites, broadcasts:

Jay Appleton – *The Experience of Landscape* (1975), Hull University Press, Hull, 1986.

Haig Beck and Jackie Cooper – *Glenn Murcutt: A Singular Architectural Practice*, Images Publishing Group, Mulgrave, 2002.

Philip Drew – *Leaves of Iron: Glenn Murcutt, Pioneer of an Australian Architectural Form*, The Law Book Company, New South Wales, 1985.

Françoise Fromonot, translated by Anning – *Glenn Murcutt: Buildings and Projects*, Whitney Library of Design, New York, 1995, pp. 62-65 (Marie Short House) and pp. 148-151 (Kempsey Guest Studio).

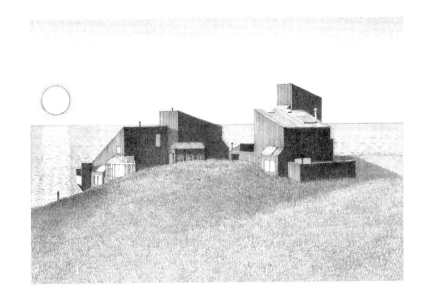

CONDOMINIUM ONE, THE SEA RANCH

'Now the aedicule, from a remote period, has been used as a subjunctive means of architectural expression. That is to say, it has been used to harmonize architecture of strictly human scale with architecture of a diminutive scale, so that a building may at the same time serve the purpose of men and of a race of imaginary beings smaller than men. It has been used to preserve the human scale in a building deliberately enlarged to express the superhuman character of a god. Perhaps this should be put another way: the aedicule has been enlarged to human scale and then beyond, to an heroic scale, losing its attribute of smallness and "cosiness" but retaining and affirming its attribute of ceremoniousness.'

John Summerson – 'Heavenly Mansions: an Interpretation of Gothic' (1946), in *Heavenly Mansions and Other Essays on Architecture*, Norton, New York, 1963, p. 4.

CONDOMINIUM ONE, THE SEA RANCH

A settlement of ten residential units on California's north coast
MOORE, LYNDON, TURNBULL, WHITAKER, 1965

My drawing above makes the setting of Condominium One appear too comfortable, too lush with trees, too calm. The Sea Ranch is a stretch of land along the Pacific coast about one hundred miles north of San Francisco. The landscape there is rugged, the rocky edge of the land beaten by crashing waves and scoured by cool northwesterly winds. The trees on the right of the drawing are part of a 'hedgerow' of cypress trees, one of many along that part of the coast planted to break the strength of the winds. Condominium One was, in the mid-1960s, the first of a series of developments to be built in this landscape. Its architects were Charles Moore, Donlyn Lyndon, William Turnbull and Richard Whitaker (MLTW). They worked in collaboration with Lawrence Halprin, a landscape designer commissioned as master planner by the developers Oceanic Properties. The overall aim of the development was to provide vacation and weekend properties. The initial intention was to do this in the form of a series of condominiums, like Condominium One, along the coast, interspersed with clusters of individual dwellings in a similar architectural language. Joseph Esherick, another architect,

'The first purpose of architecture is territorial... the architect sets out the perceptual stimuli with which the observer creates an image of "place". The architect particularizes. He selects an appropriate temperature range and builds devices for maintaining it, controls the intensity and direction of light, discriminates specialized activity patterns, organizes movement and subjects the building process to a clarifying pattern. By directing all these factors to a controlling image, he builds the opportunity for people to know where they are – in space, in time and in the order of things. He gives them something to be in.'

Donlyn Lyndon, 1965, p. 31.

built a series of demonstration houses, called the Hedgerow Houses because they sought shelter from the wind by nestling against the hedgerows, shortly after Condominium One. Subsequently the ideals of the development, which were enshrined in guidelines and policed by a design committee, began to break down and now the area does not enjoy the integrity of development that was promised by the early schemes. At times Condominium One was blamed for opening the door to such development. But its value was recognised in 2005 when it was put on the USA's National Register of Historic Places. Its quintessential image is as a small bastion of humanity standing in the face of rugged nature. Its composition is reminiscent of a clutch of farm buildings, or even a tiny traditional fishing village, set right on the edge of the continent with views across the open sea to the westernmost horizon. Its poetry is potent, evoking notions of pioneers eventually reaching the Pacific coast, timeless relationships with the land and sea, Henry David Thoreau and his ideas of independence and individuality, John Steinbeck and his heroic stories of early twentieth century working (or unemployed) life in farming communities of the far west. It also evokes ideas of simple but hedonistic lifestyles, the resources to own and enjoy a weekend home, the desire for escape from 1950s stuffiness and an aesthetic freedom associated with the decades after the Second World War and with the beginnings of the hippy generation. In their 1974 book *The Place of Houses*, the architects confessed that 'the condominium building was the initial attempt to make a community' (p. 34).

Identification of place 1

Condominium One's comparability to a group of farm buildings or a small traditional fishing village is perhaps due less to imitation and stylistic influence and more to a common focus on practicality and simplicity. The avowed aim of the architects was to identify a place in a direct and simple way, without extravagance or show, in harmony with surrounding conditions.

In *Analysing Architecture* there is a key chapter entitled 'Architecture as Identification of Place' (third edition, 2009, pp. 25-34). One of the books that influenced the thinking behind this chapter was the already mentioned book *The Place of Houses* by Charles Moore, Gerald Allen and Donlyn Lyndon. In various ways this book makes the case that the essential purpose/*raison d'être* of architecture is that it establishes a place (places). This is where architecture began, and always begins: with the need/desire for a place to sleep, to light a fire, to cook and eat, for ritual and so on. It is in this spirit that Condominium One was built. It is a way of thinking that is shared by farm buildings and traditional fishing villages – buildings built with practicality as a higher priority than the display of intellectual or aesthetic sophistication. Place identification is, *a priori*, a part of life. We cannot walk through the landscape without continually making sense of our surroundings in terms of identification of place.

Lawrence Halprin, the developer's master planner for The Sea Ranch, seems to have been in accord with this way of thinking about how people relate to the world around them. In a drawing reminiscent of the arguments put forward by Jay Appleton in his book *The Experience of Landscape* (1975), Halprin illustrated the ways we interpret and project ourselves and our activities into the world around. Though sketched in 1980 Halprin included the drawing in his own book, *The Sea Ranch ... Diary of an Idea* (2002, p. 7). It shows a stretch of the rocky coastline at The Sea Ranch, with distinctive features annotated.

Appleton argued that we interpret the landscape we experience in terms of prospect and refuge. These are aspects of survival. We feel safer if we can survey a prospect from a refuge, such as an open field from the cover of a forest or the sea from a cottage. That way we can see if strangers, possible enemies, are approaching and have an advantage over them.

In Halprin's drawing of the coast at Sea Ranch, the features he includes are given identities related to these ideas of refuge and

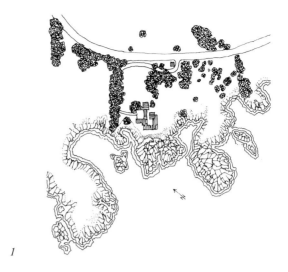

1

prospect. These identities infer an active relationship between people and the landscape. For example… Halprin's drawing depicts the view from the cliffs over two large rocks in the sea – Castle Rock and Lion Rock. The latter, the higher of the two, Halprin annotates 'Place for dominance – and protection; the head of the tribe… watch tower; King'. The twin peaks of Castle Rock he labels 'Places of Power', and the dip between them he describes as 'The place for relationships – partners'. Behind the Castle Rock he identifies a space of 'mystery, danger, withdrawal'. Smaller rocks in the sea Halprin labels respectively as 'a place to make offerings of things to the sea' and 'a place for group initiations – rites & ceremonies'. A pool he sees as a place for 'self purification, *mikveh* – Baptism' and a tunnel through the rock as 'a place for birth rituals'. On the cliff is a 'witnesses space on the bluff'; a precipitous path down to a tree by the water is 'processional down'; and at the tree one would 'end processions; enter the new'.

Such interpretation of the landscape involves recognition of the inherent characteristics of features and how they might relate to human activity and settlement. When the architects decided the site for Condominium One they worked in the same way. The composition is positioned with the same sense of place in the landscape as a small fort on a headland (*1*). It stands on sloping ground, a refuge at the top of the cliffs, open to the path of the sun from dawn to sunset, and with a prospect across the craggy rocks to the wide ocean. Its back is protected by the rising ground on the inland side of the main coast road. But Condominium One is not a military fort, so it sacrifices part of its prospect across the coastal plateau to the north in favour of some shelter from the wind, which is provided by an existing hedgerow. The building is also positioned where the

coast road comes closer to the edge of the land, easing access. A service road winds down the slope from the main road, taking a route through the cypress trees. This route prevents the service road from being too evident in the land. (One of Halprin's precepts for the whole development was that it should damage the land and its appearance as little as possible.) The trees also form a gateway or tunnel through which you pass to reach the condominium. And this 'gateway' has the effect of creating a sense of arrival, detaching the weekend residences from the hundred mile drive from San Francisco and from the everyday world. You emerge close to the edge of the cliff in another world, with your fantasy castle before you. There is an element of the fairy tale about Condominium One.

Identification of place 2

Identification of place operates at all scales. It involves not only the recognition of a suitable location for building, taking advantage of places that are already there, but also making interventions, adding elements, that modify the location in favour of the intended purpose. This involves building.

Condominium One is positioned not only in relation to the cliff edge and the existing hedgerow, but also on a patch of land that, although steep, is not quite as steep as elsewhere in the vicinity. Even so it stands next to a mound. This complex variety of ground slopes contributes to the layout of the development. The less sloping ground from the north allows easy vehicular access. The steeper slope created from the mound down to the cliff edge allows residential units at the back of the development to enjoy views over those nearer the sea.

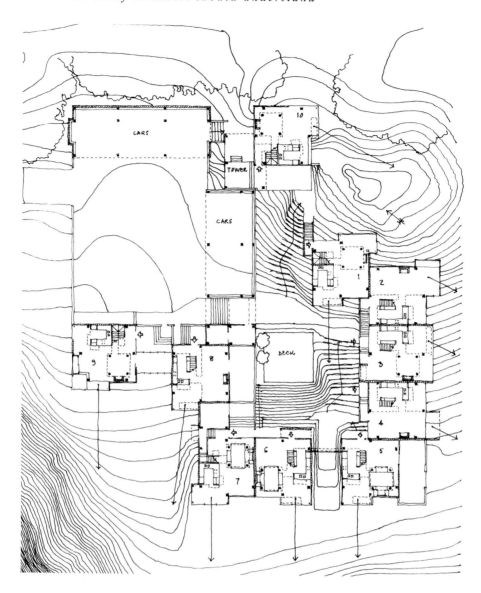

1

You can appreciate the variation in ground slopes from the contours in the above drawing (*1*). North is to the top left. The ocean and setting sun is at the bottom. The development is arranged around two courtyards, one for cars and one for people. The cars get a courtyard on the less sloping ground to the north and without a view of the sea. The ten residences for people are arranged mainly (all except one, around the courtyard to the south, tumbling down the steeper part of the ground. Their arrangement was decided initially, according to the architects, using sugar cubes. This southerly courtyard has a deck for sunbathing, sheltered from the wind, but otherwise its ground surface follows the steeper lie of the land. Notice the difference in the contours between the car courtyard and the residential courtyard. The back walls of the car

shelters act as retaining walls, allowing the ground surface to be made more level for the cars.

All the residential units receive sunlight and have views across the sea or along the coast. Units 1 and 10 at the top of the site have views over the lower units (*3*). Unit 10 has a tower alongside enhancing the condominium's image as a fairy tale castle. Even though all units have views, their privacy is maintained; they are arranged so none has a view into another.

Nevertheless, together the units form an integrated composition. This is an example of 'the whole being greater than the sum of the parts'. Scattered across the land as individual units they could not have made a courtyard. Brought together they create this extra outdoor room to be shared by all.

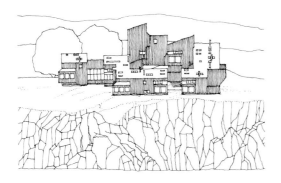

2 elevation from the sea

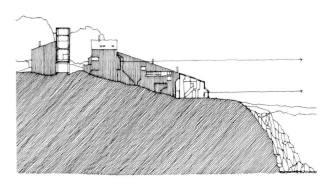

3 section through the residential courtyard

Transition, hierarchy, heart… levels of interior

Apart from the approach road and by the feet of people, the condominium does not extend its alteration of the ground surface beyond its outside walls. The natural ground comes right up to the small concrete plinth above which its unfinished (unvarnished, unpainted) rough vertical timber cladding rises. Inside this threshold between the natural and the human the architects created a hierarchy of places.

> *'For some time we had been especially concerned with making several degrees of "inside", marking first a place in the landscape, then progressively segregating places outdoors and in, so that the user could be continually aware of his location, from the altogether natural and unprotected outside to the sheltered, secluded, and protected inside.'* (Moore, Allen and Lyndon, 1974, p. 32)

These 'degrees of inside' are punctuated by sequences of thresholds. First there is the point where the driveway passes through a fence defining the car courtyard. Three of the units are entered from there; the one at the top of the site (Number 10) by passing under the tower. Next there is a covered way with steps leading through to the residential courtyard. The remaining units are entered from here, each with its own lobby or porch space. From the residential courtyard there is a gateway towards the sea, a threshold back out to nature.

But the 'degrees of inside' do not stop there. Each unit is based on an open cube of space (like the sugar cube) open to its pitched roof, and extended at the sides with outshots, lean-tos – 'saddlebags' as the architects called them. These saddlebags are in most cases sun spaces with views of the sea, and make places that are in-between inside and outside. Each cube of space with its saddlebags contains, like a large piece of built-in furniture, a small two-storey 'building', also clad in vertical timber (smooth in this case, and painted),

containing the kitchen with a bathroom above. In various patterns, each of these interior buildings has a stair attached, in some instances straight and others dog-leg.

The final element in most of the units – seven out of the ten – is a small 'temple' – an aedicule – supporting a platform for the bed(s). This too is reached by the stair, with a bridge to the bathroom (*4*). Beneath this aedicule is the heart, and the hearth, of the unit. This is the inside of the inside, the culmination of the spatial hierarchy. Some of the aedicules have sitting pits, others do not. The three units without aedicules (Numbers 2, 4 and 8) have mezzanine floors instead, also with hearths and sitting places underneath.

A vocabulary of elements

No two of the units are identical and yet all are similar. They share a language, a vocabulary of elements composed differently in each

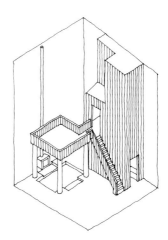

4

163

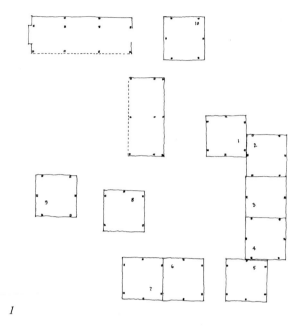

1

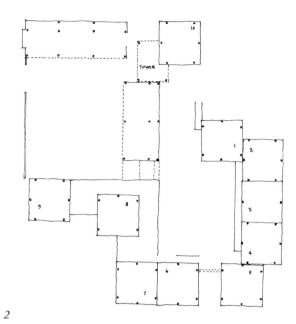

2

case. The composition is described in the diagrams above (*1-4*).

First there are the ten 'sugar cubes' of space (*1*) arranged on the sloping land. All the cubes have a basic timber frame (stick) structure based on six posts (*5*) with rails and bracing supporting the cladding. Notice that the corner posts are moved 'in-board' to allow, in some instances, corners to be open; and that some posts are shared, as between Units 7 and 6 and Units 2 and 3 and 3 and 4. The cubes do not seem to be arranged according to an underlying ideal geometry. Their form is governed more by the geometry of making. Two additional single-storey car shelters define the space of the car courtyard.

Second are the additional bits of building that join the cubes together (*2*). These comprise fences, steps, the tower, passageways and entrance lobbies and porches. There is also a panel of timber over the gateway towards the sea (dotted) making it more a frame defining the view out to the horizon and to strengthen the sense of threshold.

Third come the 'saddlebags' attached to the outside of the cubes (*3*). Charles Moore had experimented with this idea in some of his early houses, for example the Bonham House designed in the early 1960s (*6*). In Condominium One the saddlebags create in-between spaces that although 'inside' have a character of being

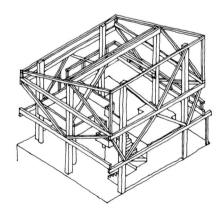

5

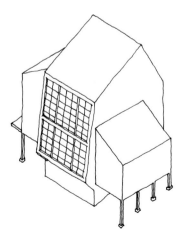

6

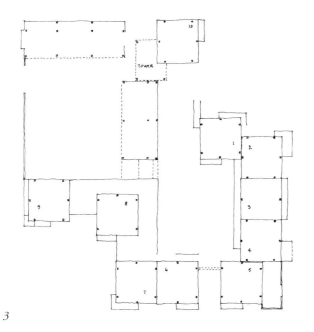

3

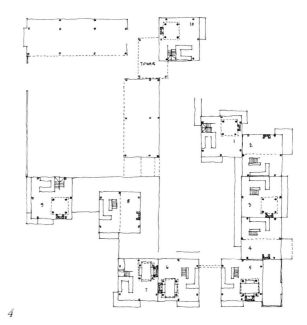

4

'outside' because they are outwith the main structure, highly glazed and with rooflights, are therefore sunny and have expansive views of the ocean and coastline. Some of the quintessential images of Condominium One show people sitting in these spaces looking out to sea. Others show the counterpoint of the protective interiors of the units.

The saddlebags with their semi-external character create a counterpoint to the aedicules which create an interior within an interior (4). This too is an idea Charles Moore had experimented with earlier, for example in the first house he designed for himself (7). In this house one of the aedicules frames the living space while the other frames the bath and shower. The aedicules in Condominium One all

frame sitting spaces adjacent to hearths or heating stoves and support bed platforms above. They are related too to the large inbuilt pieces of 'furniture' that house the kitchens and bathrooms. Together all these components constitute a vocabulary of elements (8) disposed in different arrangements and permutations in the individual units. It is as if the architects had created a small architectural language to be used in a variety of ways.

Conclusion, and a note about the dream

The form of Condominium One is clearly architecturally a 'cottage'. Generally irregular in composition its occasional regularities

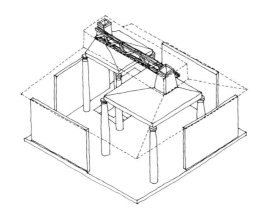

7

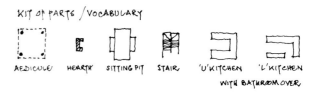

KIT OF PARTS / VOCABULARY

AEDICULE   HEARTH   SITTING PIT   STAIR   'U' KITCHEN   'L' KITCHEN
                                                                  WITH BATHROOM OVER

8

165

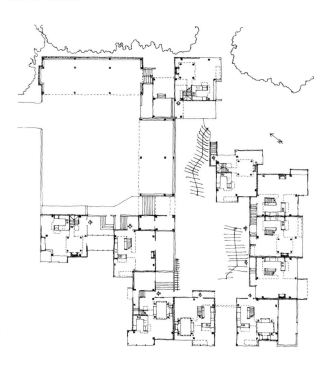

– the underlying square 'sugar-cube' plans – derive more from the geometry of making than from ideal geometry. The composition accepts the underlying lie of the land and provides for the physical and emotional needs and desires of people, sheltering them from the external elements and providing them with homely centres to which they may relate. But if 'cottages' are governed by response and 'temples' by the assertion of control then there is something of the 'temple about this building too. This is not a group of residences prompted by need and conditioned by the availability of resources. Its language was determined by its architects and policed by a de-sign committee. The only activity with which it is associated is that of leisure. If it is *like* a fishing village or a group of farm buildings then it is no more. It might be condemned as a pretence, a dream, a fantasy, a fairy tale. (It might be celebrated as such too.)

In the various published accounts of The Sea Ranch develop-ment Halprin and the architects MLTW bemoan the fact that the principles and the precepts realised in Condominium One (and in Esherick's Hedgerow Houses) have not survived the pressures from the market for individual villas dotted around the landscape each isolated in its own plot of land. Clearly their project had a social as well as architectural dimension to it, one that failed in the face of actuality. Maybe their avowed aim 'to make a community' is a step beyond what it is within the powers of architecture to achieve. Maybe architecture is more a *product* of community rather than an *instrument* by which community may be created. Discuss.

References and other relevant publications, websites, broadcasts:

Jay Appleton – *The Experience of Landscape* (1975), Hull University Press, Hull, 1986.

Kent C. Bloomer and Charles W. Moore with a contribution by Robert J. Yudell – *Body, Memory, and Architecture*, Yale University Press, New Haven CT, 1977.

Lawrence Halprin – *The Sea Ranch... Diary of an Idea*, Spacemaker Press, Berkeley CA, 2002.

Donlyn Lyndon, editor John Donat, contributing editor Patrick Morreau – 'Sea Ranch: the Process of Design', in *World Architecture Two*, Studio Vista, London, 1965, pp. 30-39.

Donlyn Lyndon – 'The Sea Ranch: Qualified Vernacular', in *Journal of Architectural Education*, Volume 63, Number 1, October 2009, pp. 81-89.

Donlyn Lyndon and Jim Allinder (with essays by Donald Canty and Lawrence Halprin) – *The Sea Ranch*, Princeton Architectural Press, New York, 2004.

Donlyn Lyndon and Charles Moore – *Chambers for a Memory Palace*, MIT Press, Cambridge MA., 1994.

Charles Moore, Gerald Allen and Donlyn Lyndon – *The Place of Houses: Three Architects Suggest Ways to Build and Inhabit Houses*, Holt Rinehart and Winston, New York, 1974.

Barry Parker and Raymond Unwin – 'Co-operation in Building', in *The Art of Building a Home*, Longmans, London, 1901, pp. 91-108.

John Summerson – 'Heavenly Mansions: an Interpretation of Gothic' (1946), in *Heavenly Mansions and Other Essays on Architecture*, Norton, New York, 1963, p. 4.

William Turnbull – *Buildings in the Landscape*, William Stout, Richmond CA, 2000.

VILLA E.1027

'There is a set of small books that are English nursery classics. Their interest for architects is in their detailed and imaginative exposition of a way of life. However, architects might be surprised at any suggestion that there was a connection between the houses of Beatrix Potter and those in the post war style of Aalto and Le Corbusier: between the house of Mrs Tittlemouse and that for Mr Shodhan in Ahmedabad… In Beatrix Potter's interiors, objects and utensils in daily use are conveniently located, often on individual hooks or nails, and are all the "decoration" the "simple" spaces need, or in fact can take… Here then, we find basic necessities raised to a poetic level: the simple life well done. This is in essence the precept of the whole Modern Movement in architecture.'

Alison Smithson – 'Beatrix Potter's Places', in *Architectural Design*, Volume 37, December 1967, p. 573.

VILLA E.1027

An architect's vacation house at Cap Martin, on the south coast of France
EILEEN GRAY (and JEAN BADOVICI), 1926-29

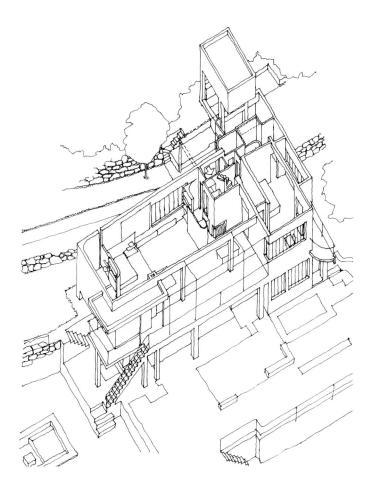

This is the villa near which Le Corbusier built *Le Cabanon* in the early 1950s. If you are reading these analyses out of order you can see the spatial relationship and the setting of Villa E.1027 in the drawing on page 94. Eileen Gray's villa, which she designed for her lover Jean Badovici (with his collaboration), was the first of the buildings on this craggy patch of land between the railway and the rocky coast of the Mediterranean. The restaurant and flats, as well as *Le Cabanon* came later.

It is sometimes difficult to relate what architects say and write to what they do in their architecture. An exception is the 'Description' Eileen Gray and Jean Badovici wrote of Villa E.1027 for a special issue of *L'Architecture Vivante* devoted to the house on its completion in 1929. (Badovici was the editor of the journal.) So clear is this as an exposition of the way in which the house was designed that it is worth including a large part of it on the following two pages.

Eileen Gray and Jean Badovici, 'Description' of Villa E.1027, 1929.

External architecture seems to have absorbed avant-garde architects at the expense of the interior, as if a house should be conceived for the pleasure of the eye more than for the well-being of its inhabitants. If lyricism can be dedicated to the play of masses brought together in daylight, the interior should respond to human needs and the exigencies of individual life, and it should ensure calm and intimacy. Theory is insufficient for life and does not respond to all its requirements. It is necessary to free oneself of a tendency with obvious failings and seek to create an interior atmosphere that is in harmony with the refinements of modern life while utilizing current technical resources and possibilities. The thing constructed is more important than the way it is constructed, and the process is subordinate to the plan, *not the plan to the process*. It is not only a matter of constructing beautiful arrangements of lines, but above all *dwellings for people...* The need to distinguish oneself, to be original at all costs, leads to suppressing the most elementary concern for practical comfort.

...

The interior plan should not be the incidental result of the facade; it should lead a complete, harmonious, and logical life. Rather than being subordinated to the external volume, it should on the contrary control it. It should not be pure convention, as in the eighteenth century, but on the contrary, as in Gothic times, a homogeneous whole built for man, to the human scale, and balanced in all its parts.

...

If in regarding the dwelling as a living organism we have been led to adopt the current formula of the "living room", we at least sought to plan the room in such a way that each of its inhabitants could, on occasion, achieve total independence and an atmosphere of solitude and contemplation. The entrance is done away with, as befits a region where the windows and doors are rarely closed; but on the other hand one has sought an architectural layout that separates the interior from the exterior. One avoids making a door when one fears that it may open at any moment, evoking the possibility of an inopportune visit. For the same reason, this arrangement has also been adopted for the rooms.

The four essential issues on which we have focused attention are:
1. The problems of windows, for which we have created three types.
2. The problem, often neglected and thus very important, of shutters: a window without shutters is an *eye without eyelids*. Otherwise, all the current combinations lead to the same result: insufficient ventilation when the shutters are closed. Our method leaves a large area for the free passage of fresh air while blocking excess light.
3. The problem of the independence of rooms: everyone, even in a house of restricted dimensions, must be able to remain free and independent. They must have the *impression* of being alone, and if desired, entirely alone. This has led us to position the walls so that the doors remain out of sight.
4. The problem of the kitchen, which should be easily accessible yet sufficiently isolated that no odors can penetrate the living spaces. We have separated the kitchen from the rest of the house: one can only go from one to the other by passing through the entry threshold, which is only possible in an exceptionally mild climate.

As to the seaside character of the house, it results inevitably from the ambiance, from the materials imposed by this ambiance, and from the views of the sea.

The Entry. – This is a large covered space: a sort of atrium; it is large, accommodating, and not like the small narrow doors that only seem to open reluctantly. Ahead is a large blank wall, suggesting the idea of resistance, but clear and distinct. To the right is the main entry, to the left the service door.

The door to the right leads to the main room: a partition screen obstructs views that might penetrate from the exterior to the interior when the door is open.

Built into the wall of the stair to the left is the *niche for hats*, a half cylinder in transparent celluloid, with its shelves made of loose-knit twine

nets, so the dust cannot settle. A tube along the length of the partition accommodates umbrellas dropped there freely and effortlessly. In a drum by the entry a system of runners carries hangers for umbrellas. Under the hat niche is a deep cupboard for storing extra chairs that one uses only for entertaining.

The Large Room. – The house has been built for a man who loves work, sports, and entertaining. Although it is very small, its layout should permit the occupant to welcome friends and entertain them. Only the "camping" style allows this otherwise exceptional difficulty to be resolved: one has resorted to it without thinking for an instant that it might result in a normative method, or that it will be the style of tomorrow, but simply as a convenient response to an exceptional circumstance.

To allow for entertaining numerous guests one has made a convertible room of 14 x 6.30 metres. Because this room is to be used for other purposes, a low wall at its end that allows the entire ceiling to be visible from any point conceals a dressing area, complete with shower, linen chest, cupboard, etc.

Against the full wall is a large divan of 2.20 x 2 metres, where one can stretch out or sit, rest or converse comfortably – an indispensable item that can be converted into a bed. The cushions can be placed around it like satellites to extend the divan by 4 cm., providing comfortable and relaxing seating.

Opposite the dressing area, an alcove shelters a small divan at the head of which is a flat storage unit containing pillows, mosquito netting, tea kettle, and books. A flexible table with two pivots allows for reading in while lying down. A white lamp mounted between two panes of blue glass provides rational light.

At the head of the small divan a double door gives access to a covered terrace sufficiently large to hang a hammock. A metal door is embedded in the thickness of the wall, as well as a shuttered door with pivoting slats, to allow practical ventilation and to give the sleeping figure the impression of being outdoors when the first door is left open. A pierced opening high in the fixed part of the glazed frame at the foot of the bed provides for excellent cross ventilation on warm summer nights.

Above the small divan, a thin cable at arm's reach allows the mosquito netting to be extended at night.

The fireplace against the window allows one to enjoy firelight and natural light at the same time.

The furnishings – chairs, screens and pile carpets, the warm leather colors, low metallic luster, and depth of the cushions – all contribute to an atmosphere of intimacy. A marine chart, lit at night, brings an ingenious note, evoking distant voyages and encouraging daydreams. Even the carpets are reminiscent of marine horizons, through their colour and form.

When viewed from within the room, the entry partition consists of a series of racks that end in a deep vertical segment of a celluloid half cylinder, which encloses a column of gramophone records. This is the music corner, and the felicitous arrangement of the partition serves to amplify the sound.

The tea table is made of tubes that can be retracted, and it is covered with a cork sheet to avoid the impact and noise of fragile cups. It includes disks for fruits and cakes, and a narrower end on which to rest the cup that one is about to offer.

The terrace adjoining the large room serves as an extension to that space when the window panels are folded up against the pillars. Its full balustrade has been replaced by one in cloth that can easily be removed to allow one to warm one's legs in the winter sun. The cloth canopy is made of four independent pieces to resist the strongest mistral winds; it allows cool shade in the summer when the sun is blazing, and full exposure to the sun's heat in winter, while being sheltered from the wind.

On this terrace, which gently slopes toward the interior and has a gutter under the glazed doors to accommodate run-off, a *heavy brush-weave carpet for the terrace garden* provides a note of gaiety. The fleeting patterns of sun and shadow play freely about, and the breeze flows in from the far horizon. It is a preferred location where one can, according to the hour and the mood of the weather, either hide from or stretch out in the full sun.

When the seas are rough and the horizon gloomy, it suffices to close the large southern windows, draw the curtains, and open the small northern window that overlooks the garden of lemon trees and the old village, to seek a new and different horizon where the masses of greenery replace the expanses of blue and gray.

The space used to serve and clear the dining room can be transformed into a bar. The bar's horizontal surface of striated aluminium, which is used for serving meals, can be folded up against a pillar, while a second serving table has pivoting drawers. The dining table is surfaced in cork to avoid the noise of plates and place settings. The table is supported on legs of tubular steel that can be extended or adjusted effortlessly.

At the end of the table, a leaf and two runners covered in leather provide a place to set down a serving tray. During the summer one can either push the table onto the terrace, or, by sliding the terrace doors open, expose the dining room to the exterior.

The bar ceiling is split diagonally in two panels, one of which is higher than the other, allowing the lighting to reach the bottles. The fixed part of the table on which one prepares the drinks is lit by a circular device fixed to the ceiling. The bar also has a box for lemons and one for plates. A pair of doors can be closed to allow the service spaces to be completely isolated from the living spaces. The maid would pass directly from the kitchen to her room on the lower level.

The Table-Units. – Each has a table that can serve as a writing desk. For entertaining, all these tables can be brought to the large room, stretched out, and – since the supports can be adjusted one inside the other – made into a very large dining table that is lightweight but perfectly stable.

The principal bedroom includes a boudoir/studio with a small private terrace on which is a daybed in the open air. A dressing cabinet in aluminium and cork conceals the washstand and, when opened, forms a screen; although very shallow, it contains all the drawers and bottles necessary for grooming oneself. A washbasin is there in case the bathroom is being used by friends. Service can be provided directly from the bathroom, which adjoins this small bedroom. From this room one can go directly to the garden via a small external stair; the independence of each room is assured, despite the small size of the house. There is a level of comfort that one would expect only in a much larger dwelling.

The room is sunny from morning to evening, and, owing to its shuttered windows, the light and air can be regulated at will, as with the shutter of a camera.

The bed, sheltered against two full walls, has colored sheets so that the mess is not noticed when the bed is unmade. Owing to the layout of this room (through shifting alignments), the doors are invisible from the interior.

In the part arranged as a studio are a writing table, metal chairs, a filing cabinet, a low hanging light diffuser of frosted glass, and a private terrace with a daybed.

This room has a small bookshelf; a bed with a plywood headboard against the wall, where there are built-in lamps, one in white and one in blue that dims to serve as a night light; a movable bedside table with two segments and a luminous watch face; electrical outlets for a kettle and bed-warmer; mosquito netting in transparent celluloid, the fabric of which extends along an extremely thin steel cable with a guy rope, which eliminates the heaviness and inelegance of ordinary mosquito netting. The linen cupboard below the window is placed at the height of the hand, so that the bottom can be reached effortlessly, without bending over. It is hung from the wall, which allows the tiled flooring underneath to be easily cleaned. Completing the furnishings for the dressing area are a waste basket, a stool, shelves, a washbasin, a disk for jewelry, and a dressing cabinet made of aluminium – a beautiful material providing agreeable coolness in hot climates.

The tile flooring is gray-black for the studio and gray-white for the room.

Although very small, the bathroom is fully fitted with useful accessories. Ventilation is assured by a slatted door, like the sleeping alcove in the large room, and by a large frame that opens above the bathtub. Above the doors are cupboards for suitcases to take advantage of the square metre of space taken up by the door. A step allows them to be reached easily.

A cupboard in the bathroom wall contains a shelf for shoes and dressing gowns (with a special system of drying racks), and a large cupboard for underwear and pajamas has a chamfered corner to facilitate ease of movement in the room.

The tub is an ordinary bathtub covered in an aluminium casing, which gives it an agreeable appearance and strikes a glistening note in the tone of ensemble. The bidet is covered with a seat of foam rubber. The toilet, located near both the living room and the bedroom, is outside under the entry canopy, in a drum; it is ventilated through the roof.

The kitchen layout has been suggested by the customs of the peasant women of the region who prepare their meals outside during the summer and inside during the winter and bad weather. It can be transformed into an open-air kitchen by a partition made of glass panels that fold flat. When this partition is opened, the kitchen is nothing more than a paved alcove in the courtyard, with a coal store, a niche for wood, a washstand, an electric ice chest, a water softener, a zinc-covered cabinet for bottles, a folding table, and an oil-fired oven. Inside is another oven for the winter.

The Stair. – The stair has been built using the smallest possible dimensions, but with large, deep steps that are grooved to be comfortable underfoot. The stair shaft is much larger than the spiral staircase, so that the volume seems light and airy. Around the spiral stair, which serves like a stepladder, are a series of cupboards that are ventilated, lit, and accessible from both inside and outside. The light pours down the glass shaft above, which provides access to the roof.

...

Lower Floor. – The guest room has been carried out with the essential concern of avoiding the mistral. Because the bed must be sheltered from the currents of air, a partition wall cuts off all air flow. The room comprises a studio and a dressing area with a lit ceiling. The lit mirror has a small satellite mirror that permits one to shave the nape of one's neck: a lamp is fixed at the center of the mirror, flaring so that all is lit equally, without shadows. There are drawers everywhere, external and internal, pivoting and sliding, to contain common objects. The guest room is independent, with doors leading directly to the garden and the terrace under the house. The bed is an ordinary divan, simply modified with a fixed headrest to be used during morning breakfasts.

...

We have tried to create the *smallest habitable cell*. Despite its extremely reduced dimensions, the maid's room provides a sufficient level of comfort. There is ease of movement, although the space has been strictly economized, and this room could serve as an example of all rooms for children and servants where one seeks only essential comfort.

The boiler room, storage and gardener's shed are equally independent.

Terraces and Gardens. – Paving crosses the entire garden up to the space under the house raised on *pilotis*. To give the garden greater intimacy, the side exposed to the wind has been closed off by a narrow storage space in corrugated sheet metal, where the gardener can store his tools. A reflecting pool, which would attract mosquitoes, has been avoided; instead there is a sunbathing pit with a sort of divan made of sloped paving stones, a tank for sand baths, a mirrored table for cocktails, and benches to either side for chatting. A small stair enables one to descend directly to the sea to bathe, fish, or sail.

This very small house thus has, concentrated in a very small space, all that might be useful for comfort and to help indulge in *joie de vivre*. In no part has a line or a form been sought for its own sake; everywhere one has thought of *man*, of his sensibilities and needs.

Translated from Gray and Badovici, 1929 in Constant, 2000, pp. 240-245.

Some comments regarding Gray and Badovici's 'Description'

Gray and Badovici are keen at the outset to establish that the house they have designed is less about appearance and more about making a place to live (to '*dwell*', which implies a more embedded, engaged, profound form of living than mere existence) and to enjoy (there is an aesthetic as well as a pragmatic aspect to their attitude. They have obviously read and been inspired by Le Corbusier's recently published *Vers Une Architecture* (published in French in 1923 and translated into English in 1927) but question and refine its polemic. Their remark about the 'play of masses brought together in daylight' refers to Le Corbusier's assertion that 'architecture is the masterly, correct and magnificent play of masses brought together in light' (Le Corbusier (1923), 1927, p. 29). They make the point that architecture is more than that; it is about 'responding to human needs', physical and emotional (aesthetic), in making habitable spaces. Le Corbusier would probably not have disagreed, but Gray and Badovici question his insistent theorising. Suspicious of abstract theory, which seems sometimes to be promulgated for its own sake, they prefer to design and to build. They also rebuke those (presumably including Le Corbusier) who strive for celebrity – 'the need to distinguish oneself, to be original at all costs'.

One particular aspect of Le Corbusier's theorising that Gray and Badovici reject is his system of 'Regulating Lines' (Le Corbusier (1923), 1927, pp. 65-83). They see this as an interest in abstractions that diverts focus away from more immediate realities of living in the world. Architecture, they say, 'is not only a matter of constructing beautiful arrangements of lines, but above all *dwellings for people*'.

This dichotomy, between abstraction and experience, has a long pedigree, stretching back at least to the philosophers of ancient Greece, Plato and Aristotle. It has always had an architectural dimension. In the first century BC, the Roman architect Vitruvius promoted the importance of 'symmetry' and its dependence on 'proportion' in architecture. 'Proportion' he wrote in the third of his *Ten Books on Architecture*, 'is a correspondence among the measures of the members of an entire work, and of the whole to a certain part selected as standard' (Vitruvius, translated by Hicky Morgan, 1914, p. 72). In the fifteenth century, Alberti, in his own *Ten Books on Architecture*, said that 'the Force and Rule of the Design, consists in a right and exact adapting and joining together the Lines and Angles which compose and form the Face of the Building' (Alberti, translated by Leoni, 1755, p. 1). In the eighteenth century, writers such as Jean Jacques Rousseau in France and Johann Wolfgang von Goethe in Germany questioned the abstract geometry of classical architecture, favouring the more pragmatically organised forms and arrangements of Gothic and traditional regional architectures. (The distinction is related to that between 'Ideal Geometry' and 'Geometries of Being' outlined in *Analysing Architecture*; and relevant too to the differences in the underlying attitudes evident in 'Temples and Cottages'.)

Gray and Badovici refer to this ancient dichotomy when they comment that the architecture (classical) of the eighteenth century was 'pure convention', and prefer to be inspired by the Gothic, which was 'a homogeneous whole built for man, to the human scale, and balanced in all its parts'. This sentence is an echo of the sentiments of the late nineteenth century artist, craftsman, philosopher and social reformer William Morris, who was a protagonist of the English movement called the Arts and Crafts. The Arts and Crafts movement has been recognised by historians as a progenitor of architectural Modernism because of the way its architects arranged their buildings according to practical needs, clear construction and aesthetic experience rather than the abstract prescriptions of classical design. But Modern architects (including Le Corbusier as well as Gray and Badovici) distinguished themselves by rejecting the Arts and Crafts movement's allusions to the past (rural cottages and farm buildings…) in favour of a clean-lined, forward-looking architecture influenced more by the availability of new materials (steel, concrete and large sheets of glass) and the heroic achievements of engineering.

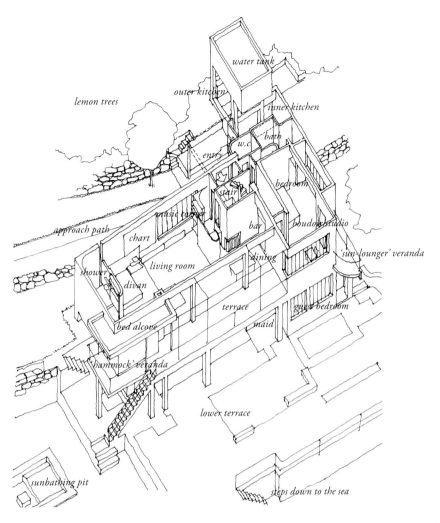

As we have seen in some of the other analyses in the present book, this predilection for the new did not stop Modern architects being influenced by the directness and practicality of traditional architectures. Remember that Mies van der Rohe was influenced by African traditional architecture and told his students to admire the 'simple and true crafts' of the 'unknown masters'. The link is evident in Gray and Badovici's comment that the entry and kitchen arrangements in Villa E.1027 had been influenced by traditional rural architecture and the 'customs of the peasant women of the region'.

Gray and Badovici make it clear that their focus in designing Villa E.1027 has been on creating what one might call a 'considerate' architecture, an architecture that gives priority to the enjoyment and comfort (physical and emotional) of the person inhabiting a building (rather than to abstract theory or the celebrity of its architect). They allude to providing for the desire for solitude and emotional peace, for finding shade and a cooling breeze in the summer, for having space to entertain friends, for the need to settle to work. They seek to achieve what Alison Smithson in 1967, in her discussion of the dwellings illustrated in the children's books of Beatrix Potter, was to call 'the simple life well done' (see the quotation at the beginning of this analysis).

Identification of place

Gray and Badovici describe their house in terms of its places (rather than its visual appearance or sculptural form). As in the house of Mrs Tittlemouse, there are places for small things: storage cupboards for suitcases and for knickers and pyjamas, racks for hats and for umbrellas, a cylinder of gramophone records, even a place for the lemons without which a gin and tonic would be incomplete. There are also specific places for activities: the usual ones such as sleeping (including a place for a hammock), eating, cooking, washing... but also for warming your legs in the sun, sunbathing, dozing, talking, reading... There is a divan in the living room, and a bed alcove.

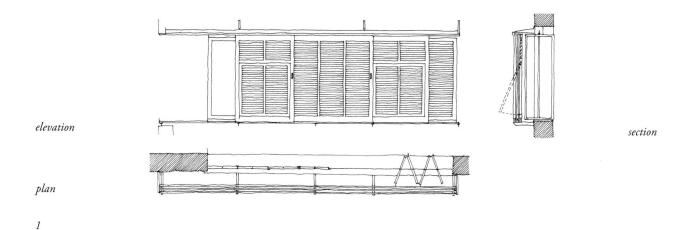

elevation

section

plan

1

The heads of the beds are designed with reading lights, and with contraptions to assist in supporting a book or having a breakfast cup of coffee.

A house designed with accommodation for a maid, for a clear zoning of service and living spaces, and with a specific place for lemons may seem irredeemably *bourgeois*. But beneath the cocktails and 'Riviera villa' privilege of Gray and Badovici's lifestyle there is in their 'Description' of Villa E.1027 a fine discrimination about how architecture and life might find a gentle (as well as genteel) humane sympathy.

Response to climate

One aspect of the gentle sympathy of Gray and Badovici's design is its sensitivity to the variable climate of the south coast of France. In ways found in traditional architecture, they were conscious of what is now, eighty years later, called 'sustainability'. The house can be changed to respond to different conditions. These include fierce sun, the vicious and mind-disturbing Mistral wind, and grey, drizzly winter days.

Badovici patented a window system (*1*) that allows all the permutations I outlined in 'A Hotel Terrace Doorway' (*Doorway*, 2007, pp. 168-169). The casements are divided into slim vertical panes that can be folded back against the jambs or pillars, leaving the opening completely clear for ventilation. On the outside of the windows there are rails on which run louvred shutters that can be slid across to provide varying degrees of shade. Some of these have hinged panels to provide even finer gradations of ventilation.

The large openings to the terrace are fitted with the folding windows so that the living space can be opened directly to the sea.

The terrace itself is provided with a slim framework of steel posts and rails onto which fabric (sail cloth?) can be stretched to provide shade.

Elsewhere (as mentioned in the 'Description') doorways are positioned to be protected from the Mistral, and windows to allow cross ventilation on sultry summer nights. Some of the doorways are provided with two or three leaves – a metal door for security, a louvre panel for ventilation and a mesh to keep out mosquitoes. These, as with the window system, can be arranged in different permutations for different circumstances.

The subtle mechanics of providing environmental comfort have aesthetic dimensions too. Gray and Badovici write of enjoying the light from the fire along with the daylight, and, on a grey drizzly day, of closing the view to the sea and opening that to the old village and dripping lemon trees on the slope immediately behind the house.

Transition, hierarchy, heart

Gray and Badovici's acknowledgement of the centrality of the person – the inhabitant – stretches to using architecture to manipulate (orchestrate) experience and to alter the way the world appears. In discussing Rem Koolhaas's *Maison à Bordeaux*, I mentioned how he used a device found also in country houses of the eighteenth century, by which a building may manipulate a visitor's introduction to the world occupied by its owner. Something similar happens in Villa E.1027.

For practical reasons it was easier to enter the house from the up-slope side (*2* and *3*); that is the direction of approach from a tunnel under the adjacent railway. But this arrangement works dramati-

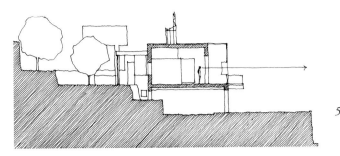

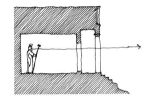

5

2 section

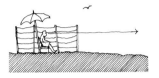

6

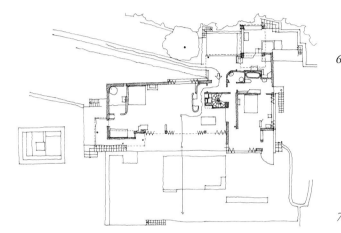

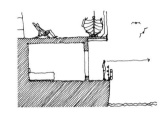

7

3 living floor

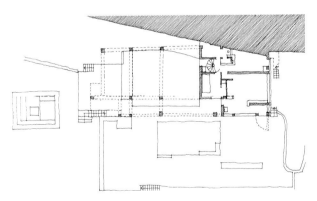

4 lower level, undercroft

cally too; and Gray and Badovici enhance the drama by making the visitor walk along the length of the shaded northern elevation before entering the house over what seems like a bridge (or the gangway onto a ship). Under a concrete canopy the visitor turns right to enter the house but is confronted not by a 'front door' but by a recessed wall. To the left is the lavatory. To the right is the door into the house. Diverted by the wall and passing through the doorway, entrance is further drawn out by a complex partition, comprising umbrella

stand and storage, which screens the living space. Negotiating the chicane created by this screen one enters the heart of the house to be confronted by a panoramic view of the sun glistening on the ocean. One has entered another world. Walking out onto the terrace, shaded by the sail cloth or not, the visitor finds him- or herself a storey above the ground, on an in-between space contemplating the horizon. This in-between space is an architectural relative of: the portico of a Greek temple (5), which intervenes between the place of the god and the outside world; the beach camp (6) which mediates between the sunbather and his or her surroundings; and, perhaps most pertinently, the deck of a cruise ship (7) from which 1920s lovers, arm-in-arm, look wistfully out to sea.

Geometry; space and structure

If the spatial organisation of Villa E.1027 is reminiscent of English Arts and Crafts and traditional forms of architecture, its appearance and the way in which is was constructed is very different.

Towards the end of the nineteenth century new building materials were developed. These included structural steel, reinforced concrete and large sheets of glass. In 1918, aware of the radical

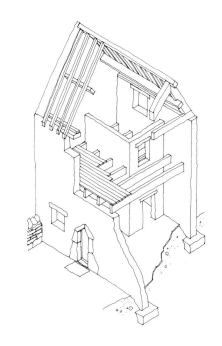

potential of reinforced concrete, Le Corbusier published his famous image of the 'Dom-Ino' house, which replaced load-bearing wall construction with a grid of concrete (or steel) columns or '*pilotis*' (see *Analysing Architecture*, p. 180). Eight years later, just as Gray and Badovici were designing and building Villa E.1027, he published his 'Five Points for a New Architecture' (pilotis; roof garden; free plan; horizontal window; and free elevation; see page 201 of *Analysing Architecture*, and Conrads, 1970, pp. 99-101) inspired by what he saw as the potential of the new methods of construction.

1

In their villa, Gray and Badovici did not follow Le Corbusier's Five Points, but they did take advantage of the constructional freedoms offered by the use of reinforced concrete. Some of the advantages are illustrated in the two drawings alongside.

The upper drawing (*1*) illustrates traditional load-bearing wall construction. It is a made-up example. It is composed of relatively small elements that have to be put together in particular ways. The walls are built of stone or brick with joints of mortar which evens out their irregularities and helps them to be stable. These heavy walls have to be supported on foundations (footings) that spread the load into the ground. They also, generally speaking, have to be built vertically so that the loads transmit directly down into the foundations. Windows and doorways into such walls have to be small because the walls above such openings have to be supported by lintels or arches. Upper floors and roofs are generally composed of layers of lengths of timber: joists supporting floorboards; trusses, purlins, rafters, battens supporting roof slates or tiles. Many buildings still are constructed using similar traditional materials and construction.

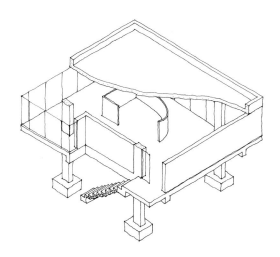

2

Reinforced concrete (*2*) is fundamentally different in that it is composed of a liquid material poured into a pre-built mould – the formwork. Its strength comes from steel reinforcement rods laid in the formwork before the concrete is poured. Floors and roofs do not need walls to support them; columns are sufficient. Floors and roofs, as well as the columns that support them, act as a single – monolithic

– element. Columns are supported on concrete pads in the ground, rather than strip foundations. The columns – *pilotis* as Le Corbusier termed them – allow floors to be free of structural walls; the ground floor may be left open; upper floors may be planned and organised using lightweight partitions that are free of any responsibility for

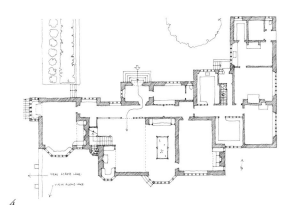

3

holding up floors or the roof above. Windows no longer need lintels; in fact, whole walls may be made of glass. Also, because reinforced concrete is monolithic and strong, floors may be cantilevered, i.e. project sideways over space.

Villa E.1027 has a flat roof (accessed by the spiral stair) but no roof garden. Its plan might be called 'free' in that the living room is open and divided by the non-load-bearing partitions of the entrance screen and that defining the shower space at the end. The openings to the terrace are also 'free' in the sense that the large folding glass wall is made possible by the reinforced concrete structure of the columns and roof.

On the lower floor (5), Gray and Badovici used *pilotis* to create a space, shaded from the sun but open to the garden. In that Gray and Badovici's emphasis was on making places for the various aspects and activities of life in their villa, the plan is related to that of an Arts and Crafts house (*4* – Blackwell by M.H. Baillie Scott, 1899). Such Arts and Crafts houses were influenced by traditional houses (*6* and *7* – Llanmihangel Place in south Wales). This last also has the main living rooms on the upper floor (*6*). But the possibilities of reinforced concrete construction are illustrated by comparing the amount of structure necessary in the lower floor of the load-bearing masonry house (*7*) with the plan of the lower floor of Villa E.1027 (*5*). In place of thick walls there are slim concrete columns.

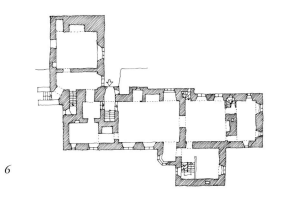

4

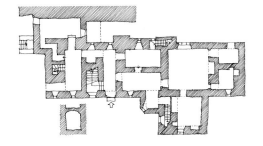

6

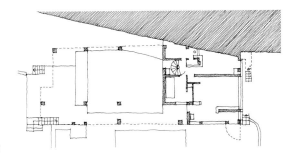

5

7

177

'A seaside villa, conceived as are these liners, would be more appropriate than those we see with their heavy tiled roofs.' Le Corbusier (1923), 1927, p. 98.

Conclusion: a note on metaphor

In the film *Il Postino* (Michael Radford, 1994), the poet Pablo Neruda (played by Philippe Noiret) tells the eponymous postman Mario Ruoppolo (played by Massimo Troisi) that the most important elements in poetry are *metafore*. The pertinent metaphor – the poetic allusion – for Villa E.1027 is that of the ocean-going liner.

The idea comes again from Le Corbusier's book *Vers Une Architecture*, which had been published in Paris in 1923. It was a collection of illustrated essays that had previously appeared in the magazine *L'Esprit Nouveau*, edited by Le Corbusier and his then friend Amédée Ozenfant. One of these essays was entitled 'Eyes Which Do Not See' and the first part of this essay, complete with photographs of ships such as the *Aquitania*, was devoted to 'Liners'. It made the point that the way in which the modern ocean-going Cunard passenger ships were designed should be seen as an inspiration to architects: for their clarity of purpose; freedom from historical 'styles'; power; and efficiency of construction using industrial materials. They were also launched into the shifting oceans. And each time they left port it was to carry passengers to distant destinations.

In their 'Description' of the house, Gray and Badovici refer to the power of the chart on the wall of the living room, which evokes in the imagination ideas of distant voyages and romantic sunsets over tropical seas. This is not the ship metaphor used by Sigurd Lewerentz in his church in Klippan (see next analysis); this is not the ship that supports you and provides you with a reference point and home on the rough and unpredictable seas of life. This is a ship that transports you, in the romantic sense of the word, to far-away places. It is like a child's make-believe ship constructed of dining chairs; a place to play 'let's pretend we're sailing to the other side of the world'. The broad open living room with its terrace, which like a ship's deck may be shaded by sail-cloth, is not only about providing a view of the Mediterranean. It is about putting the person who stands there in the presence of the horizon, the infinities of sea and sky. This is a

ship of romance and privilege, about freedom and sunshine, open fresh horizons, unlimited aspirations. It is a ship that is sailing away from the claustrophobia of the past, the dark muddy trenches of the recent First World War… and into the future.

References and other relevant publications, websites, broadcasts:

Peter Adam – *Eileen Gray: Architect/Designer*, Harry N. Abrams, New York, 1997.

Leon Battista Alberti , translated by Leoni – *Ten Books on Architecture* (1485, 1755), Tiranti, London, 1955.

Ethel Buisson and Beth McLendon – 'Architects of Ireland: Eileen Gray (1879-1976)' in *Archiseek*, available at:
http://ireland.archiseek.com/architects_ireland/eileen_gray/index.html

Ulrich Conrads, translated by Bullock – *Programmes and Manifestoes on 20th-century Architecture* (1964), Lund Humphries, London, 1970.

Caroline Constant – *Eileen Gray*, Phaidon, London, 2000.

Le Corbusier, translated by Etchells – *Towards a New Architecture* (1923), John Rodker, London, 1927.

Eileen Gray and Jean Badovici – 'De l'électicism au doute' ('From eclecticism to doubt'), in *L'Architecture Vivante*, Winter 1929, p. 19.

Eileen Gray and Jean Badovici – 'Description' (of Villa E.1027), in *L'Architecture Vivante*, Winter 1929, p. 3.

Shane O'Toole – 'Eileen Gray: E-1027, Roquebrune Cap Martin', in *Archiseek*, available at:
http://www.irish-architecture.com/tesserae/000007.html (July 2009).

Alison Smithson – 'Beatrix Potter's Places', in *Architectural Design*, Volume 37, December 1967, p. 573.

Colin St John Wilson – *The Other Tradition of Modern Architecture* (1995), Black Dog Publishing, London, 2007, pp. 162-173.

Vitruvius, translated by Hicky Morgan – *The Ten Books on Architecture* (first century BC, 1914), Dover, New York, 1960.

CHURCH OF ST PETER, KLIPPAN

*'Once our language has been declared
insufficient, room is left for others;
allegory can be one of them, like
architecture or music.'*

Jorge Luis Borges, translated by Allen – 'From
Allegories to Novels' (1949), in
Weinberger, editor – *Jorge Luis Borges, The Total
Library: Non-Fiction 1922-1986*,
Penguin Books, London, 2001, p. 338.

CHURCH OF ST PETER

A Lutheran church in the southern Swedish town of Klippan
SIGURD LEWERENTZ, 1963-66

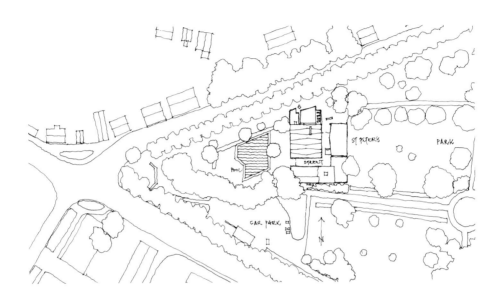

This small church in Klippan is the work of a man in his late seventies who had been working as an architect for over fifty years. Sigurd Lewerentz never explained his work in words. It is left to speak for itself. St Peter's does not look like a church. It is intense, apparently saturated with meaning but open to a variety of interpretations. It is the architectural equivalent of one of Beethoven's late string quartets; complex in its avoidance of orthodox, clear, resolved form; affecting in its dramatic and shifting effects on the emotions.

Context

Lewerentz was asked to design the church in 1963. The triangular site, by a quiet crossroads and in the corner of a municipal park, had been donated some years previously. Klippan is a small town of generally low density. The area around the site can be characterised as suburban. Nevertheless, despite its parkland and suburban setting, Lewerentz chose to make the church a small but dense cluster of buildings: the square block of the church itself; an L-shaped block of ancillary accommodation; and a street between the two. The composition constitutes a small piece of city – not a modern city but a non-specific traditional or Biblical city – a tiny fragment of what St Augustine referred to as 'The City of God'.

As a small piece of city, St Peter's is severe and surreal. There are no trees in its one narrow street though there are silent street lamps that bow politely as you pass. Its ground surface is mainly grit. (You hear your own footsteps.) All the walls are of dark, purplish-brown, bricks – cooked mud – held together with concrete and mortar – mud that goes hard. The windows are like mirrors. There is no colour except perhaps the reflection of a blue sky or the occasional glimpse of a tree, outside. This is a strange city; one to be lost in.

The building is oriented exactly with the cardinal points of the compass. There are at least six paths of approach: two along the tree-lined pavement; two across the park; one from the car park; and one, which seems more an exit than an entrance, from a garden

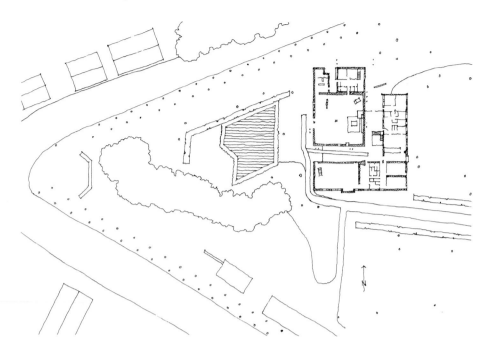

1 site plan

with a pool and fountain. Lewerentz positioned the buildings to allow room for this garden to the west. With its greenery and placid
water the garden provides the natural counterpoint to the piece of
city. The whole composition – 'city' and 'garden' is screened from
the town by the lines of trees along the pavements and by hedges
and earth banks. Lewerentz did not use or integrate his design with
what was already there so much as create a small world – city and
garden – separate from everywhere else. St Peter's is a stage set: a
discrete realm for narrative.

In my book *Doorway* (Routledge, 2007) I told the story of
my own first visit, alone, to this building. I had walked from the
train station to the south west. I found the car park first and then
walked along the pathway pointing towards a chimney. Reaching a
T-junction I turned left towards a pool of water; rounding the end
of the building I saw a tall metal fence with an open gate leading
into a street between the buildings. There was a brick path under
my feet and it led that way. Expecting to find the entrance into the
church along the street I walked through the gateway. The lower
buildings on my right were clearly secondary; the church itself
was on my left. There was no-one about. Two large panels of glass
were attached above eye level to the wall on my left; like mirrored
sunglasses they merely reflected what was outside. Above them was
a glowering brow of projecting brickwork. Next there was a small
door, but it was locked so I went on and turned the corner of the
street. The brick path stopped at the corner, leading nowhere. On

my right, steps led down into a square concrete hole in the ground;
the entrance to the church was not down there. There were offices
in the building alongside. The wall of what I took to be the church
on my left was now completely blank; not even any 'sunglasses'; just
a few more silently polite lamp-posts, standing there like (rather
unhelpful) saints. At the end of the street a freestanding wall, at a
strange angle to all the other buildings, partially blocked the view
out. Walking to the end of the street and past this wall I found
myself back on the suburban road feeling mildly rejected by this
small piece of surreal city. I felt like a thwarted Theseus trying to
find his way *into* the labyrinth.

Continuing counter-clockwise, with the church on my left, I
walked past a dingy yard which I took to be where the bins were kept,
and turning another corner found myself back in the garden with the
pool of water. Now I saw that there were two doorways, one single
and one double, in the wall of what I took to be the church. Neither
looked like a main entrance, more like doors into the boiler room.
Both were locked. Confused, I decided that if I could not enter by
the proper way (I had begun to doubt whether this church actually
had a way in!) I would try to get in by the back door. I returned to
the dingy yard to see if that door was open. It was. I had expected
to see mops and buckets but I found myself in a magical space – a
small rectangular 'cave' lit by dim light filtering through a crevice
in what seemed a very deep brick-vaulted roof (*2*). I could hear water
dripping. In the corner of this small cave was a doorway leading into

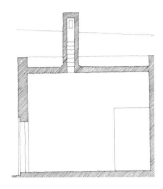
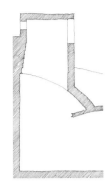

2 sections through light crevice

the larger cavern of the church itself. I had found my way in. After the sunny suburban ordinariness of the public road outside, and my experience of the surreal 'street' of the small fragment of the 'City of God', the character of this space was overwhelming.

The interior of the church (*3*) is dark, but with bright squares of glaring sunlight. One of these illuminates a huge clam shell (the font) making it shine in the darkness. Water drips silently into this shell and then overflows, drop by drop, metronomically measuring out time, into a pool of water under a rupture in the brick floor. At the centre of the church cavern a large steel T supports the brick-vaulted roof. Such is the daunting presence of this steel structure that, on my first visit, it was at least three-quarters of an hour before I realised that I had not gone near it. When I did, I tapped it and it rang like a bell.

The brick floor slopes unevenly down towards the massive brick altar under a cluster of lamps. Alongside, against the back wall, is a brick seat for the priest and a brick lectern. Past the organ is a doorway from the sacristy. The priest's entrance with the choir at

the beginning of the service is lit by light filtering through another crevice, this time in the apparently deep brick-vaulted church roof high above. This light shines a path on the floor, which the priest follows to the altar.

Light, sound, texture, scale, time...; through his building Lewerentz uses these modifying elements of architecture to intensify the drama and emotional experience of the person. With the mantle of 'architect' he designed his building as an instrument to elicit emotional responses, to organise the space for worship, to frame and protect the iconic T structure at its centre. His windows blind with glaring light; his dark interior reveals itself slowly but never ceases to daunt; his dripping water reminds you of eternity; his uneven brick floor makes you feel unsteady, even seasick; his brick walls and vaulted roof resound with organ music and singing; his steel structure rings like a bell; his altar provokes thoughts of sacrifice. This is architecture that does not stand separate from the person, consigning him or her to be a spectator. St Peter's engages, involves, includes the person as essential participant.

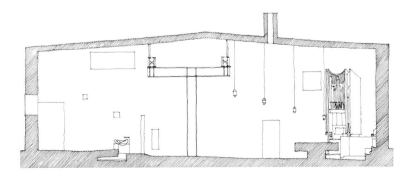

3 section through main church space

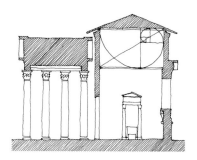

1

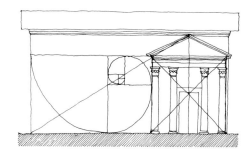

2

Ideal geometry

Throughout his career, Lewerentz used geometry and proportion to discipline his plans and sections. He designed the Chapel of the Resurrection in 1922. It was built as part of the Woodland Crematorium on the outskirts of Stockholm, which was initially designed as a collaboration between Lewerentz and Erik Gunnar Asplund. The plan, elevation and sections of the Chapel of the Resurrection (*1-4*) illustrate a geometric analysis of the building derived from drawings included in Colin St John Wilson's 1988 article in the *Architects Journal*. These suggest the building was conceived on an armature of Golden Section rectangles. (See *Analysing Architecture*, third edition, p. 162.) Other analyses are possible (see Nordenström, 1968, which suggests an analysis based mainly on √2 rectangles). Whatever his precise method, it is clear that Lewerentz sought to imbue his design with a 'genetic' integrity based in ideal geometry.

Extracting the underlying geometry from a design is fraught with difficulty. Imprecision in drawing and construction always seems to make multiple interpretations possible. The pitfalls are compounded by one's own desire to make the evidence fit a pet theory. None of this dilutes the fascination for the search, the desire to solve a puzzle, to find resolution. Lewerentz's use of ideal geometry contrasts with Mies van der Rohe's rejection of the idea that ideal geometry might hold some authority over his design.

The plan of St Peter's Church in Klippan (*5*) is perhaps even more fraught with difficulties for the geometric analyst than other buildings. A glance of the practised eye suggests a framework of ideal geometry is present; but finding it and establishing whether it is the right one are different matters. The diagram alongside (*6*) offers a possible analysis.

Lewerentz appears to have begun his design on a grid of 3.333…metre squares, marked with small crosses and coordinated A-M and 1-15 in the diagram. This grid establishes the limits of the main buildings. (It may extend outwards into the garden, but I have

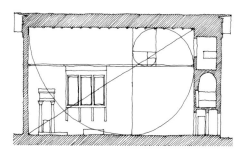

3

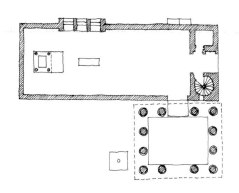

4

not explored that possibility.) The church block occupies the grid from A1 to G10. The L-shaped ancillary block has coordinates L4, L15, A15, A12, I12, I4; though its walls to the street do not align with the grid – one is slightly inside where it might be, the other apparently the same amount outside – the grid's presence seems affirmed by the nib of wall that projects to pick up coordinate I4. Within the grid the main church space occupies a perfect square, A4 to G10. This square extends diagonally to the south east by five grid units to give a larger square that includes the L-shaped ancillary block. The grid also determines the positions of some, but not all, other

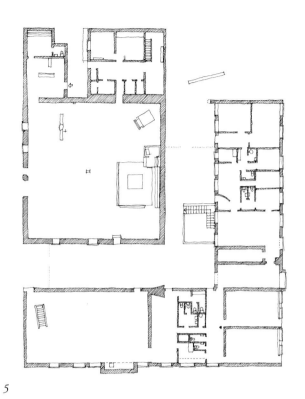

5

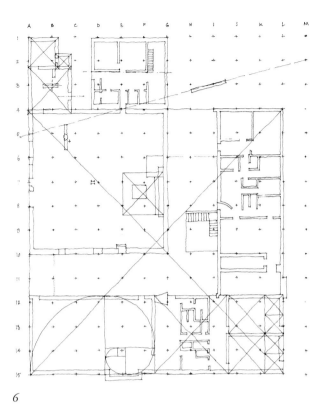

6

elements in the plan, including some of the partition walls in the office accommodation. The metal gates in the street are positioned according to grid lines B and 6; the strangely angled wall at the end of the street is on a line drawn from M2 to A5.

Having recognised the underlying rôle of the grid, analysis becomes less certain (and my attempt here is certainly not complete). There may be others hiding away but the only instance of the Golden Section appears to be in the community room with its fireplace positioned accordingly. Elsewhere, as in the case of the enclosure around the altar, the recurring figure is the square. In some areas squares interrelate in simple ways, such as in the south-east corner of the ancillary accommodation, producing 3:2 rectangles. But in the small entrance extension to the north the arrangement of squares is more complicated. Here they do not appear to conform to the grid, and they overlap by the thickness of their shared walls rather than sharing congruent sides. Their sizes do however appear to follow an arithmetic progression 3:2:1 generating a small spatial vortex or spiral. Other subtleties that become apparent during such an analysis include: the position of the font's rupture in the brick floor, which appears to relate to the diagonal of the large square and the other diagonal established by the strangely angled wall;

the entrance doorway, which seems positioned on the centre line between grid lines 3 and 4; the brick bench in the entrance lobby/wedding chapel, which is on grid line 3, and its adjacent altar, which is on grid line B; the doorway from the sacristy, which appears to be positioned on that diagonal of the strangely angled wall where it crosses grid line E; and the altar rail, which is also on grid line E. The altar itself does not line up with the grid. There are many other (possible) alignments and correspondences but I shall leave you to speculate for yourself.

One final point to notice in this geometric analysis is that the T-shaped steel structure does not stand at the exact geometric centre of the square church space. I shall return to this later, when discussing some interpretations of symbolism in this building.

Geometries of being

Most of the fabric of St Peter's is brick. Floor, walls, roof, altar, bench seats, partitions... all are made of brick. The vast majority of bricks used in building the church are uncut. To build walls without cutting bricks is not easy. One of the famous dictums of the American architect Louis Kahn, a near contemporary of Lewerentz,

185

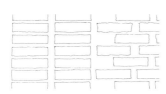

1

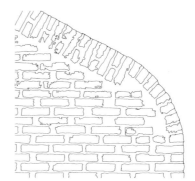

2

was that 'a brick knows what it wants to be', implying there is an accord between the uncompromising geometry of the rectangular brick and the uncompromising verticality of gravity which results in vertical rectangular walls and the geometrically curved arches. I do not know whether Lewerentz was aware of or respected Kahn's dictum but he pushed its sentiment beyond its limits. The dictum suggests, irrespective of what Kahn actually meant or did in his own work, that bricks and gravity working in harmony can, in themselves, make architectural decisions. Lewerentz asserted a more fundamental truth: that it is the architect who makes the decisions; and that, although the intractable rectangularity of the brick and the unalterable verticality of gravity constitute conditions with which the architect must work, they do not determine design decisions. Lewerentz's attitude in this is one that modifies/transcends/supersedes any authority thought to lie with the geometry of making.

The only thing the brick knew, as far as Lewerentz was concerned, was that it did not want to be cut in two. None of us would. He also refused to reject bricks if they were malformed or discoloured. The insistence on not cutting bricks seems quirky but it may, as we shall see later, have some symbolic meaning. It is an insistence that produced some unusual textures in the brickwork of St Peter's (*1* and *2*) where the usual conventions of brickwork – such as that one brick should rest on two (bonding) – are often ignored.

It is an insistence that also elevated mortar from merely being the 'glue' that holds bricks together into being an equal partner in the surface texture of walls. In some places in the walls of Lewerentz's earlier church at Björkhagen near Stockholm the mortar is smeared over the surface of the bricks – this is called 'bagging' because it is an effect achieved with the bag the cement came in. At Klippan the mortar is more often brushed to produce a neater slightly recessed but still rough-textured joint.

Lewerentz modified, subverted, even literally twisted the assumed authority of the geometry of making in other ways too. He delighted in getting bricks to do difficult things or at least things that were different from the usual. As has been said, the roof supported by the T-shaped steel structure is composed of brick vaults. These arch between smaller steel beams supported by two larger steel beams spanning across the church space. It is these two larger beams that are supported by the steel T (*3*). The smaller beams are neither parallel nor horizontal, as would be usual; their ends are up and down alternately and they meet at an undulating ridge. The brick vaults are constructed with uncut bricks too. The effect is to make the ceiling appear less substantial, like the billowing under surface of a bank of clouds.

Elsewhere Lewerentz modifies the geometry of making by subjugating it to the geometry of human form, its measure and

3

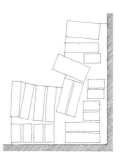

4

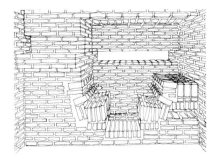

5

movement. Bricks are not flexible and 'want' (as Louis Kahn suggested) to be formed into rectangular shapes. But people are not rectangular; when they sit they need a seat that acknowledges the curvy geometry of their bottoms and backs. At various places in the St Peter's complex Lewerentz provided built-in seats constructed, as one would expect, in brick. Rather than allow the uncompromising geometry of the rectangular bricks to determine the form of these seats he asked the bricklayer to arrange the bricks in an irregular way – one that gently curves the seat to match the bottom of a human being and also provides lumbar support (*4*). In the ancillary block Lewerentz provided a pair of 'conversation' seats, also built in brick, with an eye-level view across the adjacent park (*5*). These brick details, walls and seats, were not contrived in an *ad hoc* way on site but thought through before construction, in detailed dimensioned drawings (see Wang, 2009).

Lewerentz thought about social geometry too. The brick floor of the church space has groups of parallel lines of wider mortar joints indicating the places where the lines of simple wooden chairs should be (*6*). This may seem dictatorial but clearly Lewerentz thought that, if left to themselves, the congregation might revert to organising the chairs in a conventional way – regular lines facing to the front (*7*).

His arrangement is less formal, with members of the congregation, choir and clergy sitting in a rough circle around the altar, as they might in the open landscape. And whereas in the conventional arrangement (*7*) the chairs crowd around and isolate the T structure his arrangement maintains its accessibility. Lewerentz's arrangement also allows the space to work ceremonially: there is space around the font for baptism, with the brick floor mounded up under the baptised like the ground under a saint; there is a place in front of the altar for a marriage couple, or for a coffin; and there is a processional route from the altar to the double 'exit' doorway into the garden.

'Pavements like the sea, ceilings like the sky'

St Peter's Church in Klippan is a composition of clear incontrovertible architectural elements – floor, wall, roof, column, doorway, altar…. The accomplishment of Sigurd Lewerentz in his design lies in the ways he invests these basic elements with symbolic meaning. This is a building that presents itself as being deeply poetic. But, just as when one is looking for underlying ideal geometry, it is difficult to be certain about which interpretation is right. It is probable that Lewerentz wanted his work to be enigmatic. Presented with enigma

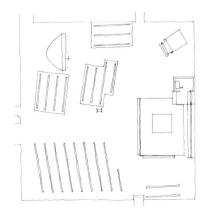

6

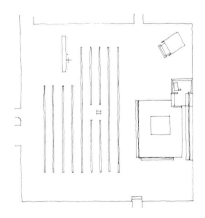

7

'The perfect temple should stand at the centre of the world, a microcosm of the universe fabric, its walls built four square with the walls of heaven... the four-square enclosure on the top of the world mountain, where the polar tree or column stands and whence issue the four rivers.' Lethaby, 1892, p. 53.

and vague allusions people try to make their own sense of things. Lewerentz, perhaps remembering Stéphane Mallarmé's saying – 'To define is to kill. To suggest is to create.' – was an architect (like a god) who refused to be explicit about the meaning of his work. Such puzzles as result engage and fascinate the mind; you sense an explanation but are unsure.

Like the world St Peter's is open to variant interpretations. It is like the world in that it is a human construct comprising 'city' – the environment dominated by human determination – and 'garden' – the environment dominated by nature. I do not know whether Lewerentz read William Richard Lethaby's book *Architecture, Mysticism and Myth*. Published in England in 1892 it may have been a text he and Asplund consulted whilst designing the Woodland Crematorium (though Caroline Constant, in her book *The Woodland Crematorium: Towards a Spiritual Landscape*, 1994, does not mention it). There are a few passages in Lethaby's book that suggest an influence on St Peter's. The first is above. Though to find allusion to the 'four rivers' in St Peter's would be tendentious, the church is certainly 'built four square with the walls of heaven', i.e. the walls of its square plan are aligned with the cardinal points of the compass. Though it stands on a flat site, the slope of the internal floor suggests a hill; and near its centre stands 'the polar tree or column' – the T structure.

In his book *Brick and Marble in the Middle Ages* (1855), an account of his architectural tour of northern Italy, George Edmund Street (who was to become an influential architect) wrote of his visit to St Mark's in Venice:

'But of all the features in this very noble interior, that which, next to the gorgeous colour of the mosaics on the walls, most attracted me, was the wild beauty of the pavement; for I know no other word that quite describes the effect it produces. It is throughout the whole church arranged in beautiful geometric patterns, just like those of the noble Italian pavement in the choir of Westminster Abbey; but these, instead of being level and even, swell up and down as though

they were petrified waves of the sea, on which those who embark in the ship of the Church may kneel in prayer with safety, their undulating surface serving only to remind them of the stormy seas of life.' (pp. 126-127)

The pavements of St Peter's 'swell up and down as if they were petrified waves of the sea' making one unsteady. Lewerentz may not have read Street but the latter's words are recalled too by Lethaby:

'Mr Street, in 1854 (sic), *described "the wild beauty of the pavement" in St Mark's as swelling up and down like a petrified sea; and he went on to suggest that this* undulation of surface *was an intentional making of the floor in the semblance of the sea.'* Lethaby, 1892, p. 201 (emphasis in the original)

In the same part of his book Lethaby quoted from John Ruskin's *Stones of Venice* (1851):

'Round the domes of (St Mark's) roof the light enters only through narrow apertures, like large stars; and here and there a ray or two from some far-away casement wanders into the darkness, and casts a narrow phosphoric stream upon the waves of the marble that heave and fall in a thousand colours along the floor.' Ruskin, 1851, quoted in Lethaby, 1892, p. 201

The 'waves' of Lewerentz's floor may be brick rather than marble but the 'narrow apertures' in his roof do create 'a narrow phosphoric stream' along which the priest and choir process on their way to the altar.

The metaphor of church as ship is old. 'Navy' and 'nave' come from the same etymological root – *navis* (Latin) = ship. And both words also suggest 'navel' – belly button – (as well as 'naval' – to do with the navy) and another sort of 'nave' – the hub of a wheel – both of which derive from a different etymological root – the northern European *nafu* (Old English), *naaf* (Dutch), *nabe* (German). As if to underline the *naval* metaphor, there is a model of a ship in the vaulted ceiling of the lobby/wedding chapel of St Peter's. And as if to acknowledge the *navel* metaphor the church with its 'polar column' establishes a 'centre' (a hub) for the world of its congregation as a

'Wounded I hung on a wind-swept gallows
For nine long nights,
Pierced by a spear, pledged to Odhinn,
Offered, myself to myself
The wisest know not from whence spring
The roots of that ancient rood.'

'Hávamál' (circa AD 800), translated by Auden and Taylor, 1981.

'And now these three remain: faith, hope and love.
But the greatest of these is love.'

St Paul, First Epistle to the Corinthians, 13.13.

'microcosm of the universe fabric'. The profound interiority of St Peter's and the blankness of the buildings' elevations suggest Lewerentz thought of his walls as limits of universal space, as flats on a stage having meaning only for their interior. For the human-made world of St Peter's there is no exterior, nowhere beyond the limits of the universe… until the gates of paradise – the doors out into the garden – are opened. The church is a ship, but it is also a primeval cave (complete with dripping water), the womb from which everyone emerges into the light.

The T-shaped structure near the middle of the church is a 'Tau cross' – *tau* is the letter T in Greek and the last letter of the Hebrew alphabet. *Tau* is thought to be one of the oldest letters. Its symbolic interpretations could fill a book of their own. (You can Google 'Tau cross' to find some of them.) Apparently Lewerentz came to this form gradually through the exploratory processes of design (see St John Wilson, 1988 and 1992). But when he 'found' it, he must have been sensible to its potent symbolism. Being a 'cross' the structure evokes ideas of sacrifice and resurrection. It stands as the presence of Christ crucified. So much is obvious.

But the T's possible interpretations have more dimensions to them than that. The structure feels primitive, even pagan. It stands like the column at the centre of a Minoan pillar crypt (see the Case Study 'Royal Villa, Knossos' in *Analysing Architecture*, third edition, pp. 228-230). And to return to the ship metaphor, it stands like the mast that penetrates below decks on a sailing ship, as if above the ceiling is a vast sail blown by the winds of heaven. The column establishes a centre – though it stands back to allow you to occupy the actual centre – but it also acts as a pivot (axis, axle) around which the space of the church, and the world outside, revolves.

The T structure is a metaphorical tree too; a steel equivalent of the real tree that stands just outside in the garden. In Norse mythology the heavens were supported by 'the Ash Tree of the World' – *Yggdrasil* – watered by the subterranean Well of Mimir (the pool beneath the font?) and with three roots stretching to the ends of the earth. *Yggdrasil* is translated as Odin's horse, a reference to the Norse god's nine-day self-sacrifice by hanging, during which he learned to read the runes, i.e. discover the secret of life (see above left). Perhaps that is why Lewerentz's T-shaped steel structure also resembles a gallows (and its off-centre position allows for the absent presence of Odin's swinging body).

Finally… A platitude heard in sermons is that 'the church is not the building but the congregation; the people are the bricks from which the church is built'. It is tempting to think this was in Lewerentz's mind when he decided that no brick should be cut in building St Peter's; to do so would be like cutting a person in two. The metaphor may be extended: the mortar that holds the bricks together represents religious belief – the *faith* that binds; the malformed or discoloured bricks represent people with physical or mental disabilities – *hope* of inclusion; and the very few bricks that were cut are those rare martyrs sacrificed for the greater good – the *love* of fellow human beings.

Not even Le Corbusier's Chapel at Ronchamp (with which St Peter's has been compared) is so replete with potential symbolic interpretation. Interpretation is another way in which architecture can engage and involve the person. Each writes their own narratives according to the clues provided by the building. Each becomes convinced that their interpretation is right. Provoked by the visitor's own creative faculties, these narratives have lives of their own.

Conclusion

Historians might try to find the truth behind Lewerentz's decisions as a matter of historical fact. (It is probable he did not quite understand them himself.) An architect is interested in understanding how architecture works and stimulating ideas for design. It would be vain to think analysis can reach into Lewerentz's mind to extract his exact intentions. It is clear he intended St Peter's to be ripe with symbolism, and it is sufficient here to note that architecture possesses that potential, not only with elements such as the T structure but also in the ways buildings are constructed and the experiences they provide. In this architecture is richer in its potential than other art forms. St Peter's is a quiet unassuming group of buildings hidden away in the suburbs of a quiet unassuming small town in southern Sweden. And yet this is one of the most emotionally powerful works of architecture anywhere. With its playful but dark brickwork it is witty and gloomy at the same time. It seems critical about the sterility of religion generated by human beings; but at the same time it seems to recognise the faith, hope and love that religion provides. It is a building that takes you on a journey: through the 'labyrinth' of the 'city street', down the apparent dead end 'back alley' of the 'bin yard'; into the 'magic cave' of the lobby, and the 'sacred catacomb' of the church with its shining clam shell. It takes you just about as far from the everyday world as you can get. Then it returns you to a paradise garden – a world of green and sunshine heightened by your descent into darkness.

References and other relevant publications, websites, broadcasts:

Janne Ahlin – *Sigurd Lewerentz, Architect*, MIT, Cambridge MA., 1986.

Peter Blundell Jones – 'Sigurd Lewerentz: Church of St Peter Klippan 1963–66', in *arq: Architectural Research Quarterly*, Volume 6, Issue 02, Jun 2002, pp. 159-173, also in *Modern Architecture Through Case Studies*, Architectural Press, Oxford, 2002, pp. 215-228.

Caroline Constant – *The Woodland Crematorium: Towards a Spiritual Landscape*, Byggförlaget, Stockholm, 1994.

Claes Caldenby, Adam Caruso and Sven Ivar Lind, translated by Krause and Perlmutter – *Sigurd Lewerentz, Two Churches*, Arkitektur Förlag AB, Stockholm, 1997.

Nicola Flora, Paolo Giardello, Gennaro Postiglione, editors, with a essay by **Colin St John Wilson** – *Sigurd Lewerentz 1885-1975*, Electa Architecture, Milan, 2001.

Carl-Hugo Gustafsson – *S:t Petri Church*, Klippan, 1986.

Vaughan Hart – 'Sigurd Lewerentz and the "Half-Open Door" ', in *The Journal of the Society of Architectural Historians of Great Britain*, Volume 39, 1996.

Dean Hawkes – 'Architecture of Adaptive Light', in *The Environmental Imagination*, Routledge, Oxford, 2008, pp. 129-141.

William Richard Lethaby – *Architecture, Mysticism and Myth* (1892), Dover Publications, New York, 2004.

Gordon A. Nicholson – *Drawing, Building, Craft: Revelations of Spiritual Harmony and the Body at St. Petri Klippan*, unpublished Master of Architecture dissertation, McGill University, Montreal, 1998, available at: http://digitool.library.mcgill.ca:8881/R/?func=dbin-jump-full&object_id=29806&local_base=GEN01-MCG02 (July 2009).

Pierluigi Nicolin – 'Lewerentz-Klippan', in *Lotus International* 93, 1997.

Hans Nordenström – *Strukturanalys : Sigurd Lewerentz' Uppståndelsekapellet på Skogskyrkogården : en Arkitekturteoretisk Studie*, Institutionen för Arkitektur 2R, KTH, Stockholm, 1968.

John Ruskin – *Stones of Venice* (1851).

George Edmund Street – *Brick and Marble of the Middle Ages*, John Murray, London, 1855.

Nicholas Temple – 'Baptism and Sacrifice', in *arq: Architectural Research Quarterly*, Volume 8, Number 1, March 2004, pp. 47-60.

Colin St John Wilson – 'Masters of Building: Sigurd Lewerentz', in *Architects Journal*, 13 April, 1988, pp. 31-52.

Colin St John Wilson – 'Sigurd Lewerentz: the Sacred Buildings and the Sacred Sites', in *Architectural Reflections: Studies in the Philosophy and Practice of Architecture* (1992), Manchester UP, 2000, pp. 110-137.

Unknown author, translated by Auden and Taylor – 'Hávamál', from 'The Poetic Edda' (circa AD 800), in *Norse Poems*, Athlone Press, 1981.

Wilfred Wang, editor – *St. Petri Church*, University of Texas at Austin, 2009.

VILLA BUSK

'We must again find a dialogue with the earth… The rampart is the ultimate trade with the landscape.'

Sverre Fehn – 'Has a Doll Life?', 1998.

'I have found a paper of mine among some others, in which I call architecture "petrified music". Really there is something in this; the tone of mind produced by architecture approaches the effect of music.'

Johann Wolfgang von Goethe, recorded by Eckermann (1836), translated by Oxenford (1906), March 23, 1829.

'(Architecture) is music in space, as it were a frozen music.'

Friedrich Wilhelm Joseph von Schelling, translated by Stott – *Philosophy of Art* (1804-05).

VILLA BUSK

A musician's house south of Oslo, Norway
SVERRE FEHN, 1987-90

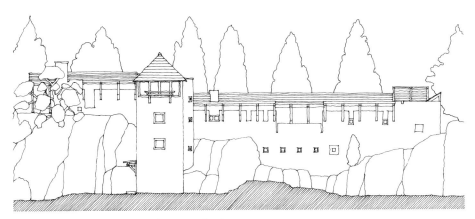

1 the Villa Busk stretched along the edge of a natural outcrop of rocks

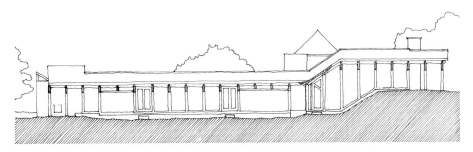

2 the Villa Busk from the other side, the elevation one approaches across the rocky plateau

Sverre Fehn's Villa Busk stands on the edge of a rocky outcrop with a distant view of the sea. It was built for a musician. With its resemblance to a romantic fortress, and standing on the edge of a precipitous cliff, it has the appearance of a house made to accommodate a poetic sensibility. But underlying its appearance, this is a building that offers an architectural equivalence to music; it is an instrument that, like music, plays with emotions, a work that orchestrates the person's experience of and relations with their surroundings.

Elements of architecture; using things that are there; identification of place

The Villa Busk is site specific. It could not be the same anywhere else. In beginning his design Fehn had the opportunity to choose the exact location. This choice was his first architectural (design) decision. He chose a position on a natural outcrop of rock, amongst mature trees, and with a view of the sea. He recognised this as a place with architectural potential, a *place* in embryo. It was a location

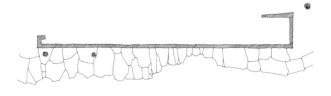

1

with dramatic possibilities. The purpose of his architecture was to enhance and exploit the inherent potential of this place.

The house has a clear composition, an intellectual organisation that may be readily deconstructed into its component parts. Many works of architecture, especially houses, begin with the idea of a box, four walls with a roof on top. Sverre Fehn begins further back, his approach is more elemental. In the first quotation at the beginning of this analysis, Sverre Fehn claims 'the rampart is the ultimate trade with the landscape'. That is how the Villa Busk begins. Fehn does not merely plonk a box on top of the cliff. His first move, in an interplay with the site's rocks, trees and level changes, is just to make a wall. Fehn's 'rampart', his 'trade with the landscape', is made of concrete, poured *in situ*. It stretches roughly east-west along the crest of the exposed rocks. This is the conceptual starting point for everything that follows.

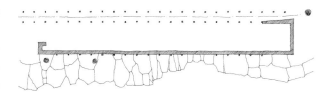

2

As soon as it comes into being, even in the imagination, the wall begins to reinforce the identity of the place. It defines and protects the place from the danger of the edge. It divides – like a castle wall divides 'friends' (insiders) from 'enemies' (those others outside) – the dwelling place of the house from the world 'out there'. It makes the refuge that is appreciated for its prospect.

Fehn also uses this wall to begin the more detailed identification of subsidiary places that a house needs. At the western end the wall turns back on itself to create a hearth (surmounted by a chimney stack). At its eastern end the wall similarly turns back on itself to make a place that will eventually become a small plunge pool adjacent to the master bedroom. In this way, two of the 'rooms' of the house have begun to be identified by the line of the wall. The living room at the western end (which is on higher ground than the rest of the house) relates to the setting sun and the view of the sea. The pool and master bedroom relate to the rising sun.

The next move in the design is to make two lines of columns parallel with the wall (*2*). These define a pathway that will become the main circulation spine of the house. At the eastern end this

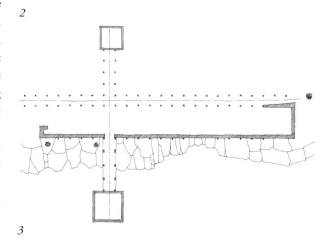

3

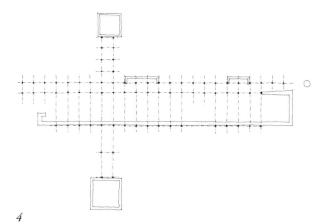

4

'*The route from boat to hearth is mediated by a tower. The daughters of the house have their rooms in the tower, and at the foot of it are the shower and cloakroom. The tower is completed by a communal room which captures all four directions of the sky.*'

Sverre Fehn, 1992, p. 6.

pathway relates to the return of the wall around the pool, and to an existing tree growing out of the rocks. At the western end the columns extend beyond the end of the wall with its hearth to make a porch leading onto the bare rock. The concrete wall – the 'rampart' – defines the edge of the house along the precipitous edge of the rock. The columned pathway, glazed along its length (except where

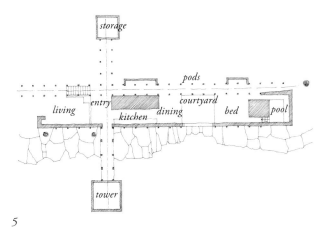

5

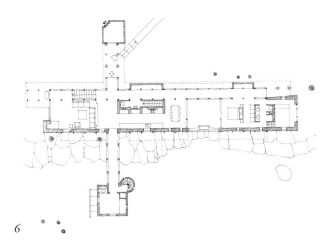

6

it protrudes out into the landscape) defines the edge to the safer plateau on top of the rock outcrop. One wall is heavy and protective; the other is light and visually open.

The third move is to make an axis at right angles to the wall and columned pathway (*3*), just where the rocks are highest. This axis too is defined by two parallel lines of columns. Where they cross is the main entrance into the house. Terminating each end of this axis there is, on the plateau side of the house, a small square storage building and, on the other, a tower reached across a bridge. The tower, dedicated to the children's bedrooms and to a study on its uppermost floor, adds to the drama and the romantic character of the house. It allows the person to go through the wall that protects the edge, to launch out into space. Approaching the house your feet are on the solid rock. Following the transverse axis and crossing the bridge you find yourself three storeys above the ground.

As well as defining the pathway – the circulation spine of the house – the columns support the roof (*4*). The structure follows a regular grid based in the geometry of making. On the south side it is supported by brackets fixed to the concrete wall.

The subsidiary places of the house occupy the space between the wall and the circulation spine (*5*). From right to left, west to east, there are: the living space, on a higher level with its views to the sea, its hearth and, over a wall, a view down to the entrance hallway; the kitchen, screened from the spine by a block containing a lavatory and stairs down to a lower level (a music studio); the dining space; a courtyard open to the sky; the master bedroom, separated from the pool by a block containing a lavatory and shower. Two storage pods are attached to the outside of the circulation spine.

All these places, together with the approach path across the rocks and the tower's spiral stair, may be seen in more detail in the plan (*6*). Subtleties may also be seen: the corner nibbled from the storage block to accommodate some existing trees; the outside face of the wall of the pool angled towards the tree; the rock left near the entrance to deflect the visitor towards the front door.

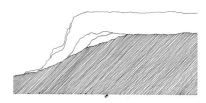

A similar analysis may be made of the house in section. The first element is the site (*1*) with its potential for a place on top of the rocks. The introduction of the wall changes the site fundamentally (*2*); it defines the habitable place on the top of the rocks and protects it from the danger of the edge. This is an ancient way of making a place.

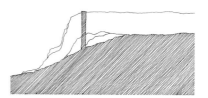

To make the place more easily habitable the ground is levelled into a platform, using the wall as a retainer, holding in the earth (*3*). If the ground slopes sufficiently, and there is space behind the wall, it is possible, as happens in some parts of the Villa Busk, to make two levels – an entrance level from the plateau at the top of the rocks, and a level below (*4*).

Finally, the lightweight roof structure shelters the interior of the house (*5*).

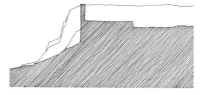

The storage block and the tower terminate the transverse axis as it enters and passes through the house (*6*) taking the person from solid ground at the entrance, up slightly onto the platform of the house, across entrance hallway and the bridge, to the third storey of the tower.

Orchestrating relationships with the landscape

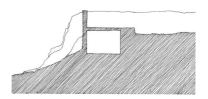

Following the transverse axis of the house is one of the 'musical' lines the house provides. These lines involve the movement of the person through the frame provided by the house, like the line of a melody against the rhythmic beat in a piece of music. What is aural in music is spatial in architecture. And, while a listener sits still as the music moves, in a building it is the person that moves while the architecture stands still (usually). You can dance to architecture as you can dance to music.

The 'beat' in the Villa Busk is provided by the structural grid. Music stimulates emotion. The emotional stimulus the Villa Busk provides lies in the relationships that the house sets up between the person and the landscape. The transverse axis through the house

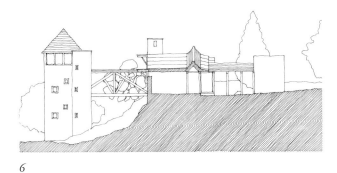

6

8

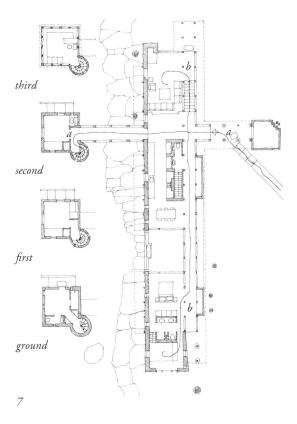

third

second

first

ground

7

(*7, a–a*) involves: approaching across the rocky plateau; stepping down under the covered way between the house and the storage block; stepping up into the porch and entrance hallway; noticing the steps up to the living area on the right and the parallel lines of columns stretching to the left; crossing the hallway to pass through the doorway in the concrete wall; finding yourself on a glazed bridge, up in the air; and then crossing into the tower with its spiral staircase leading up to the study on the uppermost floor.

The other principal musical line of the house runs along the circulation spine (*7, b–b*). If you turn right after entering, you climb some steps that follow, almost exactly, the rising ground line of the rocks outside, taking you up to the elevated living area with its hearth and distant views westward. Turning left at the entrance you go down the pathway between the columns, past the dining area and courtyard on your right, with the plateau like a Japanese rock garden through the glass wall on your left, to the master bedroom and the pool. While on this journey, the tree – one of the starting (reference) points for the house – stands as a focus outside in front of you, with the angled wall canted towards it.

The Villa Busk is not merely an object in the landscape, it is an instrument that modulates your experience of and relationship with that landscape. This is one of the powers of architecture.

Conclusion: architectural references in the Villa Busk

The Villa Busk suggests that Sverre Fehn learnt from the architecture of others.

With its defensive wall, its barbican tower and its small loop-hole like windows over the craggy cliff, the house has a clear resemblance to a romantic medieval castle. Even the way the timber roof projects over the wall, supported on brackets, is reminiscent of the timber hoardings built on the battlements of fortresses, as illustrated in Viollet-le-Duc's book *The Habitation of Man in All Ages* (*8*). (Viollet-le-Duc was a French architect of the nineteenth century who was interested in medieval architecture. His ideas on structural honesty and the use of iron were influential in the development of modern architecture.)

'Japan has a word for finding the pleasantest point in an interior... We are all on a journey through the great space of nature, and if you are capable of revealing your temperament, the place will find you and keep you there.' **Sverre Fehn**, 1992, p. 6.

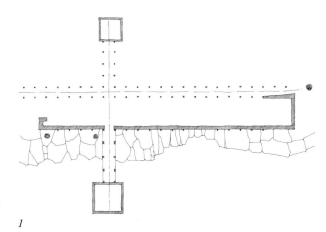

1

Fehn also acknowledged his debts to some of the twentieth century's pioneers of modern architecture. The house's underlying rectangular grid and crossed axes (*1*), for example, together with the lining of pathways with columns, is reminiscent of some of the houses designed by Frank Lloyd Wright (*2*). And Fehn's assemblage of services – lavatories, kitchen equipment, showers etc. – into cores (*3*) separated from the external walls is reminiscent of the work of Mies van der Rohe, as in the Farnsworth House (*4*).

The concrete wall of the Villa Busk, if all else were removed, would stand on the rocks like a piece of eroded ruin (*5*). The roof is attached to the wall as if added later (*6*). This illusion of layered history – of fragments from the past reused and reinterpreted – is a reminder of the actual layered history of Carlo Scarpa's refurbishment of the Castelvecchio in Verona (*7*).

Wright, Mies and Scarpa were all influenced by Japanese traditional architecture. So was Sverre Fehn. The Villa Busk is like a Japanese pavilion with its aesthetic interplay with the landscape: its exploitation of existing topography and trees; and its framing of portions of the landscape as pictures. The framing of the trunk of the tree in the rectangular frame of the window at the end of the circulation spine is a Japanese device (*8*). The exterior, framed, becomes a decoration for the interior.

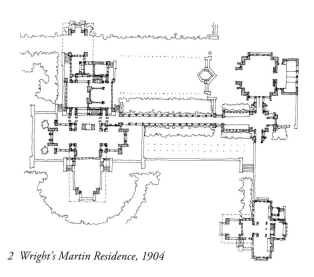

2 Wright's Martin Residence, 1904

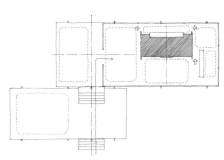

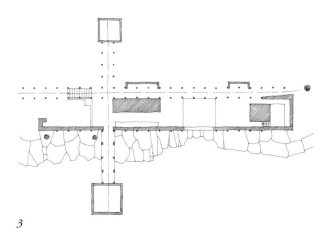

4 Mies van de Rohe's Farnsworth House, 1950

3

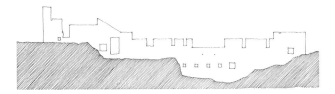

5 *the verticality of the concrete wall…*

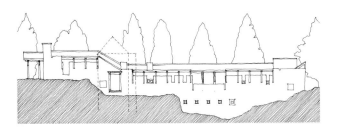

6 *and the horizontality of the roof create a geometric foil to the
irregularity of the rocks*

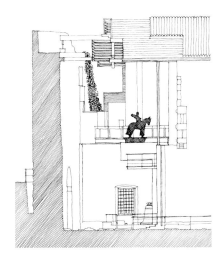

7 *Scarpa's Castelvecchio, 1950s and 1960s*

The Villa Busk's relationship with the ground has Japanese nuances too. In traditional Japanese houses there is often an interplay between the natural ground and an artificial platform. The kitchen may have the earth as its floor, while the more formal parts of the house will be on a platform supported on posts and lined with tatami mats. The stratification has poetic dimensions and emotional effects. The poetry refers to the dual state of the human being as part of and separate from nature, or at least it celebrates the subtle differences between the two states of being. The emotional effect derives from the phenomenological recognition that one feels different standing on the ground or solid rock and standing on a timber platform. The vibrations, sounds, textures, sense of stability and solidity, are different in each case. And in the former situation one is 'at large'; in the latter, framed by the structure of the platform.

The ways in which one steps onto or off a platform is handled carefully in Japanese architecture too. It may be a step, or perhaps a naturally flat stone, but always there is an intermediary stage between the natural ground and the platform, a place to leave one's shoes and the dirt of the ground behind as one steps onto a more refined domain. This happens too in the Villa Busk.

Both the Villa Busk and traditional Japanese architecture play with the in-between in other ways too. In the analysis of the Farnsworth House I mentioned the *engawa* – a veranda – that provides a traditional Japanese house with a space that is neither inside nor out, maybe for contemplation of a rock garden. In the Villa Busk the *engawa* is created by the combination of the circulation spine and a timber platform attached outside its glass wall (9). This relates to the natural rock 'garden' on the plateau.

8 *the tree at the end of the circulation spine*

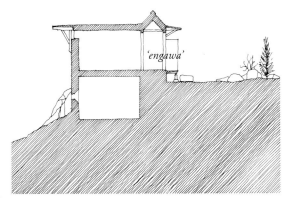

9

'The straight lines of poetry are found in the concrete mass's confrontation with the mountain, and the regular rhythm of wooden pillars is slipped down into the earth like responses to the static slide-rule of the roof construction.' Sverre Fehn, 1992, p. 7.

1 *in traditional Japanese architecture there is a functional and aesthetic difference between places where the floor is the natural ground and those that are on platforms (from Morse, 1886)*

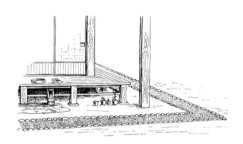

2 *as in the Villa Busk, the posts of traditional Japanese buildings have different ways of touching the ground; Japanese houses also have verandas –* engawa *– between inside and out (from Morse, 1886)*

Other Japanese nuances in the Villa Busk include the way in which the columns of the circulation spine continue outside the walls of the building for a few bays at each end. Inside, the columns are part of the integrated structural frame of the house; outside, their feet rest either on the natural rock or on padstones. By this device the stark separation of the house from its surroundings is lessened… in two ways: spatially, by the small porches that are created; and structurally, by the admission of the natural ground as part of the house's structural system (*2*).

In the Japanese way, the thoughtfulness put into the design – such subtleties as the framing of fragments of the landscape as pictures, the provision of natural blocks of stone as steps between outside and in, and the creation of in-between spaces – transfers to the person who experiences such a building. The house becomes a receptacle of consideration (considerateness), which is a powerful factor in aesthetic response. Those who experience buildings enjoy and appreiciate the feeling that they and their aesthetic sensibilities have been taken into consideration by the designer… rather more than if they feel intellectually excluded by enigmatic and arcane ideas (though the latter have been used in architecture, as in other art forms, to create and appeal to cliques).

This dimension of consideration, engagement, communication between the architect and the person is evident in the Villa Busk. It has (at least) three levels: that of *intimacy*, in which one interacts with the building and its materials closely by touching; that of *distance*, in which one contemplates the remote – the sea, the forests, the clouds in the sky, the stars; and that of the *intermediate*, in which one moves around, sits and talks to friends, cooks and eats dinner, sleeps and maybe immerses one's body in a pool of cool water.

References and other relevant publications, websites, broadcasts:

'Villa Busk, Bamble, Norway 1987-1990', in *A+U: Architecture and Urbanism*, January 1999, pp. 122-141.

Johann Peter Eckermann, translated by Oxenford – *Conversations of Goethe* (1836), 1906, available at:
http://www.hxa.name/books/ecog/Eckermann-ConversationsOfGoethe.html

Sverre Fehn, edited by Marja-Riitta Norri and Marja Kärkkäinen – *Sverre Fehn: the Poetry of the Straight Line*, Museum of Finnish Architecture, Helsinki, 1992.

Sverre Fehn in conversation with Olaf Fjeld – 'Has a Doll Life?', in *Perspecta* 24, 1988, reprinted in Norberg-Schulz and Postiglione, 1997, pp. 243-244.

Miles Henry – 'Horizon, Artefact, Nature', in *Architectural Review*, August 1996, pp. 40-43.

Edward S. Morse – *Japanese Homes and Their Surroundings* (1886), Dover Publications, New York, 1961.

Christian Norberg-Schulz and **Gennaro Postiglione** – *Sverre Fehn: Works, Projects, Writings, 1949-1996*, Monacelli Press, New York, 1997.

Eugene Viollet-le-Duc, translated by Bucknall – *The Habitation of Man in All Ages* (1876), Arno Press, New York, 1977.

Friedrich Wilhelm Joseph von Schelling, translated by Stott – *Philosophy of Art* (1804-05), Minnesota Press, Minneapolis, 1989.

VILLA MAIREA

*'The curving, living, unpredictable
line which runs in dimensions
unknown to mathematics, is for me the
incarnation of everything that forms a
contrast in the modern world between
brutal mechanicalness and religious
beauty in life.'*

Alvar Aalto – 'The Hill Top Town' (1924),
quoted in Schildt, 1997, p. 49.

VILLA MAIREA

A house in the woods of western Finland
ALVAR AALTO, 1937-39

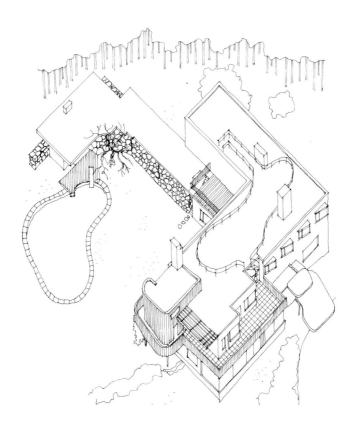

All architecture involves the in-between. Buildings mediate between us and the world; they frame us, our possessions and what we do. At its most rudimentary – such as, for example, when we make a camp on the beach – architecture involves drawing a boundary between ourselves and our surroundings, even if that boundary is no more than the edge of a towel. It is hard to think of a building that does not begin, conceptually, like this, even if it does not have walls. (See, for example, my description of the temporary mosque in Nazareth in the Introduction to *An Architecture Notebook: Wall*.) Architecture involves framing; and framing involves defining, subtracting, an inside from the general outside.

Often buildings establish a precise unambiguous division between inside and out. A fence or wall with a thickness of no more than a few centimetres or inches makes a sharp incision in space, cutting one area off from another. Crossing the threshold of an opening in such a barrier takes no more than a split second; in an instant you are transported from one place into another.

In other buildings the division between inside and out is made less clear. Architects open up a zone that is neither inside nor out, creating places that might be called transitional or in-between. Examples include the *engawa* of a traditional Japanese house, the terraces of Wright's Fallingwater or the portico of a Greek temple.

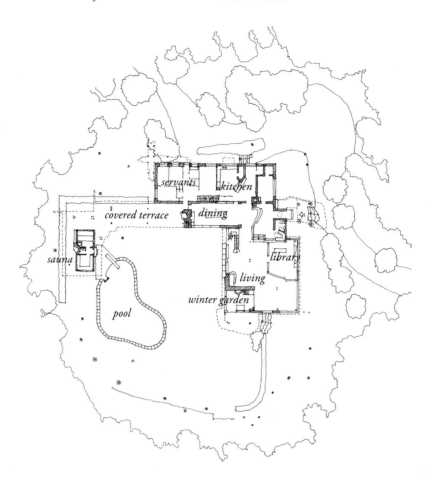

1

In the Villa Mairea Alvar Aalto creates in-between places by organising the house according to overlapping layers. Not only does Aalto blur the division between inside and out, he also tries to blend the artificial into the natural, like a painter smudging one colour into another and into the background character of the canvas.

Identification of place; overlapping layers

The Villa Mairea (*1*) was designed as a house for a wealthy client. It is situated in a clearing in the woods. The house has servant quarters and kitchen, a living space, dining space, winter garden, library. The bedrooms are upstairs. Above the winter garden is a studio. Outside is a pool and sauna attached to the main house by a covered terrace facing approximately south. There are hearths in the living space, the dining space, and in the covered terrace.

The house has a rectangular core (*2*). This contains the main spaces. The entrance is to the east, with the approach along the drive through the woods. A right-angled low wall stretches out

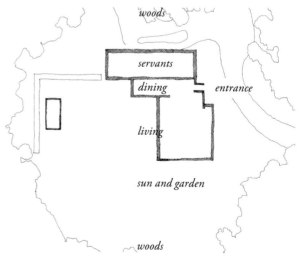

2

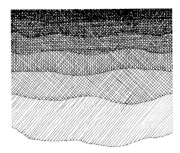

3

4

westwards from the main body of the house to embrace the small rectangular sauna.

The rectangular core of the house establishes what could be a sharp division between inside and out. But it is only the conceptual starting point for Aalto's architectural play. He sets about camouflaging its severity with overlapping spaces.

The natural world can be perceived as made up of overlapping layers. Think of the shallows of the sea, with one small wave overlapping the next and the next and the next (*3*). Particularly in wet countries one often finds rich layers: a pool of rainwater; the mud around it darkened by dampness; dry earth around that; grass; maybe leaves scattered across the water and ground; and all under the layer of shade of a nearby tree. Add to this the layer of sky and cloud reflected in the surface of the water (*4*).

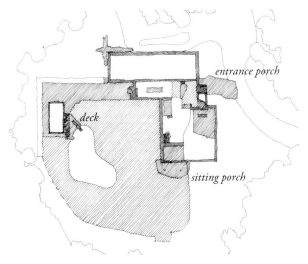

entrance porch

deck

sitting porch

5

Aalto seems to have thought of his design for the Villa Mairea like this. It too is composed of layers, some of which are clearly human because they are regular in their geometry; some of which attempt to be natural in form by being apparently free of geometry.

Some of these layers of space are shown in *5*. The first layers are natural or existing: the trees, the ground, the clearing and presumably the driveway. The next layer is the rectangular core of the house. From its wall, which divides inside from out, Aalto projects subsidiary spaces both inwards and outwards. Outwards from the house is the garden: domestic nature in contrast to the wild nature of the woods around. Layered onto this is the covered terrace and the pool. Attached to the sauna is a step down onto a small wooden deck with a diving board: more layers. Attached to the house is an irregular porch sheltering steps made of irregular stones. And over the winter garden the studio has a curved outer wall overhanging the square core to make a sunny sitting porch beneath.

The overlap of spaces continues inside. One might interpret tables and the stairs as overlaps but there is also the place where the dining space seems to spill into the entrance hallway, stopped by a curved wall. Both the winter garden and the library are layers superimposed onto the general square of the living space, the floor of which is 'layered' into different surfaces – timber floorboards and clay tiles (indicated by the curved line) – like the shallow surf lapping the sand. And the hearths are small layers added to their respective spaces. There is also a trellis, cross-shaped in plan, attached to the north-east corner of the servant quarters, presumably to camouflage its geometric harshness.

The composition is not without hierarchy and focus. Its gravitational core (the heart of the house) is the dining table, with other layers becoming more diffuse (more affected by nature) as they fan out from this centre.

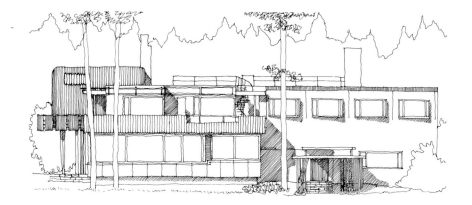

1 entrance elevation

The whole house is an abstract composition in which one layer overlaps others, confusing or blurring boundaries. This painterly attitude to composition is apparent too in the elevations (*1*). Layers of light and shade, tree foliage and trunks, bushes, and the different colours and materials, reflection and texture, of the building itself overlap like blocks of paint and fabric in an abstract collage.

There is layering and blurring of edges in the detail of the house too. The porch at the main entrance (*2*) is a blend of regularity and irregularity. The hearth under the covered terrace (*3*) is an irregular composition of irregular blocks of stone attached to the regular end wall of the dining space. And the bottom step of the main stair up from the living space (*4*) is squiffy against the sober regularity of the other steps in the flight. The edges of the main hearth in the living space (*5*) are also softened by breaks in the plastering, kerbs of irregular stones, and a strange 'bite' taken out of the edge against the window. Even the flat roof has a rail with the plan of a contour or pool (see the drawing on page 203).

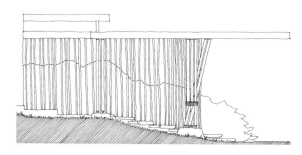

2 side elevation of main entrance porch

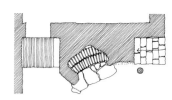

3 plan of hearth in covered terrace

4 stairs in living space

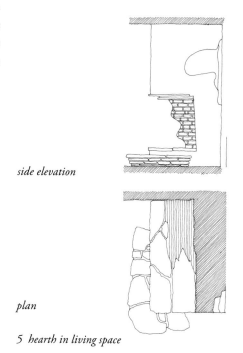

side elevation

plan

5 hearth in living space

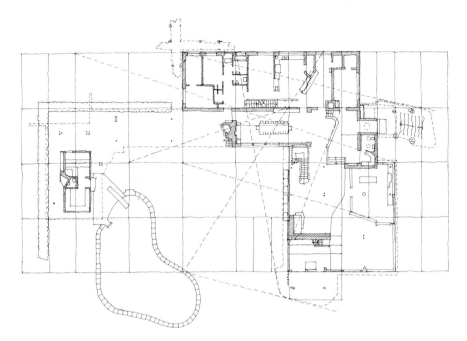

6

Geometry

When asked what was the module he used in his office Aalto replied, 'One millimetre or less'. This implies that Aalto eschewed ideal geometry in his architecture in favour of a finer grained attitude to deciding dimensions. Perhaps his reply was disingenuous. The plan of the Villa Mairea is regulated according to an underlying matrix of squares, divided into halves, thirds and quarters (6), though as usual the thicknesses of walls allow different interpretations of exactly where the grid lines fall. It appears also, as in Lewerentz's later plan for St Peter's in Klippan, that elements that deviate from the orthogonal are aligned with diagonals between grid nodes (some of these are indicated in 6). Such elements are not as free in their

geometry as they appear. Even the curve of the swimming pool can be interpreted as following the discipline of the grid.

The alignment of diagonals too is a painters' device. It offers a way of bringing a visual integrity to a two-dimensional layout. Aalto's plan is comparable to the composition techniques used by landscape painters, such as the seventeenth century French artist Nicolas Poussin. His painting of *The Funeral of Phocion*, for example (7) is organised according to diagonals linking specific points on the picture surface. Poussin's intention was to draw the observer's eye to the two stretcher-bearers in the foreground. Aalto's appears to have been no more than to find some reason (spurious or not) for the angles and dimensions of the various parts of his plan. For both Frank Lloyd Wright and Alvar Aalto the underlying grid was a framework that helped in making decisions. It cut short deliberation. If an element aligned with a grid line or a diagonal between grid nodes then it acquired some degree of rightness. A grid can be an authority against indecision and arbitrariness. Whether it imbues a design with aesthetic worth is a moot point.

Conclusion

The history books report that Aalto was influenced by Wright's Fallingwater, which had been completed and published while Aalto was beginning to think about his design for the Villa Mairea. Early designs for this house had deep cantilevers. As he developed it, and without a waterfall to work with, Aalto's design matured. Wright's imitation of overlapping geological layers in the terraces of his house

7

became in Aalto's design a more subtle layering of human presence over nature. For both architects inspiration came from the traditional architecture of Japan, as has been illustrated in some of the other analyses in the present book. Much classical 'temple' architecture presents a sharp division between the natural and the human. In rudimentary architecture the human presence can seem subject to the domination of nature. (Remember the quotation from Ruskin at the beginning of the chapter 'Temples and Cottages' in *Analysing Architecture*.) Aalto's Villa Mairea, as do traditional Japanese houses and gardens, suggests a more subtle relationship, a blending of the human and the natural. But the architect remains in control, so the appearance of blending is more an aesthetic (poetic) effect (a privilege of wealth and technical ability) than a practical or moral actuality.

References and other relevant publications, websites, broadcasts:

Alvar Aalto – *'The Hill Top Town'* (1924), in Schildt, 1997, p. 49.

Alvar Aalto – 'From Doorstep to Living Room' (1926), in Schildt, 1997, pp. 49-55.

Sarah Menin and Flora Samuel – *Nature and Space: Aalto and Le Corbusier*, Routledge, London, 2003.

Juhani Pallasmaa – *Alvar Aalto: Villa Mairea 1938-39*, Mairea Foundation and Alvar Aalto Foundation, Helsinki, 1998.

Juhani Pallasmaa – 'Villa Mairea: Fusion of Utopian and Tradition', in Futagawa, editor – 'Alvar Aalto: Villa Mairea, Noormaku, Finland, 1937-39', *GA*, 1985.

Nicholas Ray – *Alvar Aalto*, Yale University Press, 2005.

Göran Schildt – *Alvar Aalto: the Early Years*, Rizzoli, New York, 1984.

Göran Schildt – *Alvar Aalto Sketches*, MIT Press, Cambridge MA, 1985.

Göran Schildt – *Alvar Aalto: the Decisive Years*, Rizzoli, New York, 1986.

Göran Schildt – *Alvar Aalto in His Own Words*, Rizzoli, New York, 1997.

Richard Weston – *Villa Mairea*, Phaidon (Architecture in Detail), London, 1992.

Richard Weston – *Alvar Aalto*, Phaidon, London, 1995.

Nobuyuki Yoshida – 'Alvar Aalto Houses: Timeless Expressions', *A+U* (*Architecture and Urbanism*), June 1998 (Extra Edition), Tokyo.

THERMAL BATHS, VALS

'Every touching experience of architecture is multi-sensory; qualities of space, matter and scale are measured equally by the eye, ear, nose, skin, tongue, skeleton and muscle. Architecture strengthens the existential experience, one's sense of being in the world, and this is essentially a strengthened experience of self.'

Juhani Pallasmaa – *The Eyes of the Skin* (1996), Wiley, Chichester, 2005, p. 41.

THERMAL BATHS, VALS

A bathing complex attached to a hotel in a Swiss valley
PETER ZUMTHOR, 1996

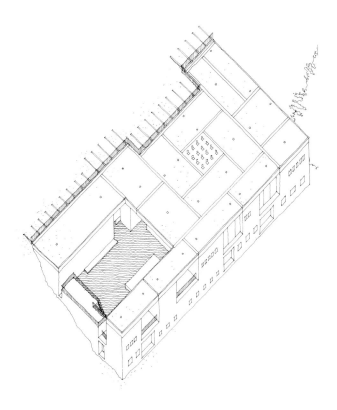

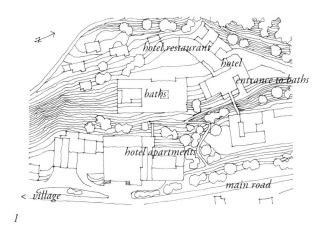

Architecture is often conceived in terms of addition but it may be generated by subtraction too. A wall is built by adding bricks onto bricks, a house by adding room to room. But space can be won by excavation, by taking away material from solid matter. Caves, for example, are made by running water wearing away rock. Troglodyte houses are made by people cutting away at soft rock – maybe expanding natural caves – to make rooms. So architecture may be made by taking away as well as adding. Peter Zumthor's thermal baths at Vals are not excavated from natural rock but they are conceived as if they were.

The thermal baths at Vals are attached to an older hotel built in the 1960s. They emerge out of the steep hillside on which the

1

211

1

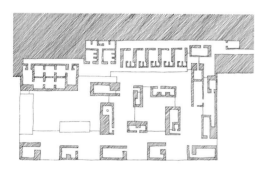

outdoor pool   pool

2

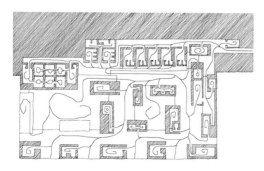

3

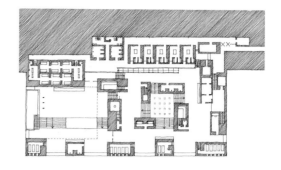

4

5

212

hotel stands, near the village of Vals beside the river that flows along the floor of a deep valley between the high Alps in the Graubünden canton of eastern Switzerland. The hotel and baths face east across the valley. In the early morning shafts of sunlight strike high across the valley, between the peaks opposite. At midday and in the afternoon the short clipped grass of the opposite hillsides, bathed in sunlight, is bright green. In winter the landscape is grey and white. On cool days vapours from the baths' warm outdoor pool join the mists in the valley.

Excavated space

The baths exploit water from a natural hot spring. You enter the building down a tunnel under the hotel, as if you too were a molecule in a flow of water, come to join the waters that are there already.

The baths building is a massive rectangular block bedded half into the slope (*1*). Though conceptually monolithic, this block is built of thin slices of locally quarried quartzite stone. Its perfect geometry emerges straight from the grass of the hillside and is capped by a perfectly horizontal concrete slab. Grass grows on the top.

The architecture begins with this geometrically perfect piece of geology. The spaces that accommodate the baths are scoured from within this block, not by water but by Zumthor's designing mind (*2*). This is an artificial cave system made not by mindless processes but, like one of George MacDonald's fairy tales, obeying the laws imposed by its own fantastic imagination.

The mind as instrument of erosion enters, as do bathers in the finished building, through the tunnel at the top right of the plan. It finds its way through crevices in the rock gradually making them wider, but always obeying the authority of its own orthogonal geometry. Spaces that are tight and small near the source become

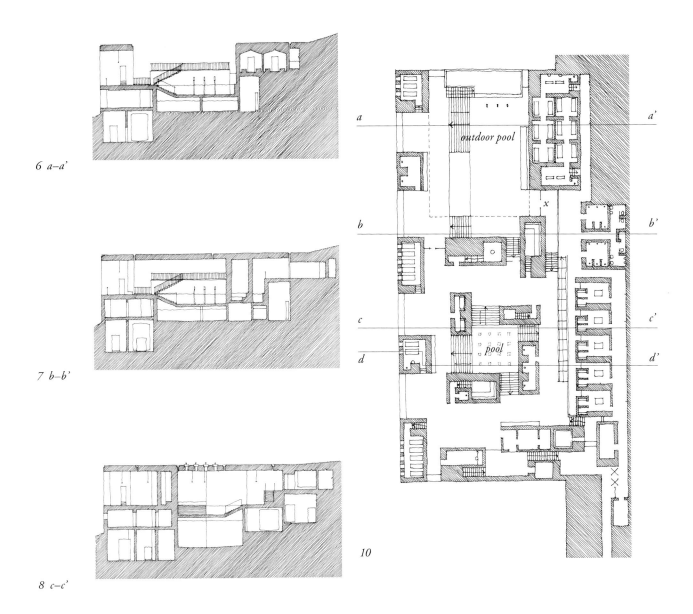

6 *a–a'*

7 *b–b'*

8 *c–c'*

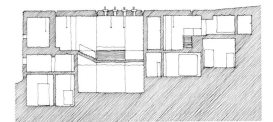

9 *d–d'*

10

wider and more generous towards the opposite corner – as they do in natural cave systems. Water collects in depressions in the floor. Light enters through the 'cave's' mouths, and through cracks in the 'rock' ceiling. Great pillars of rock left by the scouring are themselves excavated, making small secret places inside (*3*). Bathers pass through the five changing rooms to wander and swim amongst the pillars and seek out the secret places to soak and relax (*4*).

The sections (*6-9*) show how the spaces flow down and open out from the north to the east and south. The concrete slab roof is

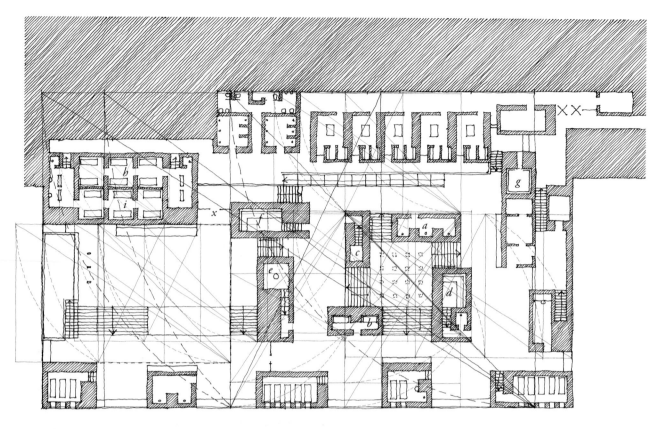

1 the geometric matrix on which the plan of this building is based is complex

cut away over the outdoor pool (at the top of the plan above, *10*). Around it are platforms for sunbathing. The outdoor pool extends under an overhang and inside. You can swim through a doorway at (*1, x*) between inside and outside.

Ideal geometry

Of course, the laws Zumthor's fantastic imagination follows are those of ideal geometry. Like the geometry of a sophisticated piece of music, that of the thermal baths in Vals is complex and many layered. It is too complex and has too many layers to give a complete account here. As in other buildings analysed in this book, it appears to be based on the square, the √2 rectangle and the Golden Section rectangle (*1*). The only obvious square is that of the indoor pool with its four by four square of sixteen small roof lights. This centres two slightly larger squares of different dimensions. One of these gives the outer extents of two of the great pillars containing the secret

places: (*a*) high powerful showers that crash on your back; and (*b*) a dark and quiet room for meditation lying on a bed listening to simple music made by striking rocks. The extent of a Golden Section rectangle generated from this square coincides with the outer edge of the building. The other slightly larger square determines the outer extents of the another two of the great pillars, containing: (*c*) a freezing cold pool; and (*d*) a pool of warm water covered with perfumed flower petals. (There is a shower to wash off the petals when you get out.) A √2 rectangle derived from this square determines the position of the inner face of the great pillar containing the fountain from which you can taste the spa water (*e*).

The whole building is based on a large square and Golden Section rectangle, but with a bit added to the northern end to accommodate the stairs down to a lower floor which is chiefly for the plant and maintenance areas. The extent of this added bit seems to have been determined by another Golden Section rectangle. The area of roof cut out over the outdoor pool is a √2 rectangle attached

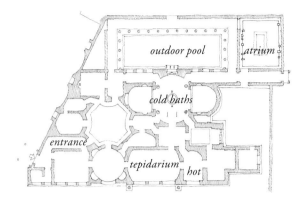

2 a reconstruction of the women's baths at Tivoli, near Rome

to the southern side of the large square on which the large Golden Section rectangle is based. And so on. The matrix of ideal geometry on which this building is based is too intricate to describe in words or even as a diagram. The thermal baths at Vals is a cave system made by a mathematician.

Modifying elements

Other great pillars contain secret places for different experiences. There is very hot bath in (*f*) and two sets of steam baths in (*h*) and (*i*). Maybe these were intended for male and female but they are used for those who wear their swimming costumes and those who do not. At (*g*) is a small but lofty rock chamber that you reach by going through a tunnel in the water. This is the chamber where you find people humming, making the sounds from their vocal chords resonate with the acoustic of the space.

The focus on sensual experience in the thermal baths at Vals is reminiscent of that in the bathing complexes built by the ancient Romans (*2*). Roman baths had pools of different temperatures: hot, tepid and cold. They might also have an outdoor pool. In his baths, Zumthor adds further sensual experiences: the perfumed pool with flower petals; the chamber where people hum; the small chamber where you can drink the spa water; the chamber where you can lie in the dark and listen to rock music; the chambers where giant showers crash water onto your back, and so on. This is a building that provides for all the five senses – sight, touch, hearing, smell and taste – but it provides for other senses too. Zumthor said there should be no clocks in the baths so that bathers would be unaware of time. But the building does not obliterate time; it replaces clock

time with other sorts of time: the movement of the sun and clouds across the sky; the movement of other bodies around the internal spaces; the movement of land workers and animals on the hillside opposite; your own explorations of the secret places in the great pillars. It is a building that caters for other senses too: the sense of slight trepidation each time you cross the threshold into one of the secret places; the sense of self-consciousness when you emerge from the changing rooms at the higher level in front of the other people in the pool; or, alternatively, the gratified sense of exhibition if you enjoy showing off your body to others.

Conclusion: content and context

There are sixteen small roof lights over the indoor pool at Vals. For each, on the grassy roof, there is a small light, lit at night; the shade of each light is black and like a narcissus flower; it looks down into the pool chamber below and at its own reflection in the glass of its roof light. Narcissus was the god who fell in love with his own image reflected in a pond. His story is told by the Roman poet Ovid in his *Metamorphoses*.

Though the building is much photographed, the thermal baths at Vals is more powerful as an instrument that manipulates the person's experience than as a visual object. It is a building that mediates between people and the surroundings – landscape and climate. It provides a frame within which people indulge privately in sensual pleasures, a refuge from which they may watch the landscape and changing weather, and a stage on which they may display themselves. Through history these have been some of the fundamental purposes of architecture. Zumthor's building is itself less narcissistic and more one that shows consideration for its context and content. It is interested in what it does as well as how it looks. In providing for the people who use it and in responding to the setting the building makes a bridge between the two. The entrance tunnel cuts visitors off from the surrounding landscape only to reintroduce them in the special circumstances of being unclothed in a labyrinth carved from inside a huge artificial and geometrically ordered rock boulder. If the thermal baths at Vals is a 'temple', it is a temple to the sensual human being.

References and other relevant publications, websites, broadcasts:

Peter Davey – 'Zumthor the Shaman', in *AR Architectural Review*, October 1998, pp.68-74.

Lars Muller, translated by Oberli-Turner, Schelbert and Johnston, photographs by Helene Binet – *Peter Zumthor: Works – Building and Projects 1979-1997*, Birkhäuser, Basel, 1998.

Raymund Ryan – 'Primal Therapy', in *AR Architectural Review*, August 1997, pp. 42-49.

Steven Spier – 'Place, authorship and the concrete: three conversations with Peter Zumthor', in *ARQ Architecture Research Quarterly*, Volume 5 Number 1, 2001, pp. 15-36.

Nobuyuki Yoshida, editor – 'Peter Zumthor', *A+U Architecture and Urbanism*, February 1998 Extra Edition.

Peter Zumthor – *Therme Vals*, Scheidegger & Spiess, Zürich, 2007.

Peter Zumthor – *Thinking Architecture*, Birkhäuser, Basel, 1998.

Peter Zumthor – *Atmospheres*, Birkhäuser, Basel, 2006.

ENDWORD

These twenty analyses affirm that there is no one right way to do architecture. Like music and philosophy, architecture is a matter of composition and proposition. And both depend on ideas. But the analyses also show that buildings designed according to different attitudes and techniques may be studied and understood according to a consistent conceptual framework. One of the reasons for preparing these analyses has been to test the applicability of the conceptual framework offered in my previous book *Analysing Architecture*. As a tool for analysis, it has, broadly speaking, stood up to the task. Though they should be used selectively and intelligently rather than as a mindless checklist, the themes identified and illustrated in the earlier book do provide 'ways into' analysis and help in gaining understanding of the general workings of architecture as well as of the underlying architecture of particular buildings. Use of a tool, however, prompts refinement.

At the outset I said that the buildings chosen for analysis had been selected according to two criteria: the range of different kinds of architectural space they exemplified; and their differing suggestions about the relationship between architecture and the person. A couple of additional themes have emerged particularly strongly. The analyses expand and refine the discussion of the different attitudes architects have to geometry and how it might be used. They also illustrate, even in what appear to be radically original works, the debt owed by their architects to traditional architecture and architecture of the distant past.

Architects and geometry

Architectural uses of geometry are discussed at length in *Analysing Architecture* under the chapter headings of 'Geometries of Being' and 'Ideal Geometry'. The twenty analyses in the present book suggest there is more to say about architects' relationships with geometry. The architects whose work has been analysed here have used geometry – geometries of being and ideal geometry – in different ways.

Wright (Fallingwater), Fehn (Villa Busk), Aalto (Villa Mairea), Le Corbusier (Villa Savoye), Lewerentz (St Peter's, Klippan) and Moore Lyndon Turnbull Whitaker (MLTW, Sea Ranch) evidently used geometry to provide a framework upon which to compose their drawn plans. In most this took the form of a grid. MLTW used sugar cubes instead. Of these only Fehn and Le Corbusier, and to some extent MLTW with their sugar cubes, related their underlying grid to the geometry of making, i.e. the structural discipline of their buildings. Even then, Le Corbusier deviated from his underlying grid when it got in the way of what he wanted to do (for example, around the central ramp). Wright and Aalto, by contrast, used grids that were more obscure – abstract grids that were not directly related to the structural geometry of their buildings. In both cases the grid was an aid they kept to themselves but which is apparent in their plans. They used the grid as a frame to help them make decisions about the positions and dimensions of things. Presumably they felt that the controlling discipline of the grid lent aesthetic integrity to their drawings. The benefit that might accrue to those who would experience their buildings is not clear. Aalto also used his grid to determine occasional diagonals and curves to modulate his otherwise orthogonal plan (i.e. to help its blending with its irregular natural surroundings. Lewerentz constructed diagonals on his grid too, though to a lesser extent. His design suggests that the mathematical underpinning of architecture has a spiritual dimension. The concealed grid St Peter's Church may be interpreted as emulating the hidden order of all things – described by the religiously minded as the 'mysterious way' in which God works and found by scientists since before Newton to be susceptible to mathematical formulation. It is appropriate (or intended by Lewerentz) that, as with nature, the underlying geometric discipline of his building should not be overt but discoverable only with some effort and, even then, open to variable interpretation.

The grid is a matrix that holds things together conceptually. It is satisfying to the architect's mind that things have some underlying order. Sometimes architects work on the basis that sophistication comes with complexity. Pawson and Silvestrin (Neuendorf House) make a relatively simple matrix consisting of overlaid squares. Kahn (Esherick House), Terragni (*Danteum*) and Zumthor (Thermal Baths, Vals) make their geometric matrices more complicated by introducing √2 and Golden Section rectangles. They also overlay matrices of different scales to achieve even greater complexity. Analysing their plans produces bewildering tangles of lines. Decisions are made about the dimensions and positions of elements according to this tangle of lines, suggesting that geometry lends a 'genetic', if complex, integrity to the whole. As mentioned at the outset of this book, George MacDonald – the writer of fairy tales and 'The Fantastic Imagination' – argued that stories need an armature of 'laws' to hold them together and, however fantastic they may be, to give them their own internal plausibility. Many architects, working in line rather than words, find that armature in geometry.

In some of the analyses I have drawn an analogy with music. Centuries of music have been composed using what was in Bach's time called the 'well-tempered' scale. From the range of sound frequencies available, this scale extracted twelve tones (A to G# including half-tones) related in geometric proportion. Doubling and halving the frequencies added octaves. Music was composed using intervals and harmonies held together by mathematics. Some architects clearly believe, as apparent in the examples analysed in this book, that geometric proportion applied to dimensions rather than sound frequencies can give their work a harmonic integrity equivalent to that possible in music composed using the well-tempered scale. Whether or not such is the case is a moot point.

Not all architects believe that ideal geometry should have authority over architecture. Märkli tries it in *La Congiunta* but neither Gray (Villa E.1027) nor Dewes and Puente (*Casa del Ojo de Agua*) bother. They prefer to depend on a different sort of geometry, one that derives from human inhabitation (geometry of being). Murcutt (Kempsey Guest Studio) is content with the discipline of the geometry of making (with timber components) and of that traced by the path of the sun in the sky. Mies (Farnsworth House and Barcelona Pavilion) asserts a fusion of ideal geometry and that of making, giving the latter the authority and status of the former. In the Farnsworth House he takes one component – a floor slab of travertine – rather than a perfect geometric figure such as a square or Golden Section rectangle, and uses that as the module to give geometric discipline to the composition as a whole. In the Barcelona Pavilion there is an extra subtlety in that the geometry of one component is in counterpoint with those of others – i.e. the geometries of the floor slabs, columns, the glazed screens and wall cladding are in interplay with each other rather than in resolved agreement.

Le Corbusier (*Le Cabanon*) proposes another hybrid geometry. His Modulor system formulates 'laws' for composition using dimensions derived from the human figure governed by series of numbers related to the Golden Section and authorised by the drawn construction of a geometric diagram. Le Corbusier suggested that using this system of dimensions *his* work would be in accord with that 'mysterious way' governing all creation. Koolhaas (*Maison à Bordeaux*) pays homage to Le Corbusier by using the Modulor diagram as a framework for the plans of his house but alters the foundations of Le Corbusier's framework by increasing its scale to that of a god rather than a human being.

By contrast with those architects who use right angles and straight lines, Kiesler (Endless House) and Findlay and Ushida (Truss Wall House) avoid Cartesian grids and Euclidian geometry. They prefer shapes based on free curves, movement, growth – of the hand and arm's movement when drawing, of the body dancing, of shells growing. Kiesler argues that it is this approach which brings *his* design closer to the source of original creation. These architects disregard the authority of the geometry of making too. They relish shapes that are difficult to make, refusing to accept ease of construction as a limitation on their imagination or on architecture's claim to transcend the mundane.

Reinterpreting architecture of the past

Even amongst buildings which at first sight appear original it is hard to find works of architecture that owe no debt to ancient and traditional architecture.

La Casa del Ojo de Agua is influenced by Mayan or Inca temples; the Neuendorf House by Moorish courtyard houses. Even the Barcelona Pavilion, considered one of the most innovative buildings of the twentieth century, is apparently influenced by the ancient Minoan hall and Greek megaron. The Truss Wall and Endless Houses, two of the most determinedly unorthodox buildings, emulate the amorphous spaces of troglodyte houses (cave dwellings) and shells. The Farnsworth House is a reinterpretation in steel and glass of a Greek temple and of a rudimentary African hut on stilts; it also seems to borrow its proportions from the ancient temple of Aphaia at Aegina. La Congiunta rearranges the components of a Romanesque church. Le Cabanon takes a lead from an ordinary garden shed but is conceptually equivalent to the hermit's cell, Elisha's room on the wall or the cabin of an ocean-going liner. The Esherick House with its detached end chimneys is a geometrically perfect settler house. The Maison à Bordeaux is a deconstructed chateau. Il Danteum draws on such ancient precedents as the Egyptian hypostyle hall, the Minoan pillar crypt and labyrinth, and the Greek Telesterion. The Villa Savoye is Le Corbusier's Parthenon and twists a Pompeian house into a spiral. Sea Ranch imitates local traditional timber barns and classical aedicules. Villa E.1027 acknowledges a debt to traditional French peasant architecture. And both the Villa Busk and the Villa Mairea owe something to their architects' interest in traditional Japanese architecture (as of course does the work of both Wright and Mies) and their inspiration by nature. St Peter's, Klippan evokes the 'anti-nature' of a barren city street, the promise of the timeless 'City of God', the labyrinth and the atmosphere of pagan worship in caves. And Fallingwater and the Thermal Baths at Vals find inspiration in geological formations.

Kinds of architectural space

Architects organise, order, mould… space in different ways. Many of these are evident in the buildings analysed. Finding words to label the different kinds of architectural space is sometimes tricky.

The spaces of La Casa del Ojo de Agua are sequential, ranged along a line like the parts of a sentence punctuated by doorways. Its dining room is a raised platform open to the trees around on three of its four sides and has no roof. The bedroom below is a staging point on the route from the top of the slope down to the river. It too is a platform open, though veiled by mosquito net, on three of its four sides. The floor of the dining room above gives the bedroom a roof. Because of this it has a horizontal emphasis. The back wall of the house and its relation to the slope give direction to both rooms. So, even in this small house different kinds of architectural space are evident: 'sequential'; 'punctuated'; 'elevated'; 'open' (in various degrees); 'veiled'; 'horizontal'; 'directional'.

The Neuendorf House also frames a punctuated sequence. Its long approach pathway is a space for movement – 'dynamic'. Like a crescendo in music it builds to a 'climax' at the 'constricted' entrance into the courtyard. The courtyard is 'enclosed'. Being open only to the sky it has a 'vertical' emphasis. The loggia is a space that 'frames' a view. It also 'projects' an axis over the swimming pool to the horizon.

Where La Casa del Ojo de Agua and the Neuendorf House provide a certain route, the Barcelona Pavilion offers choice and uncertainty. It is the seminal example of space that is said to 'flow' between separated walls (like a stream between rocks). Where both La Casa del Ojo de Agua and the Neuendorf House focus on clear 'centred' spaces – 'hearts' – that of the Barcelona Pavilion (if it has a heart) is less clear. Its space is 'uncentred', 'not focused' (except at the statue). Without its walls the Barcelona Pavilion would have space 'structured' by its columns; but the columns and walls make space in different 'overlapping' ways. In Sea Ranch spaces are defined by use and by structure, as they are too in the Villa Busk. In both there are spaces that are 'in-between' inside and outside.

The Truss Wall and the Endless House 'choreograph' space, emulating the movement of dance. The sequence in the Endless House has no beginning nor end; its architect called it 'endless'. The Farnsworth House's relationship with 'endlessness' – the infinite – is different. It frames a 'centred', though 'asymmetric', space hovering slightly above the infinite curved surface of the earth. Its space is 'raised' and with a 'horizontal' emphasis. Inside, its places – for sleeping, eating, cooking… – are 'implied' rather than defined by enclosure.

On the lowest floor of the *Maison à Bordeaux* there are spaces that are 'excavated' out of the ground. The spaces of both the Endless House and *La Congiunta* can be interpreted as 'excavated' too, but from space itself rather than from solid matter. The walls of St Peter's, Klippan also excavate space from space itself, making the interior, though orthogonal, like a cave. The spaces of the Thermal Baths, Vals, are excavated from a large constructed rectangular block of rock.

We have seen that the spaces of many of the buildings analysed are ordered mathematically. The mathematical order of the Esherick House is abstract where that of *Le Cabanon* is formulaic and related to 'human scale'. The Esherick House illustrates Kahn's notions of 'served' space and 'servant' space.

The mathematical space of *Il Danteum* is, like the Esherick House, abstract too. Its sequential spaces are 'narrative' – they relate the story of Dante's *Commedia*. This is a form of 'dynamic' space. The Villa Savoye frames a quintessential example of dynamic space – the architectural promenade – sequential, punctuated and possibly narrative. It plays with mathematical space and spaces with horizontal and vertical emphases.

Villa E.1027 and Sea Ranch concentrate on making space into *places* for 'inhabitation'. Christian Norberg Schulz, in his book *Existence, Space and Architecture* (1971), called this kind of space

'existential'. Martin Heidegger, in his essay 'Building Dwelling Thinking' (1950), called it space for 'dwelling'. Space for inhabitation provides psychological and physical comfort for the person. In the case of the Kempsey Guest Studio this is done by 'reinterpreting' the space of an existing building. Both the Villas Busk and Mairea add to this a 'poetic' relationship with their landscape. The Thermal Baths, Vals, offers spaces that are 'sensual'. And St Peter's, Klippan makes spaces that are 'emotionally charged'.

These very brief descriptions do not account for the full range of kinds of architectural space. There are grand classifications, such as: inside, outside and in-between; static, dynamic; focused, unfocused; horizontal, vertical; punctuated, flowing; enclosed, open; structured, unstructured and layered; axial, asymmetric; excavated, constructed… But within these there are as many subtle nuances as there are in the ways music may be composed and played. This is the art of architecture.

Architecture and the person

Perhaps the curse of architecture is that essentially it is about making frames but some architects want their work to be the picture. There is a desire to make buildings photogenic. Architecture frames the lives and activities, possessions and beliefs of people. And as people occupy, inhabit, use, perform in the space of buildings, the various kinds of architectural space relate to them and affect them in different ways. Architecture manifests and symbolises human presence and will to change the world. It also manipulates, orchestrates and manages people's experience.

Some architecture is conceived as if it were sculpture, as if the three-dimensional form and visual appearance of buildings were its paramount subject. But as the preceding analyses illustrate, architecture has more dimensions to it than the visual. Juhani Pallasmaa (see the quotation on page 210) makes the point that architecture involves smell, sound, touch and even taste. But this argument does not go far enough. Architecture involves other senses too, emotional senses: curiosity; uncertainty; trepidation; fear; contradiction; refuge; humour; well-being; secrecy; display; transition; arrival; exclusion; welcome; entertainment and many others. All these reside in the person. All these and more are part of our experience and enjoyment of buildings. They depend not just on the information received from our five senses. They depend on interpretation. Architecture mediates between people and their surrounding. Architecture is also a mode of communication between the mind of the architect and that of the person, a gift from one to the other.

Le Corbusier uses the person, human form, as the basis on which he constructs the Modulor. He also makes architecture that takes a person on a walk from the earth to the sky. Dewes and Puente give the person a temple in the jungle. Pawson and Silvestrin use the wall to accompany, challenge, enclose and then reveal the horizon to the person. Mies lifts the person onto a higher plane, and makes a place in which to wander. Märkli offers a cave in which the person may encounter, divorced from the landscape, tortured sculptures. Terragni uses architecture to tell a story. Koolhaas tells jokes. Wright puts the person next to a hearth on a rock by a waterfall. Murcutt, Moore (*et al.*), Gray, Fehn and Aalto offer a 'simple life well lived' in harmony with nature. From the person, Lewerentz elicits emotional responses. And Zumthor stimulates and soothes the body's sensuality.

All is done through the medium of architecture. Physically, sensually, psychologically, socially, emotionally… architecture is, without doubt, the richest of arts.

ACKNOWLEDGEMENTS

Thanks are due to: Tom Killian (New York), who has unflinchingly provided challenging debate and invaluable information on some of the American examples included in this book; The Austrian Frederick and Lillian Kiesler Private Foundation in Vienna, and Tatjana Okresek in particular, for granting me permission to use the Kiesler drawing on page 57; Leena Pallasoja at the Museum of Finnish Architecture in Helsinki for sending me some useful material on Sverre Fehn.

I am grateful too to the team at Routledge: Fran Ford for her good humoured encouragement; Laura Williamson for her support; and Faith McDonald for seeing the book through production.

As always I depend on the support of Gill, and the occasional interest of Mary, David and Jim. But now I have another generation to thank – Emily, daughter of Mary and Ian – though at only a few months old she is sublimely unaware that merely by coming into existence she makes the work involved in putting together a book worthwhile (not that I expect her to have the slightest interest in architecture).

INDEX